1

Writing Processes

Many people assume that professional writers find writing easy, that when they sit down at a keyboard, the right words just flow. But, in fact, these writers know that writing is hard work. They don't expect to achieve perfection in one draft or at one sitting, but instead they approach writing as a series of steps or activities, known as the writing process. Learning to use this process can help you to express your ideas well and to succeed at the writing you will do in college and during your career.

INSTANT ACCESS

WRITING PROCESSES

prewriting	deciding on the subject, considering the needs of the reader, gathering information
planning	choosing a preliminary thesis and organization
drafting	writing a first draft to develop the main ideas and discover new ones
revising	making changes in the thesis, structure, content, paragraphing, and sentences
finishing	proofreading for grammar, mechanics, and spelling errors and preparing the final copy

Listing these writing activities one by one may imply that writers complete them in chronological order, but the process is not so clearly segmented. After you have begun to draft a paper, for example, you may decide that you need more information—and return to prewriting. You may need to do more planning after you finish a draft. It is through this recursive process that experienced writers move from a topic to a finished product.

INSTANT ACCESS

The **Pocket Handbook** for **Writers**

Michael L. Keene
The University of Tennessee, Knoxville

Katherine H. Adams
Loyola University New Orleans

McGraw Hill

Boston Burr Ridge, IL Dubuque, IA Madison, WI New York
San Francisco St. Louis Bangkok Bogotá Caracas Kuala Lumpur
Lisbon London Madrid Mexico City Milan Montreal New Delhi
Santiago Seoul Singapore Sydney Taipei Toronto

The McGraw·Hill Companies

McGraw Hill Higher Education

INSTANT ACCESS: THE POCKET HANDBOOK FOR WRITERS, 2003 MLA/CMS Update
Published by McGraw-Hill, a business unit of The McGraw-Hill Companies, Inc., 1221 Avenue of the Americas, New York, NY, 10020.

This book is printed on acid-free paper.

3 4 5 6 7 8 9 0 BAN/BAN 0 9 8 7 6 5

ISBN 0-07-310493-0

Editor-in-chief: *Emily Barrosse*
Publisher: *Lisa Moore*
Director of development: *Carla Kay Samodulski*
Development editor: *Anne Stameshkin*
Marketing manager: *Lori DeShazo*
Project manager: *Jennifer Mills*
Production supervisor: *Carol Bielski*
Designer: *Jean Mailander*
Art editor: *Emma Ghiselli*
Cover design: *Laurie Anderson*
Interior design: *Linda Robertson*
Typeface: *9/11 New Century Schoolbook*
Compositor: *Thompson Type*
Printer: *The Banta Book Group*

Library of Congress Cataloging-in-Publication Data
Keene, Michael L.
Instant access : the pocket handbook for writers / Michael L. Keene, Katherine H. Adams.
p. cm.
Includes index.
ISBN 0-07-310493-0 (spiral : alk. paper)
1. English language—Rhetoric—Handbooks, manuals, etc. 2. English language—Grammar—Handbooks, manuals, etc. 3. Report writing—Handbooks, manuals, etc. I. Adams, Katherine H., 1954- II. Title.
PE1408 .K428 2004
808'.042—dc21 2002038654

www.mhhe.com

MLK: To Sewanee

KHA: For Gerald

HOW TO USE THIS BOOK

Instant Access was written and designed to help writers get answers to their questions as close to *instantly* as possible.

ORGANIZATION

The book is organized into three parts so that you can get to the *kind* of information you need as quickly and easily as possible: Part One (blue tab) provides **how-to guides** for writing processes and various types of writing; Part Two (orange tab) provides comprehensive and quick coverage of how to avoid or solve the **most common problems** for both native and non-native English-speaking writers; and Part Three (white tab) provides an alphabetically arranged list of **terms** central to grammar, mechanics, and punctuation, all with clear explanations and useful examples.

Part One, Writing Processes and Products contains step-by-step guides to

- writing processes for essays, research papers, various kinds of professional communication, and Web pages;
- MLA, APA, *Chicago Manual of Style,* and CSE documentation styles;
- document design—for short papers, long papers, and Web pages;
- and oral presentations.

Part Two, Common Writing Problems provides quick but intensive help with the ten most common problems writers encounter. This part also includes a separate section that covers the key trouble spots for writers whose first language is not English. Each of the eleven sections in this part opens with an "Instant Access Overview", a guide to understanding and solving these common problems, and is followed by a detailed discussion.

Part Three, Grammar, Punctuation, and Mechanics from A to Z presents terms central to English grammar, mechanics, and punctuation, all alphabetically listed for quick and easy reference. Each term is briefly defined, clearly explained, and illustrated with examples.

The Glossary of Usage concludes Part 3 and provides alphabetically arranged help covering how to correctly use commonly confused words (such as *affect* and *effect*).

The Index follows the Glossary of Usage and presents the entire handbook's contents listed alphabetically by topic and followed by the page numbers where the topics are covered.

Elements Specially Designed to Speed Up Your Search
This book includes numerous features to help you find and use the information you need as quickly as possible:

- The **Instant Access Contents** listing on the inside front cover provides an immediate overview of the topics this book covers.
- **Instant Access Boxes** INSTANT ACCESS appear throughout the book to provide the fastest—the most concise and easy to find—answers to your questions.
- **Instant Access Overviews** 8A INSTANT ACCESS OVERVIEW open each chapter in Part 2, Common Writing Problems. These orange-screened pages present the key points to remember for each of the ten most common problems so that you can identify and avoid the problems in your writing. The rest of each chapter explains the key points in more detail and offers more examples.
- **ESL Icons and Cross-References** 324–26 appear in the margins next to sections that address topics of interest to writers whose first language is not English. The page numbers accompanying the icons indicate where you can find further information on related topics.
- The **Directory of Instant Access Boxes** on pages 309–10 will help you to locate these boxes and overviews as quickly as possible, so that you don't have to flip through the book looking for them.

- The **List of Figures** on page 311 shows you at a glance where you'll find all of the book's illustrations (for example, diagrams, sample Web pages, sample business letters).
- The **Checklist for Finishing Documents** on page 312 can quickly guide you through the necessary step of making sure that your paper is ready to turn in.
- On the inside back cover flap you'll find a chart of **Revision and Correction Symbols** that identifies the symbols' meanings and the page numbers where you'll find corresponding explanations and examples.
- On the book's back cover, you'll find a listing of **Frequently Asked Questions (FAQs).** The order of these questions follows the book's organization. The FAQs are a good review of the kinds of questions this book can answer—as close to instantly as possible.

1a Prewriting

To start work on a paper, you need to choose a topic and select the information you want to present about it. The following questions and invention techniques should help you with this first stage of the writing process, called prewriting.

QUESTION ONE: WHAT IS THE ASSIGNMENT?

Begin by carefully reviewing the writing task. What do you need to know about the assignment? If you were asked to write about capital punishment, for example, you might ask yourself the following questions to see whether you understand your teacher's expectations:

- Who is the **intended audience** for the paper? Is it your teacher, fellow students, residents of your state, the governor, or a news magazine?
- What types of **research materials** should you use? Will you be relying on course materials or your own opinions? using articles and books? searching the Web? conducting interviews?
- What type of **thesis** should the piece have? Should it state your opinion about capital punishment? evaluate the strengths and weaknesses of several articles on the subject? discuss recent cases in which new evidence led to the overturning of past convictions?
- What **organizational structure** would be appropriate? Should you refute other opinions before you state your own? discuss two articles fully and then compare them? review recent court cases and then predict their impact on future legislation?
- What is the assigned **length?** When is the paper **due?**

QUESTION TWO: WHAT SHOULD I WRITE ABOUT?

Frequently in writing classes, you will be assigned a paper type, such as comparison or argumentation, but not be given a topic. After you feel that you understand the assignment generally, you will need to consider your interests to choose your subject.

- What subjects do you know well?
- What subjects would you like to know more about?

- What interests you in your classes? at your job? from your hobbies? in the choices and activities of your friends and family? in books and magazines? in movies and television shows?
- What are your favorite places?
- What are your best and worst memories?
- What lively debates have you participated in recently?
- What political or ethical positions matter to you?
- What are your career goals?

If your teacher asks for a comparison essay, for example, you might write about two bosses you have worked for, two Internet auction sites, two film versions of *Hamlet,* or two television networks' coverage of the same news event: your own preferences should guide your choice.

QUESTION THREE: WHO ARE THE READERS OF MY PAPER?

Writing involves not only your topic and purpose but also your readers' needs. If you're going to instruct them about how to do something, whether it be sewing, skiing, or job hunting, you must consider their skills and preferences. If you want to persuade them to agree with you on a controversial topic like school discipline, capital punishment, or gun control, you should analyze their values and knowledge of the subject.

As part of your prewriting, then, consider the following list of questions about your readers.

- What age are my readers?
- How much education do they have?
- What do they value most?
- What do they fear?
- Will they be seeking my information, or will I have to convince them of its importance?
- How do they feel about my topic? How does it affect them?
- How much do they know about my topic?
- What vocabulary concerning my subject will they already know? Will their definitions agree with mine?
- What examples will they find most disturbing or inspiring?

INVENTION TECHNIQUES FOR DEVELOPING YOUR IDEAS

After considering the three questions, you will be ready to decide on the specific facts and examples that will supply the content of your paper. You are not yet starting a draft or deciding on a specific outline. Instead, you are gathering all the information that may help you to write convincingly. As you proceed, *write as much as you can,* using the invention techniques that seem most helpful to you. You can then choose the best ideas when you write your rough draft.

INSTANT ACCESS

GUIDELINES FOR COLLEGE WRITERS: IDENTIFYING YOUR AUDIENCE

In college you will sometimes be writing for a general academic audience and sometimes for the teacher as audience. In either case, you should consider the reader's needs and interests carefully. The following points should help you to address the reader.

- Both a general academic audience and a teacher as audience have a basic knowledge of politics, history, entertainment, and other fields, but you should not expect them to be experts on your subject. Thus for both audiences you will need to define specialized terminology, explain the historical background of a problem, or summarize the plot of a story.
- Neither audience may already be interested in your subject—assume that you'll need to create an interest.
- These readers will consider your points carefully and critically.
- They appreciate clear writing and a tone that is neither extremely formal nor extremely informal.

COMPUTER NOTE: PREWRITING ON THE COMPUTER

If you prewrite on a computer, you may later be able to paste some of your notes directly into a rough draft. As you work, don't worry about the mistakes marked by grammar and spelling checkers—just write. If these functions break your concentration, turn them off.

Listing

Do you make reminder lists of assignments, errands, or friends' birthdays? Lists can also help you develop your ideas. If you are writing about your father, list thirty of his habits.

If you are arguing against capital punishment, write down all the reasons you oppose it. Lists can be made quickly; they allow you to consider all kinds of facts and possibilities.

Carl Michowski, for example, began work on a paper about a cherished hobby—skateboarding—by creating the following list:

> stance on the board
> doing wheelies and spinning 360s
> the lingo: aerials and ollies, board flips, grinds
> logo shirts and baggie shorts
> skate parks
> half pipes
> almost all skaters are boys and men?
> places to skate
> conflicts with business owners about using sidewalks and parking lots

By doing this quick exercise, Carl discovered many possibilities for specific topics and details.

Freewriting

Put your general topic at the top of a sheet of paper or at the beginning of a new word-processing file, and then freewrite about the topic for at least five minutes. Don't begin a rough draft; just write down in any order—in sentences or in phrases—all the ideas that come to mind. You can decide later where they will go and how to connect them.

To begin work on a paper about starting first grade, Jaime Garcia recorded everything that he could remember:

> O.K., the subject is my first day in first grade. I remember entering the yard to see all these other first graders that I knew from kindergarten, but we were up here with the bigger kids, through a new gate where we would soon line up for a flag ceremony. My mother held my hand tightly because she was much more nervous than I was, I think. I was with my friends (and my mother, who still hadn't left) when I heard a cry, "Where's Jaime?" It was my friend, Micah, from day care, who was new at my school. . . .

Using these remembered details in his final draft will help Jaime create a clear impression for his readers.

Reporters' Questions

Write down your topic, and then ask yourself the six questions reporters rely on in their investigations: *who? what? when? where? why?* and *how?*

Peter Mackey posed the following questions, for example, when he began writing about an Internet auction site:

> *Who* shops at this site? *Who* owns it? *Who* sells the goods? *Who* regulates it?
>
> *What* does the site sell? at *what* prices?
>
> *When* do people visit this site? *When* was the site created?
>
> *Where* do the items come from? *Where* did the site originate?
>
> *Why* is this site popular?
>
> *How* are the items paid for and shipped? *How* are complaints dealt with? *How* profitable is this site?

These questions helped Peter to discover different facets of his topic and possibilities for research.

INSTANT ACCESS

PEER REVIEW QUESTIONS FOR PREWRITING

In class, perhaps in a small group, either tell your classmates about your topic and your prewriting or let them read what you have written. Then, together, consider the following questions:

1. Has the writer chosen a good topic? Does it interest him or her? fit the assignment? seem manageable within the assigned length of the paper? seem appropriate for the audience?
2. What information has the writer gathered? What are the best ideas and details? What other information will be needed to convince readers? What sources might provide these key details?

Reading

You should also investigate your topic by reading about it in books, journals, newspapers, and pamphlets and on the Internet. Even if the teacher did not ask you to write a research paper, relevant statistics or quotations may strengthen your arguments. (For suggestions about secondary research, see **2a, Do Your Research,** pages 30–35.)

Internet Browsing

In addition to using the Internet to locate particular articles and Web pages, you may want to browse a large number of Web sites to get a range of opinions, especially if you are writing on a current social issue. To begin, you can type the appropriate keywords into the text box of a search engine like Yahoo! and then travel through the various links you find.

Some sites won't seem trustworthy and some will repeat the same news, but you will quickly find out what people all over the world believe and desire. (For more on doing research on the Internet, see **2b, Doing Part of Your Research on the Web,** pages 36–40.)

Brainstorming and Peer Review

As you investigate your subject, you might talk through your developing ideas with your classmates. Discussing your progress will help you to focus on what you know and don't know and will enable other students to offer suggestions—as your first readers.

1b Planning

While you are gathering information, you may want to create a preliminary plan for your paper. This section focuses on choosing a main idea and making a visual map or an outline. You can adjust both of these later, as you write.

CHOOSING A MAIN IDEA OR THESIS

A **thesis** is a sentence that presents the main idea of a paper, an idea that every fact and detail should support. Although you may alter your thesis after you write a first draft, formulating it now will help you to organize your ideas.

A good thesis has two qualities:

It states the paper's **topic.**

It states a specific **point of view** concerning that topic.

Topic	**Thesis Statement** *(Topic + Opinion or Attitude)*
1. Waiting tables	Anyone who is thinking about waiting tables should first get acquainted with all the psychological games involved in restaurant work.
2. The law school admissions process	To complete the law school admissions process successfully, students need to give adequate time to choosing schools, preparing for the LSAT exam, and completing the applications.
3. Residence hall visitation policies	To keep students from leaving the residence halls, the university should revise its new visitation policies.

These writers have chosen three of the most common forms of thesis statement:

1. A thought-provoking statement
2. A preview of the essay's structure
3. A call to action

To create a specific thesis, you may need to consider several possibilities and make revisions. The box "Revising Your Thesis Statement" gives examples of how thesis statements can be strengthened.

INSTANT ACCESS

REVISING YOUR THESIS STATEMENT

Thesis: College can teach students so many lessons.

[This thesis may be too big and vague to develop in a short paper. A narrower choice might work better.]

Revision: Our sociology department's new requirement of three hours of community service allows students to apply lessons they learn in their classes.

Thesis: This paper is about capital punishment in our state.

[The writer's viewpoint is unclear.]

Revision: Our state should substitute the sentence of life without parole for capital punishment.

Thesis: The women's soccer team has strengths and weaknesses.

[So does everything—a more specific focus will work better.]

Revision: Key changes in personnel and institutional support will make the women's soccer team the best in our conference this year.

Thesis: More than eight million children are taking Ritalin; prescriptions have quadrupled in the United States since 1990.

[These are facts; the writer needs to state a viewpoint concerning them.]

Revision: Ritalin is being overprescribed to American elementary school students.

CHOOSING AN ORGANIZATIONAL PATTERN

After you have collected your information and written a preliminary thesis statement, you should begin organizing your ideas, a process that will continue as you write a first draft.

Your subject matter and audience will help you to determine which organizational structure will be best for your paper.

Chronological: You may decide to present events or details in a time sequence, from first to last or from past to present. This structure might be appropriate for explaining the law school's admission process.

Spatial: A spatial order helps create an exact picture and thus enables readers to envision a scene: from left to right, top to bottom, or inside to outside. This choice might be best for explaining the appearance of a new athletic training facility for soccer players.

Emphasis or order of importance: You may want to order your details or examples from least important to most important so that your readers encounter your strongest points or recommendations—about capital punishment, for example—right before the conclusion.

General to specific: You may choose to begin a paper with your general judgment—perhaps of current residence hall policies—and then move through the specific cases or points of evidence that support your judgment. This choice provides readers with a clear presentation: an overview of a situation and the thesis concerning it, the details that develop the thesis, and a concluding statement that restates key points and further analyzes the subject's meaning or impact.

Specific to general: You may decide to discuss several Internet auction sites and then move to your general opinion of them. Instead of encountering the thesis first, readers will be actively reviewing the data and coming to the same conclusion that you state.

CREATING A PLAN FOR THE PAPER

After deciding on a thesis and considering possible methods of organization, you may want to create a preliminary structure. Your decisions may change as you write, but a plan will help direct your work. After you have finished drafting, you may decide to make a second plan or outline—to evaluate your product and determine the necessary revisions. (For more on outlining, see **1d, Revising,** pages 18–19.)

To plan your paper, read over your prewriting materials and your thesis, and then try one of the following planning devices: clusters, topic outlines, and formal outlines.

Clusters

To create a cluster, write the main idea or thesis sentence in the middle of a sheet of paper and draw a circle around

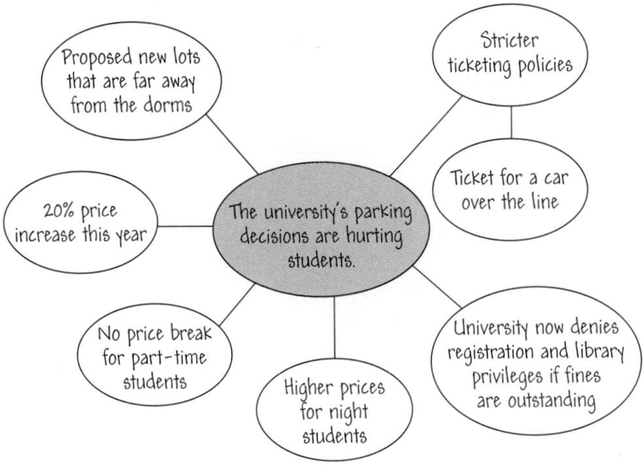

FIGURE 1. Clustering Diagram for Thesis about Campus Parking

it. Then draw lines out from that circle to smaller circles and write in them the major points that will prove or develop that main idea. Repeat this process to list your supporting evidence for these points.

When you finish, you can decide whether you've placed each example or fact under the right topic and whether you have enough detail supporting each major topic. A cluster can also help you decide on the best order for your ideas.

Crystal Jones, for example, created the cluster shown in Figure 1 for a paper on campus parking. After she completed the cluster, she realized that she needed more information about the location of the new parking lots. She also saw that several of her complaints concerned pricing, and thus they might be grouped together in a paragraph.

Outlines

If you feel fairly sure about the order of your main points, you may prefer simply listing them instead of creating a cluster. A topic outline, which you can create quickly and modify as you write, provides a general plan to follow.

The more details you include, the clearer your course will be. Win Tran, for example, made this quick outline before she started writing a paper on the women's soccer team.

```
Thesis: Key changes in personnel and institu-
tional support will make the women's soccer team
the best in our conference this year.
A new coach
   Coach Haskins's success at other schools
   Her defensive strategies
New players
   Trudy Parnell at halfback
   Carmen Garcia at forward
The athletic department's increased commitment
   The new scholarship program
   A better practice facility
   Better arrangement of the playing schedule
```

INSTANT ACCESS

PEER REVIEW QUESTIONS FOR PLANNING

Along with sharing your prewriting with your peers, you may also want to show them your preliminary cluster or outline, talking them through each level. Then they can consider the following questions:

1. Does the outline cover the points necessary to support the thesis?
2. Should anything be added, moved, or omitted?

You can use your word processor's outline template to make an outline others can read easily.

1c Drafting

Once you have considered your subject, audience, thesis, and organization, you will be ready to write a rough draft. In the first draft, your goal should be to develop the main idea of the paper, to put the major points in order—and not much more. Try to write quickly, getting down lots of words and not worrying over each paragraph and sentence. You want to produce not a finished product but a draft (from an Anglo-Saxon word meaning "to draw or sketch"), a preliminary version that you can enlarge upon through revision.

"How can I know what I think until I see what I write?" asked novelist E. M. Forster. By taking chances with this first draft and letting the writing flow, you can find out what you think and how best to say it.

FINDING THE BEST TIME AND PLACE

Before you begin your draft, think about what will help you complete it in one sitting. Does some background noise—perhaps a radio playing in your room—help you concentrate? Or do you like the quiet of a library carrel or a secluded area of the park? Do you need an early-morning burst of energy or late-night solitude? Think back to where and when you wrote a successful paper: early morning in your room, late afternoon in the back booth at McDonald's, or late night at the computer lab. If possible, return there to draft your next paper.

Whatever your favorite writing spot and time, give yourself enough uninterrupted time—at least an hour—to complete the draft. If you have to stop without finishing, you may forget some of what you planned to say.

COMPUTER NOTE: DRAFTING ON THE COMPUTER

If you began by taking prewriting notes on a word processor, you may find that you can start a rough draft with those notes. By cutting and pasting, you can easily move sections of your prewriting into a draft or into an outline in your word processor.

As you write a draft, you should be concentrating on your ideas. You might want to turn off your word processing program's grammar and spelling checkers so that you don't become distracted by them and begin focusing on individual words. You might also try dimming your screen or looking away from it, down at the keys or at your notes, so that you can keep thinking about the flow of ideas instead of fiddling with individual sentences.

STARTING YOUR FIRST DRAFT

Although you are trying to produce a complete draft, you don't have to begin at the beginning and write to the end. If you are most confident about some of your supporting data, you can skip the introduction and plunge in at the second or third paragraph. If you have a strong message for the reader, you can begin with the conclusion.

WRITING QUICKLY

As you proceed, use your plan or outline but don't be controlled by it. If new ideas occur to you that don't seem to fit, write them down anyway to ensure that you don't forget them. In fact, try to get down every point that supports your thesis.

As you work, try to enjoy the writing. This time is for you to explore creative options; nothing you write can be wrong. Ignore the voice inside that says "This is too short," "This sentence sounds stupid," or "This part isn't clear"; revising and proofreading will come later. Your product may be—even should be—uneven and imperfect.

INSTANT ACCESS

OVERCOMING WRITER'S BLOCK

If you have trouble putting words on paper, you might consider the following advice:

Don't expect perfection. View a drafting session as a chance to write whatever comes to mind, without expecting a finished product.

Try to imagine your audience. Speak to them informally, directly, in your draft.

Avoid staring at the blank page. Look instead at your notes and outline.

Don't make yourself start at the beginning. If you feel more sure about a later paragraph, start there.

Try soft music. Something rhythmic may get you into the flow of writing.

GETTING UNSTUCK AND RESTARTED

You may be able to keep writing smoothly, without any breaks. Or you may get stuck and feel unable to go on. To get unstuck, return to your prewriting and outline notes or reread what you have written so far—to jar your memory or reveal a new angle.

If you realize you don't have enough information about a particular point, leave a dash—or write down the question that you will need to answer—and keep going. But if this missing fact or opinion could change the entire paper, write down the rest of your ideas quickly and then return to the prewriting stage to continue investigating your topic.

**COMPUTER NOTE:
USING FORMAT OPTIONS WHILE DRAFTING**

When you draft on a computer, you can use capital letters, italics, or highlighting to note questions you still need to answer or points you have not yet covered.

BEFORE LEAVING THE DESK

Before you leave your first draft, you might make some notes to guide your revisions. Jot down the points that need more research, possible changes in organization, or another good idea that has just come to you.

Then, rejoice. You have created a complete draft of the paper. You are not still pondering the second sentence of the introduction or avoiding your assignment by sharpening pencils or doing your laundry. You will make changes—there is more work to be done—but you should feel a real sense of accomplishment.

1d Revising

Revising means "reseeing" your work with the purpose of making a draft into the best paper possible. To improve your work, you should begin with the larger issues of meaning and structure and then move to each paragraph and sentence. (See **1e, Finishing,** pages 27–29, for more on when and how to proofread.)

**COMPUTER NOTE:
REVISING ON THE COMPUTER**

Computers make the mechanics of revising easy. You can add, delete, and move pieces of text without any retyping. Before you start, make a file copy of your original draft in case you find that you want to return to something that you have deleted. If you are having trouble evaluating your argument, you might try printing the draft and reading the paper copy: some writers have difficulty analyzing the overall structure when they can only see a few paragraphs at a time.

REVISING: THESIS AND STRUCTURE

The first step in revision is to reread the whole, without stopping to make corrections. Try to read as though you are your intended readers, imitating their knowledge and interest level. You can also use the questions in the box "Peer Review Guidelines for Revision" to start evaluating and revising your own draft, as well as those of your classmates.

Evaluating Your Thesis and the Supporting Information

Let's suppose that your rough draft has a general thesis, like this one chosen by Lyn Hartsell for the purpose of informing other students about planning a beach vacation:

> **Original Thesis:** `To have a good beach vacation, tourists need to consider changing environmental conditions during the summer.`

As Lyn reviewed her draft and worked with her peer group, she recognized that she was not writing about beaches generally, but about North Carolina beaches. And, although she had written a few sentences about the entire summer, most of her information concerned late August. She thus chose a new, more specific thesis:

> `Because of environmental changes that have occurred in the past three years, tourists should avoid the North Carolina beaches in late August.`

Lyn's next step was to decide whether she had all the information she needed to support this revised thesis. If more details seemed necessary, she could return to the prewriting questions and invention techniques discussed in **1a, Prewriting,** pages 5–10.

Evaluating Your Organizational Pattern and Outline

After evaluating your thesis, you may need to reorganize your information, deciding on the best order for your main ideas. (See **1b, Planning,** pages 10–14, for more information on organizational patterns and outlines.)

As Lyn continued her revising work, she omitted a few undeveloped paragraphs about other months and about tourism generally and then began considering how to organize all the details that would support her new thesis. When she reviewed the organizational patterns listed on page 12, she decided on a general-to-specific pattern, placing her main assertion in the introduction and creating paragraphs to develop each supporting point:

Thesis: Because of environmental changes that have occurred in the past three years, tourists should avoid the North Carolina beaches in late August.

Paragraph 1

The beginning of the hurricane season has in recent years brought huge clumps of seaweed to the shore in late August.

Paragraph 2

Mosquitoes, spawned in standing water at coastal construction sites, also come out en masse at that time.

Paragraph 3

Stinging jellyfish, called sea nettles, come into shallow waters in late August to feed on plankton, a food source that has been greatly increased by recent beach dredging.

REVISING PARAGRAPHS

Along with the thesis and the overall structure, you will want to consider each paragraph of your paper. In the first draft, some paragraphs may consist of one undeveloped idea or several ideas placed together without a clear connection. When you revise, you will need to make sure that each paragraph clearly presents information about one part of your argument. You may need to work on

choosing a clear topic sentence,
developing that main idea thoroughly, and
presenting the supporting information in a unified format.

INSTANT ACCESS

STRATEGIES FOR WRITING INTRODUCTIONS

Describe a general problem.
Provide historical information.
Tell a relevant story / cite a particular case.
Address your readers directly.
State the sides of a debate.
Use a relevant quotation.

INTRODUCTIONS TO AVOID

1. Avoid the flat announcement that "The purpose of this essay is . . ." or "This paper will be about . . .". Stating the obvious will not engage your reader.
2. Don't start with "According to Webster . . ." or another form of dictionary definition. This type of lead-in has been overused, and it rarely adds much to the essay.
3. Don't apologize for your opinions or level of knowledge with a phrase like "I'm not sure, but I think . . .". State your ideas with confidence.

Choosing and Placing the Topic Sentence

A topic sentence presents the paragraph's main idea and controls the rest of its contents: every sentence in the paragraph should support this main assertion. Your revisions may involve strengthening each topic sentence to ensure that it states one main idea, eliminating details that don't support that idea, and including more details to back up that one assertion per paragraph.

Most frequently, the topic sentence begins the paragraph, giving the reader a clear idea of what will follow, as in this paragraph about settling America. (The topic sentence is italicized for emphasis.) Notice how each sentence focuses on the specific topic, the role of women in the new settlements:

> *Women were an integral part of the permanent settlements in the New World.* When men traveled alone to America, they came as fortune hunters, adventurers looking for a pot of gold; such single men had no compelling reason to establish communities. Women acted as civilizers for men living alone in the wilderness. Where there were women, there were children who had to be taught. There was a future—a reason to establish laws, towns, churches, schools. The organizers of Virginia understood as much when they sought to attract

women to their colony so that the men who came "might be faster tied to Virginia." The labor provided by a wife and children also helped transform the forest into farmland. In the early days of the Georgia settlement the proprietors advertised for male recruits with "industrious wives."

—Carol Hymowitz and Michaele Weissman, *A History of Women in America*

Sometimes the topic sentence comes last, to sum up the paragraph's contents. The reasoning proceeds from facts or examples to the main idea that they all support, as in this paragraph about campus parking (the topic sentence is italicized for emphasis):

When students returned to school this fall, they were greeted by new pricing policies for parking. All students found that prices had increased twenty percent even though the university had added no new lots or lighting that might explain an increase. Night students and part-time students, who are usually just on campus for three or four hours at a time, now must pay as much per day as full-time day students. Those who live on campus are being charged an additional ten percent for guaranteed parking near their residence halls. If they choose to skip this fee, they have to pay a dollar to take a shuttle from a faraway lot to their room, a necessity at night when the campus is not safe. *All of these measures prove that the university's only concern is making a profit from students, not offering them a fair price or a safe service.*

—Crystal Jones, student

In other paragraphs, the writer implies but does not specifically provide a topic sentence. Here, Naomi Wolf never directly states her strong dislike for the intimidation of women at department store cosmetics counters, but each sentence supports that claim.

On either side of her are ranks of angels—seraphim and cherubim—the "perfect" faces of the models on display. Behind them, across a liminal counter, stands the guardian angel. The saleswoman is human, she knows, but "perfected" like the angels around her, from whose ranks the woman sees her own flawed face, reflected back and shut out. Disoriented within the man-made heaven of the store, she can't focus on what makes both the live and pictured angels seem similarly "perfect": that they are both heavily lacquered. The lacquer bears little relation to the outer world, as the out-of-place look of a fashion shoot on a city street makes clear. But the mortal world disintegrates in her memory at the shame of feeling so out of place among the ethereal objects. Put in the wrong, the shopper longs to cross over.

—Naomi Wolf, "Faith Healers and Holy Oil: Inside the Cosmetics Industry"

INSTANT ACCESS

STRATEGIES FOR WRITING CONCLUSIONS

Discuss the results or future impact of your subject.

Provide a call for action or an attitude change.

Use a relevant quotation.

Return to the story or case with which the essay began.

CONCLUSIONS TO AVOID

1. Avoid the flat statement "In conclusion . . .".
2. Don't simply restate your thesis or introductory paragraph. Your conclusion should refer to material presented in your body paragraphs—and its larger meaning.
3. Don't start off in an entirely new direction: the conclusion should further develop the content of the essay.

Developing the Main Idea

As you revise each paragraph, you may want to rely on the following development strategies:

Describe a person, place, or scene.

Provide facts and statistics.

Give examples.

Make comparisons.

Discuss causes and effects.

REVISING SENTENCES

Your first draft probably contains awkward or wordy sentences that reflect your initial attempt to get ideas on paper. After working with your thesis, organization, and paragraphing, you can focus on sentence structures and word choices that will make your writing more vivid and exact, more effective for the reader.

Prefer Active Voice

When you write a sentence in the **active** voice, the subject does something and the verb tells what the subject did. The action is straightforward through the sentence, from beginning to end.

Active Structures

Subject	*to verb*	*to object*
The girl	hit	the ball.
The student	reviewed	her course notes.

The **passive** sentence is the reverse of the active. In the passive sentence, the verb explains something that is *done to* the subject. The doer may or may not be named in the sentence. The flow of the passive sentence is backward.

Passive Structures

Subject	*having something done to it (verb)*	*by agent (sometimes omitted)*
The ball	was hit	by the girl.
The course notes	were reviewed	by the student.
The application	was filled out.	

All passives consist of a form of the verb *to be* (am, is, are, was, were, being, been) plus a past participle. (A *past participle* is the form of a verb that can fill the empty slot in this sentence: "I had ________ it.")

A passive verb may be acceptable if the actor or agent is either well known or unimportant:

➤ **Bill Clinton *was reelected* president in 1996.**

➤ **Sidney *was buried* in the family plot next to his wife.**

Additionally, you may choose the passive if you want to avoid casting blame:

➤ **Three bicycles and a skateboard *were left* in the yard.**

Generally, however, you should avoid passive structures because they make writing wordy and confusing. Active voice produces vigorous and direct statements.

Once you recognize a sentence as passive and decide to change it, you can create an active sentence by finding the doer (or inserting one) and turning the sentence around:

Changing Passive to Active

Passive	*Active*
Houses *were destroyed* by the storm.	The storm destroyed houses.
Your proposal *has been turned down.*	Our committee turned down your proposal.
The cake *was eaten* by me.	I ate the cake.

Avoid *It . . . That* Sentences

Some sentences wander aimlessly, taking too long to make a point and thus destroying the flow of ideas. These sentences often contain unnecessary *it . . . that* constructions:

➤ **~~It seems to be the fact that t~~** *T* **his dog ~~has~~** *seems to have* **worms.**

➤ **~~It is true that t~~** *T* **he residence halls are no longer popular with juniors and seniors.**

Eliminate Forms of *Be* and Other Weak Verbs

In first drafts, writers often choose constructions containing weak verbs, especially forms of *be* (*am, is, are, was, were, been, being*). But in a final draft, a succession of sentences with *be* verbs can be vague and monotonous.

You can easily eliminate one use of *be* that wastes words and delays the action: the *there is* structure.

➤ **~~There is o~~** *O* **ne camper ~~who~~ hates milk.**

➤ **~~There was a~~** *A* **man ~~lurking~~** *lurked* **in the shadows.**

You can eliminate other *be* verbs by making more specific choices. If you say that "the man was in the gym," your reader knows very little. Did he hang from the ceiling? slump in a chair? Think of the different impressions you can create with *strolled, ambled,* and *limped along* to describe the man walking in the gym. Many writers pick the most obvious choice in a first draft but decide on more specific verbs as they revise.

Eliminate Nominalizations

To make your sentences more concise, remove nominalizations—nouns created from verbs—because they can lead to wordiness and a plodding tone:

➤ **The two leaders ~~held a discussion concerning~~** *discussed* **several peace alternatives.**

➤ **The director ~~made a recommendation~~** *recommended* **that the student assistant be rehired.**

Other common nominalizations include *give encouragement, make a payment, have admiration,* and *make a judgment.*

Use a Noun after *This*

You may want to use the word *this* to refer to ideas that you have mentioned in previous sentences or paragraphs. But *this* should not be used by itself; instead, it should always be followed by a noun so that the reference cannot be misunderstood. When *this* is the first word of a sentence, you may be able to incorporate the entire idea of that sentence into the preceding one (as in the second example):

➤ **That dealership charges high prices for repairs and doesn't stock parts for older cars. This** ^*poor service* **has caused many loyal customers to consider a competitor.**

➤ ^*Chandra's refusal* **~~Chandra refuses~~ to bring her boyfriend over for dinner~~. This~~ has insulted her family.**

Eliminate Empty and Wordy Phrases

You can also write more effectively by avoiding long phrases that provide little information. In the list that follows, the single words on the right can replace the wordy expressions on the left:

Wordy Phrase	Replacement
along the lines of	like
at all times	always
at this point in time	now
because of the fact that	because
by means of	by
due to the fact that	because
for the purpose of	for
for the reason that	because
have the ability to	can
in a great many instances	often
in order to	to
in spite of the fact that	although

INSTANT ACCESS

PEER REVIEW GUIDELINES FOR REVISION

Just as your classmates can help you as you prewrite, plan, and begin revising, they can also read your second or third draft. Ask the students who read your paper in class or lab sessions to respond to the following questions that will help you assess your work.

REVISION CHECKLIST

A. Thesis and Structure

- What is the thesis? Does it clearly state the writer's subject and an attitude or opinion concerning it? Will it be clear and convincing to the reader?
- Does the body of the essay support this thesis? Does the supporting evidence seem to be in an effective sequence? Should any information be moved, added, or omitted?
- Would any other organizational structure be a more effective choice?

B. Paragraphs

- Does the introduction explain the thesis, involve the reader in the subject, and provide necessary background information?
- Does each body paragraph clearly relate to the thesis? Does each paragraph have a clear topic and topic sentence?
- Does each body paragraph contain enough details, examples, or reasons to support its topic sentence?
- Is each paragraph unified?
- Does the conclusion state a judgment, provide a call to action, or forecast future events?

C. Sentences

- Has the writer avoided using ineffective passives and *it . . . that* sentences? Should the writer eliminate nominalizations, *is* verbs, and wordy phrases?
- Are the sentences clear and vivid?

1e FINISHING

Once you have completed your revisions, you will be almost ready to turn in your work. At this stage, you are probably tired of everything about your paper and unwilling to do much more work. But don't get impatient, or you may turn in work with good content and organization that receives a low grade because of errors in grammar, spelling, and typing. Finish your work by proofreading carefully and preparing an attractive manuscript.

PROOFREADING

Before you turn in your paper, proofread it carefully to make sure that the text is error-free.

When to Proofread

Begin to proofread when you are finished writing and revising. You may want to take a break first so that you can return to the task as though you were another person, reviewing a piece of writing you had not seen before.

Allot enough time for proofreading, at least half an hour for a short paper. If you wait until five minutes before class to do a quick proofreading, the teacher will probably return the paper to you with at least several errors marked. Instead of rushing, you should take proofreading seriously.

How to Proofread

To proofread successfully, quit thinking about the ideas and focus on the grammatical correctness of each sentence and the spelling of each word. Try the following techniques to turn yourself from writer into proofreader.

Read Out Loud

If you read the paper silently, you will be remembering what you *meant* to say and will imagine you see words on the page that aren't there. Reading the material out loud slowly will help you to focus on what is really there, on each word and each mark of punctuation.

Read Paragraphs Out of Order

Another helpful technique is to read paragraphs out of order: perhaps the third and then the second or the fifth

INSTANT ACCESS

COMPUTERIZED PROOFREADING TOOLS

USE COMPUTERIZED GRAMMAR CHECKERS—CAUTIOUSLY

You can check your grammar by using a computerized grammar or style checker. These programs usually isolate spelling errors, grammatical errors, and poor stylistic choices such as passive constructions and overly long sentences. Some also explain grammar rules.

Grammar programs have limitations, however. Even if you agree with the program's analysis of an error, perhaps in subject-verb agreement, you may want to choose another method of correcting it: the checker may suggest changing the subject and verb to the singular, for example, when you meant for them to be plural. You may have purposely chosen to express a complex idea in a lengthy sentence and thus may decide to keep a sentence that the program flags as incorrect. You should also realize that these checkers do not recognize every error. You will still need to review your sentences carefully.

USE COMPUTERIZED SPELLING CHECKERS—CAUTIOUSLY

If you use a computerized spelling checker, you need to recognize its limitations as well as its strengths. Instead of identifying all errors, a spelling checker points out words that are not in its dictionary. If the computer tells you that a proper noun is "misspelled," it may simply mean that the term is not in its dictionary. Verify these spellings in another source. If any other word is tagged that you think is correct, look it up in a dictionary.

Because the spelling checker tells you only whether a word is in its dictionary, it cannot determine whether you have used the wrong word, such as *affect* for *effect* or *there* for *their.* After you use a spelling checker, you should also proofread for this type of error. (For help with spelling, see **19s, Spelling** in Part Three, pages 273–77.)

paragraph. This method will force you to look carefully at the actual words and sentences instead of at your ideas.

Use a Ruler or a Pencil as a Marker

Place a ruler or a pencil below a sentence and then look at that one sentence before moving the marker down the page to the next one. This technique will stop you from reading and thinking ahead and thus will help you to concentrate on sentence structure and words.

INSTANT ACCESS

PEER REVIEW AND PROOFREADING

You may have noticed that you can more easily locate errors in someone else's paper because you do not know what the writer intended to say—you are reading what is really there. You may, therefore, want to exchange papers with a classmate or see a tutor—after you have checked everything yourself.

PREPARING THE FINAL MANUSCRIPT

When the paper is finished, you should present it to the teacher as the polished work that it is. The final paper layout, like the proofreading, should indicate the care you have taken. Teachers don't like to receive papers that are written on spiral pads, in illegible handwriting, or in a very faint computer print; that have no page numbers; or that have writing on the back of the page. They want manuscripts to show that students have taken the assignment seriously. For help with preparing your manuscript, see Sections 3 to 5 on documentation styles (MLA, APA, and *Chicago Manual of Style*) as well as **6a, Document Design Principles,** pages 110–13.

2

RESEARCH WRITING

For many assignments, you may need to do research on the Web or in the library. The following sections will help you to find, evaluate, quote, and cite these sources.

2a Do Your Research

USE GENERAL AND SPECIALIZED REFERENCE TOOLS

You may want to read several overviews of your subject—to learn about its history, the key facts, the major controversies concerning it, and principal figures involved with it. The following discussion will acquaint you with some of the most helpful reference tools available either in the library or on the Web.

Specialized Encyclopedias

You can often find helpful information in general encyclopedias such as *World Book* and *The New Encyclopedia Britannica,* which are written for a general audience and cover a wide variety of subjects. The full text of *Encyclopedia Britannica* is available online at <http://www.britannica.com/>; the *Columbia Encyclopedia* is available at <http://www.bartleby.com/65/>. There are also encyclopedias devoted to one specific field, era, or country. These specialized encyclopedias, including the ones listed here, provide background information, an overview of current debates, and bibliographies:

Encyclopedia of Beaches and Coastal Environments
Encyclopedia of Black America
Encyclopedia of Chemistry

Encyclopedia of Computer Science and Technology
Encyclopedia of Management
Encyclopedia of World Art
International Encyclopedia of Social Sciences
McGraw-Hill Encyclopedia of Science and Technology

Many specialized encyclopedias are available on the Internet. You can find ones that deal with traditional academic topics, such as religions, computing, or authors' lives, by typing "encyclopedia" and your topic into the text box of any online search engine, such as Google or AltaVista.

Biographical Dictionaries

Biographical dictionaries contain brief accounts of well-known figures, listing such information as family history, educational background, major accomplishments, and significant publications. To find information about the people who played important roles in the events you are studying, you might look them up in biographical reference works such as the following ones:

Current Biography covers people of various nationalities and professions, providing a biographical sketch, a short bibliography, a picture (with some entries), and an address.

Dictionary of American Biography contains short biographies of over 15,000 deceased Americans representing many professions.

Dictionary of National Biography contains biographies of deceased notables from Great Britain and its colonies.

Who's Who offers brief biographies of notable living people. The three major volumes are *Who's Who in America, Who's Who* (primarily British), and *The International Who's Who.* The first two have companion volumes for the deceased: *Who Was Who in America* and *Who Was Who.*

The "who's who" label has also been used on a variety of other biographical and critical sources:

Who's Who in American Art
Who's Who in Economics
Who's Who in Faulkner
Who's Who in Horror and Fantasy Fiction
Who's Who in Military History

On your library's Web site, you may want to use indexes such as Biography Index or Biography Resource Center to locate additional biographic sources. You can also search biographical Web sites such as <http://biography.com>.

Almanacs and Statistical Sources

For the facts and statistics necessary to substantiate your claims, almanacs are an invaluable source. Their tables, charts, lists, and thorough indexes give the researcher quick access to all kinds of data. Here are two examples:

The World Almanac and Book of Facts contains such diverse data as annual gasoline use, college graduation rates, and divorce rates by state. It includes historical as well as current information.

Statistical Abstract of the United States, which is published by the U.S. Bureau of the Census, contains information gathered each year under such categories as energy, education, income and wealth, and parks and recreation. The *Statistical Abstract* and other statistical sources can be found online at <http://www.census.gov/statab/www/>. The U.S. Census Bureau's home page is at <http://www.census.gov/>.

Dictionaries

Unabridged dictionaries enable you to check the meaning of key terms. The *Oxford English Dictionary* explains the derivation of words and their meanings in earlier centuries as well as their current meaning. The complete *OED* is available online at <http://www.oed.com/>. Specialized dictionaries, such as those in the following list, provide full explanations of the specialized terminology of a particular academic discipline or career:

A Dictionary for Accountants
Dictionary for Computer Languages
Dictionary of American Art
Dictionary of Battles
Dictionary of Genetics
Dictionary of Mathematics
A Dictionary of Psychology
A Dictionary of Science Terms

SEEK INFORMATION IN BOOKS

Besides looking in various reference works to get an overview of your topic—and perhaps to narrow it somewhat—you may want to turn to other types of books for more detailed information. The steps outlined in the following discussion will help you find relevant data from books in your library or online.

Find the Subject Heading for Your Topic

You may waste time and miss sources if you head straight to the library catalogue, trusting in your own label for your topic. You should first consult the *Library of Congress Subject Headings,* found in book form, on microfiche, or online by doing a subject search of the Library of Congress catalogue at <http://lcweb.loc.gov/>. This guide will tell you the wording that libraries use to name various topics.

If you looked under *movies,* for example, you would find that the term is not in the system: all entries are under *motion pictures.* If you were looking up *horse racing,* you would see that it is indeed a subject heading and that you could also try narrower terms, such as *doping in horse racing, chariot racing, racetracks, women in horse racing,* and *horse racing—betting.* Consult a librarian if you need help finding the applicable subject headings.

Use the Library Catalogue

After choosing the correct subject terms, you are ready to head to the library catalogue and begin building a list of possible sources, a working bibliography. If the catalogue is computerized, ask a librarian if you will need to use the card drawers to search for older books.

The catalogue lists books by *author, title,* and *subject heading.* For most searches, you will be relying on the subject heading entries, which begin with Library of Congress subject labels. You can save time—and find the best materials—by studying the entries carefully. Each card or computer entry, like the sample in Figure 2, contains a great deal of information that should help you decide whether to choose a book or not.

Here are some of the questions you should ask about each potential source. You may not be able to answer all of them, but the answers you generate will help you decide whether the book will be worth reading.

- **Author's name:** Do you know who the writer is? Have you read or seen entries for other books or articles by the writer? Is he or she a well-known expert?
- **Title:** Does the title seem related to your topic?
- **Publisher and date of publication:** Does the publishing house specialize in serious scholarship, popular how-to books, religious materials? Is it well respected? When was the book published?
- **Number of pages and contents:** How long is the book? Does it contain illustrations, a bibliography, and an index?

Source:	State College Library Catalog
Author:	Thomas, Brian J.
Title:	The World Wide Web for scientists & engineers : a complete reference
Imprint:	Bellingham, Wash. : SPIE Press ; New York : IEEE Press, c1998.
Call No.:	Q179.97.T48 1998
Description:	xv, 357p. : ill. ; 26 cm.
Contents:	Essential tools & applications -- Web authoring & publishing --Searching & researching on the Web -- Science & engineering resources -- Appendix: search engine comparison chart
Subject:	Science -- Computer network resources. Engineering -- Computer network resources. Online data processing. Electronic publishing World Wide Web
Bibliography:	Includes bibliographical references (p. 351-354) and index
Variant title:	World Wide Web for scientists and engineers
ISBN:	0819427756 (softcover) 0780334523 0852969392
Holdings:	Main Library stacks Q179.97.T48 1998
Status:	Checked in

FIGURE 2 Online Catalogue Entry

By studying catalogue entries carefully, you can write down or print out information on only those sources that could be valuable instead of wasting time looking for books that are really brief pamphlets, are outdated, or are hard to use because they don't contain indexes. Many online catalogues can also tell you whether a book is already checked out.

LOOK FOR CURRENT PERIODICAL AND NEWSPAPER ARTICLES

Besides finding relevant books, you should also search for pertinent material from magazines or journals. Magazines include publications such as *Time, The New Yorker,* and other general-interest periodicals that might be sold at a newsstand. Journals—such as the *Journal of Nursing* or *College English*—contain scholarly articles intended for experts. Both types are called periodicals. You may also want to look for newspaper articles to get information on current events and to consider various editorial viewpoints.

To find relevant periodical articles, use the online indexes provided by your library. Each one covers a specific discipline and specific years of publications. Like online library catalogues, indexes like those listed below can be searched by subject keywords as well as by author and title:

ABI/Inform (business)
American Chemical Society Journals (chemistry)
ATLA Religion Database (religious studies)
BasicBIOSIS (biology)
CINAHL (nursing)
ComAbstracts (communications)
ERIC (education)
MEDLINE (medicine)
MLA Bibliography (literary studies)
Philosopher's Index (philosophy)
PsycINFO (psychology)
Sociological Abstracts (sociology)

Along with these specialized indexes, you might try out general indexes or online subscription services such as ProQuest, FirstSearch, LOUIS, and InfoTrac.

To find newspaper articles, use the National Newspaper Index or Lexis-Nexis Academic Universe, which also indexes business and law periodicals.

READ CRITICALLY TO EVALUATE YOUR SOURCES

As you begin reading the books and articles that you gather, carefully evaluate the arguments they present. Consider the following questions to become an *active, critical reader:*

The author: What qualifies the author to speak on the subject? Is the author likely to have a particular bias or be neutral?

The source: Is the publication reputable? biased? Is it recent or out of date?

The audience: To whom does the author seem to be writing? How does the author deal with the audience's opinions and level of knowledge?

The arguments: What points is the author trying to make? Are they all clear, or are some relatively hidden?

The evidence: What evidence is offered in support of each point? Is the evidence sufficient?

2b Doing Part of Your Research on the Web

START WITH SUBJECT TREES

A special Internet resource that works much like an encyclopedia is a *subject tree* (also called a *subject guide*), such as the Virtual Library at <http://vlib.org/>. Subject trees are hierarchical indexes of topics that allow you to begin with a broad category and follow the subject tree's branches down to a specific file. Subject trees can be good places to start your research because you can get an idea of the different types of information available on your topic. In the Virtual Library, there are at least three ways to search: by using the Subject Index on the main page, by searching the Category Subtree, or by searching the Top Ten Most Popular Fields. The Virtual Library's subject tree is shown in Figure 3. To use it, you simply pick the category closest to your topic and follow where the tree's branches lead you.

Today most major search engines have added subject trees to their start pages. If the subject tree on the first search engine you try does not offer a good place to start, you can try the subject trees on other search engines.

MOVE ON TO SEARCH ENGINES

Search engines are large computer programs that allow you to find information through keyword searches. The search engine provides a text box into which you type keywords associated with the information you seek. Most search engines also offer more complex searches with the aid of AND, OR, NEAR, and AND NOT. (Some search engines let + stand for AND and – stand for NOT.) Some offer even more advanced searching, such as limiting a search to specific dates or ranking keywords in order of appearance within the document.

Alta Vista <http://www.altavista.digital.com> indexes sites thoroughly, so it is especially useful for finding sites that contain information on obscure subjects or terms.

Excite <http://www.yahoo.com> ranks the relevance of sites and provides lists of sites similar to ones you have found useful.

Google <http://www.google.com> is one of the most extensive search engines, listing the largest number of Web sites.

HotBot <http://www.hotbot.com> allows you to customize your search by date and domain type (like .edu, .org, or .com)

Infoseek <http://www.infoseek.com> is one of the fastest search engines on the Web.

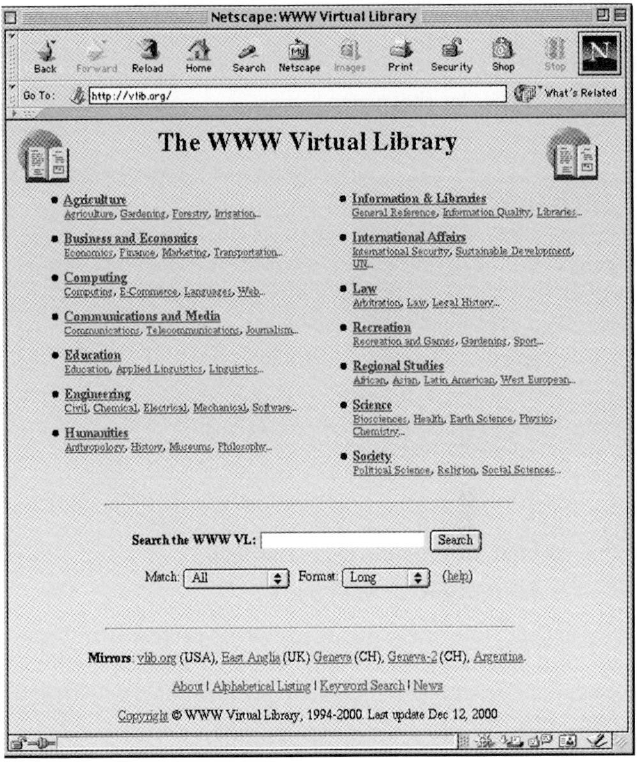

FIGURE 3 The Virtual Library's Subject Tree <http://vlib.org/>. There are more entries under each main heading than the tree's first screen shows. *(Image courtesy of Virtual Library.)*

WebCrawler <http://www.webcrawler.com> is a fast engine that provides summaries of your searches.

Yahoo! <http://www.yahoo.com> offers detailed subject directories, which can help guide your searches, and it allows you to restrict your search by date.

You may also want to try meta-engines, like Dogpile <http://www.dogpile.com> and Metacrawler <http://www.metacrawler.com>, which search many search engines at once.

CAREFULLY JUDGE THE RELIABILITY OF WEB SOURCES

There is no centralized regulating body that concerns itself with the reliability of what is on the Internet. Although the Internet can seem like a really big library, it is much more like a huge open-air market. There's a saying in Latin, *caveat emptor,* or "let the buyer beware." When it comes to doing research on the Internet, the saying should be *caveat internauta,* or "let the surfer beware."

INSTANT ACCESS

EVALUATING WEB SOURCES

Ask these five questions about your Web sources:

- What *kind* of information is on this page?
- What is the *source* of the information on this page?
- How well done is the *design* of this page?
- How *current* is the information on this page?
- How *verifiable* is the information on this page?

What *Kind* of Information Is on This Page?

What Is the Purpose of the Page?

Why is this material being posted? Is it posted as information, as a public service, as a news source, as a research tool for academics, as a personal ax to grind, or as a way to gain attention?

Is the Information on the Page Primary *or* Secondary?

Primary sources, such as a medical researcher's article counting cases of "mad cow" disease in England, report facts directly. Secondary sources, such as an Internet news-group discussion about "mad cow" disease, report and talk about the results of others' research. The papers and reports you write for your college classes need to be based on reliable information. The further your sources are from original research studies, the less reliable the information is.

What Is the *Source* of the Information on This Page?

Who Is the Author or the Sponsor of the Page? Is Contact Information Provided?

A page sponsored by a reputable person or organization should contain various ways to verify the sponsor's identity, such as an e-mail or postal address at the bottom of the home page. A page put up by a person or an organization that does not want to be identified is probably not a good source to cite.

You may also be able to tell something about the reliability of the page by the kinds of links it has. Are they to reputable sources, or are they to biased or anonymous ones? Note also that a tilde (~) in the page's address usually indicates a personal home page and thus may require you to look further to find out about the author's credentials.

Are There Obvious Reasons for Bias?

If the page is presented by the Society for the Preservation of Contact with Martians, you must be suspicious of its claims for the existence of Martians. Is there any advertising? If the page is sponsored by Acme Track Shoes, you may want to be suspicious of its claims concerning these shoes' performance.

How Well Done Is the *Design* of This Page?

How Well Written Is the Page?

Does the page read as if it was created by someone who can speak with an authoritative voice on the topic? Look at the page's grammar—are the language and the style geared toward the intended audience? Who is the intended audience?

How Well Organized Is the Page?

Does the page look as if it was created by a mature, responsible adult? Although the slickest page is not necessarily the most reliable, if the page looks as if it was put up by a twelve-year-old, chances are it was. Is the page easy to navigate? Is the page complete? When was it last updated? Is the information on it current? Are the layout and the design good? How good are the links it provides, and what kinds of sources or links are being used?

How *Current* Is the Information on This Page?

Watch Out for Zombie Pages

Avoid pages that are considered "walking dead" because the person who posted them no longer maintains or updates them. Even though the information is "alive" in that it is still accessible, it is "dead" because it could well be several years old!

How *Verifiable* Is the Information on This Page?

Can You Verify the Information?

Is there some other way to verify the Web page's content? For example, can you check the page's bibliography (if there is one) against your library's holdings or check the information against a source in the library?

Does the Information Lack Credibility?

If you believe that the information lacks credibility, check with a source that is recognized as reputable. For example, if you have to do a project on the latest in cancer research, you can verify your information at major cancer research institutes, such as Mayo Clinic in Rochester, Minnesota, at <http://www.mayo.edu>.

INSTANT ACCESS

TIPS FOR INTERNET SEARCHES

1. **Finding names, words, and phrases:** Remember to use double quotation marks to lock together the parts of a name or the words in a phrase. Otherwise, when you search for, say, *Vanity Fair,* you may get 52,000 hits: all the occurrences of "vanity" and all the occurrences of "fair."
2. **Narrowing a search:** If you are *getting too many hits,* try adding more key words, joining them to the original search with AND (or a + sign).
3. **Broadening a search:** If you are *not getting enough hits,* delete some of your more specific keywords or substitute other, perhaps broader, keywords. If searching using "Kokopelli" does not yield enough sources, try broadening the search to "Hopi religion" or just "Hopi."
4. **Using more than one search engine:** No single search engine searches even half of the Web. So if Yahoo! does not find your information, try AltaVista. If that does not work, try Google. If that does not work, try a meta-engine, such as Dogpile.
5. **Using a specialized search engine:** One interpretation of the future of search engines suggests there will be more and more subject-specialized ones. Try putting "specialized search engines" into the text box of a couple of general search engines and see whether one of the resulting options might be right for your needs.

2c Use Your Sources Effectively

As you work on a paper, you need to decide when to quote directly and when to paraphrase your research sources.

LIMIT YOUR USE OF DIRECT QUOTATIONS

Direct quotations should be used in only three cases:

- when you want to provide a sample of a writing style or dialect,
- when a point is particularly well stated, or
- when the exact phrasing of a policy or a law is important to your argument.

In the following paragraph on the continuing struggle for civil rights, for example, the dialect and speaking style make the quotation powerful:

> Someone said recently to an old black lady from Mississippi, whose legs had been badly mangled by local police who arrested her for disturbing the peace, that the Civil Rights Movement was dead, and asked, since it was dead, what she thought about it. The old lady replied, hobbling out of his presence on her cane, that the Civil Rights Movement was like herself, "if it's dead, it shore ain't ready to lay down."
>
> —Alice Walker, *In Search of Our Mothers' Gardens*

The following excerpts from an essay on bear management at Yellowstone Park provide two examples of effective use of quotations. The first uses a quotation to emphasize a point; the second uses a quotation to explain official policy:

> Shortly after the study team began its real research, disturbing trends began to surface. The life expectancy of bears was dropping, possibly due to poor nutrition as well as human predation. The average life expectancy of bears studied by the Craigheads was more than twenty-five years. But the team was finding no older animals in Yellowstone Park. "Our bears," the report concluded emphatically, "are dying before they reach sixteen and no one knows why."
>
> A bear injury often resulted in a tort claim against the Park. So when a bear hurt someone, the bear was removed, to prevent further liability. The new policy, as described by Starker Leopold and Durward Allen, both of the National Parks System Advisory Board, was to be one that "protects the people from the bears; protects the bears from the people; and protects the National Park Service from tort cases in the event of mishap."
>
> —Alston Chase, "The Last Bears of Yellowstone"

Keep Direct Quotations Short

When you have decided that a quotation will be effective because it meets one of the three criteria, choose as short an excerpt as possible to keep the quoted material from overwhelming your own developing argument.

If you are writing a paper criticizing college testing methods, for example, you might want to quote some of this paragraph written by a college professor who opposes final exams:

> I suspect that most of us have little conviction that six years or six months after the completion of this or that course, its graduates could pass even a vastly simplified examination on its content. What we might call the "retention quotient" is, in most cases, very low indeed. There is much to suggest that because the final examination presents both a frightening hurdle and an obvious terminus, it actually inhibits retention of the course content. Students at least believe so and often speak cynically of final examinations as a kind of intellectual purge by which the mind is evacuated of all the material that has been stored in it during the course.
>
> —Page Smith, *Dissenting Opinions*

Instead of using the entire excerpt, quote only the part that is essential to your argument and then continue with your own writing, as in these examples employing MLA documentation:

> Final exams generally call on students to recall the most basic factual material covered in the course. Perhaps they will make some judgments, but nothing very taxing. One critic has suggested that the traditional exam "actually inhibits retention of the course content" because it focuses on memorizing facts quickly and not on thinking critically (Smith 42).

> Educators have to face the fact that exams do not help students master the material: "what we might call the 'retention quotient' is, in most cases, very low indeed" (Smith 42). The student may not even remember the material several days or weeks later.

(For a full discussion of MLA documentation, see **3, MLA Documentation Style,** pages 54–71. For help with using both longer and shorter quotations, see **19q, Quotation Marks,** in Part Three, pages 264–68.)

Paraphrase Sources When Appropriate

Because you should choose direct quotations only in the three situations mentioned on page 41, you will generally use a paraphrase when you discuss ideas and facts from sources. To summarize or paraphrase, put the author's ideas completely into your own words instead of creating some odd combination of the text's original wording and your own. Such "plagiaphrasing" should be avoided because it is a form of plagiarism. Consider the differences between the adequate and inadequate paraphrases of this direct quotation:

> The new women's social history focuses on the lives led by the majority of women in all strata of society, using material from a wide range of sources, from diaries to demographics.

Inadequate Paraphrase

```
Today's new social history
of women focuses on how
women lived in all segments
of society, using a wide
range of research
materials (Brod 266).
```

Adequate Paraphrase

```
In women's studies classes,
the concern is not with a
few famous historical or
literary women but with the
daily lives of all types of
women, something previously
given very little attention
(Brod 266).
```

A good method of paraphrasing is to read the source material, put the book or article down, think through the information, and then write your own version of it.

INTRODUCE QUOTATIONS AND PARAPHRASES PROPERLY

One method of introducing a quotation or paraphrase is with a *signal phrase,* which explains to the reader the author's authority or intentions and thus makes the excerpt more meaningful. Signal phrases, like those preceding or following the quotations in the following sentences, commonly appear in research papers.

```
"It could not have been worse for local
businesses," wrote economist Marcia Todd of
the World Trade Center bombing.

    Ronald Dore contends that workers are
treated well in companies employing Japanese
management theories: "To equate hierarchy
with domination and exploitation is clearly
illegitimate" (112).
```

> At the conclusion of his editorial, Mayor Giuliani noted a dramatic increase in local traffic and maintained that a new bridge must be built on Hester Street (6).

> In seeking causes for Republican victories in 1994, the Cryer Report argues that "voters who rejected the Democratic party did not necessarily endorse the Contract with America" (4).

When you want the subject matter to remain central, you can also use the *dropped-in quotation or paraphrase* and give the author's name only in the parenthetical reference.

> Young workers "will find the social security system bankrupt when they need it" (Santayana 237).

> More than two-thirds of today's college students feel that graduate study will be necessary for a successful career (Cremedas 92).

INSTANT ACCESS

VERBS TO INTRODUCE QUOTATIONS AND PARAPHRASES

When using signal phrases to introduce source materials, you might choose a more specific verb than *said* to indicate the author's attitude or approach. The following verbs create different meanings that may suit your purposes more specifically:

For an Objective Observer

describes	observes	points out
explains	notes	sees

For Making Conclusions and Defending an Interpretation

analyzes	concludes	maintains
alleges	contends	predicts
assesses	insists	suggests

For Agreement

agrees	concurs	grants

For Disagreement

condemns	derides	opposes
criticizes	objects	warns

AVOID PLAGIARISM

Careful note taking will help you to avoid any possibility of plagiarism in your papers. Failing to cite a source, either intentionally or unintentionally, is called plagiarism. It is a form of stealing because it involves pretending that another person's work is your own.

When you work with source materials, whether they come from the library or the Internet, you must provide a note or citation for the following types of borrowings:

- direct quotations
- paraphrases
- the author's opinions and data
- visuals and graphics

Citations for all four should give appropriate credit to the authors and enable your readers to locate the source. Correct documentation also requires that all direct quotations, placed in quotation marks, be the author's exact words and that all paraphrases be completely in your own words and sentence structure.

The only exception to the requirement to cite all source materials occurs when you decide that a certain fact is common knowledge in the field you are researching. Examples include a president's birth date, a shared definition of a scientific process, and the weight of a certain molecule. If you are in doubt about whether to give credit, however, go ahead and cite the source: no teacher will fault you for being overly careful. (See **2d, Document Your Sources Correctly,** pages 45–53, for more help with citing sources.)

2d Document Your Sources Correctly

If you incorporate quoted and paraphrased materials into a paper, make sure you document those borrowings correctly. (See **2c, Use Your Sources Effectively,** pages 40–45, for a full discussion about avoiding plagiarism.)

WHEN AND WHAT TO DOCUMENT

Here are four guidelines to help you decide when and what to document:

1. If you use the exact language of your source, you must use quotation marks and cite the source.
2. If you decide on a paraphrase and thus put the information completely into your own words, you don't use quotation marks but you do cite the source.
3. If you use information that is not common knowledge, you must cite the source. If the information would not be familiar to someone who has not researched the subject, it is not common knowledge, and you must cite its source, whether you are quoting or paraphrasing.
4. Cite sources for all kinds of borrowings, not just for words and facts. You need to cite the source for anything that is not yours, including drawings, photos, artwork, ideas, and music.

DIFFERENT DOCUMENTATION STYLES FOR DIFFERENT FIELDS

The method for citing sources varies from field to field; different disciplines, even different teachers within the same discipline, have different requirements. In this book we include detailed coverage on three commonly used documentation systems: the MLA (Modern Language Association) style for the humanities, explained in the *MLA Handbook for Writers of Research Papers* (6th ed.); the APA (American Psychological Association) style for the social sciences, explained in the *Publication Manual of the American Psychological Association* (5th ed.), and the *Chicago Manual of Style* (*CMS*), two note styles used in business, history, and many of the hard sciences.

Professors in higher-level classes or classes in other disciplines may expect you to use some other style. One is the Council of Scientific Editors (CSE) style (formerly called the Council of Biology Editors, or CBE style), which is used in the life sciences and described in *Scientific Style and Format: The CBE Manual for Authors, Editors, and Publishers* (6th ed.). Descriptions of many of these documentation styles may be found on the Web simply by typing the name of the style in your favorite search engine's text box. For more on these documentation styles, see the remainder of this section—especially the Instant Access boxes of each style on pages 47–53.

INSTANT ACCESS

MLA STYLE <http://www.mla.org/>

CITATIONS IN THE TEXT (SEE 3, MLA DOCUMENTATION STYLE, pages 55–61)

For Paraphrases and Short Quotations

Enclose short quotations (under five lines of prose or under four lines of poetry) in double quotation marks in your paragraphs. Separate lines of poetry with slashes (/). Cite the author's last name either in your text or in parentheses with the page number (or line numbers of poetry) after the quotation marks and before the period: (Quarles 19).

For Longer Quotations

Double-space longer quotations (over four lines of prose or over three lines of poetry or verse plays) and block-indent them one inch from the left margin, without quotation marks. Each line of poetry should appear on a new line. If the author's name is not given in the text, cite it in parentheses with the page number (or line numbers of poetry) one space after the final punctuation mark.

FOR THE BIBLIOGRAPHY—ENTITLED "WORKS CITED" (SEE 3, MLA DOCUMENTATION STYLE, pages 61–69)

Book

Junger, Sebastian. The Perfect Storm: A True Story of Men against the Sea. New York: Norton, 2000.

Essay or Article within a Book

Faludi, Susan. "The Backlash against Feminism." Connections: A Multicultural Reader for Writers. Ed. Judith Stanford. 2nd ed. Mountain View, CA: Mayfield, 1997. 391-403.

Periodical Article

Stewart, Doug. "Kudzu: Love It—or Run." Smithsonian Magazine Oct. 2000: 64-70.

Newspaper Article

McKinley, James C., Jr. "Performance Enhancers and Baseball." New York Times 11 Oct. 2000: A1.

Electronic Source

Brown, Janelle. "The New, Improved Steve Jobs." Salon.com 11 Oct. 2000. 11 Dec. 2000 <http://www.salon.com/tech/books/2000/10/11/deutschman/index.html>.

INSTANT ACCESS

APA STYLE <http://www.apastyle.org>

CITATIONS IN THE TEXT (SEE 4, APA DOCUMENTATION STYLE, pages 73–77)

For Paraphrases

Cite the author's last name either in the sentence or with the publication date in parentheses after the first reference to the material. Place a comma between the name and the date: (Carlson, 2001).

For Short Quotations (Less Than Forty Words)

Enclose short quotations in double quotation marks in the text: do not indent them separately. If the author's name is mentioned in the text, place the publication date in parentheses after it. Cite the page number(s), using *p.* or *pp.,* in parentheses immediately after the quotation marks. If the author's name is not mentioned in the text, include it with the date and the page number in the parentheses: (Harrelson, 2000, p. 32).

For Longer Quotations (More Than Forty Words)

Double-space long quotations and block-indent them five spaces from the left margin, without quotation marks. Place the page reference in parentheses after the final period, along with the author's name and the date if they did not appear in the text.

FOR THE BIBLIOGRAPHY—ENTITLED "REFERENCES" (SEE 4, APA DOCUMENTATION STYLE, pages 77–85)

Book

Holmes, E. R., & Holmes, L. D. (1995). *Other cultures, elder years.* Thousand Oaks, CA: Sage.

Essay or Article within a Book

Wilkinson, D. (1997). American families of African descent. In M. K. DeGenova (Ed.), *Families in cultural context* (pp. 35-51). Mountain View, CA: Mayfield.

Periodical Article

Tuan, M. (1999). Neither real Americans nor real Asians? *Qualitative Sociology, 22* (2), 105-125.

(APA Style, continued)

Newspaper Article

Sydney Olympics cost $3.5 billion. (2000, October 12). *Sydney Morning Herald*, p. A4.

Electronic Source

Crispell, D. (1996, July). Empty nests are getting fuller. *The Numbers News*. Retrieved July 17, 2000, from the World Wide Web: http://www.demographics.com/publications/fc/96_nn/9607_nn/9607NN11.htm

As section 5 explains, the *Chicago Manual of Style* (*CMS*) presents two documentation styles. Both are briefly reviewed below, and explained in more detail in the full CMS section, which begins on page 88.

INSTANT ACCESS

CMS STYLE 1

CITATIONS IN THE TEXT (SUPERSCRIPT NUMBERS PLUS FOOTNOTES OR ENDNOTES)

Citing Printed Sources

Entry in the Text

Mussolini and Hitler were "natural bedfellows" because they opposed communism and thought alike about socialism.[1]

Footnote or Endnote

1. Harriette Flory and Samuel Jenike, *The Modern World* (White Plains, N.Y.: Longman, 1992), 150.

Subsequent references to the same text need only a partial citation:

Footnote for Subsequent Reference

2. Flory and Jenike, *The Modern World*, 381.

There is a footnote or an endnote entry for every numbered reference in the text.

(continued)

(CMS Style 1, continued)

Citing Electronic Sources

Web documents are cited in the text like print sources, except the footnote or endnote entry also contains the Web address and the date of access.

Entry in the text

According to the *Occupational Outlook Handbook*, employment opportunities for technical writers will be good at least through the year 2006.[1] Therefore, students who. . . .

Footnote or Endnote

1. Bureau of Labor Statistics, "Writers and Editors," in *1998-99 Occupational Outlook Handbook*, (1998), http://stats.bls.gov/oco/ocos089.htm#outlook (accessed June 22, 2002).

The footnote/endnote entry shown above gives full information on the source. If your paper or report is going to include a bibliography (where the entries would also include full information on each source), your instructor may allow you to shorten the footnote/endnote entries.

BIBLIOGRAPHY

Citing Printed Sources

For a Book

Deist, Wilhelm. *Germany and the Second World War*. Oxford: Clarendon Press, 1990.

For a Periodical Article

Jones, Clarence. "Memories of a Confidant." *Journal of Interdisciplinary History* (May 1992): 21-34.

Citing Electronic Sources

For a Book

Bureau of Labor Statistics. "Writers and Editors." In *1998-99 Occupational Outlook Handbook*, 1998. http://stats.bls.gov/oco/ocos089.htm#outlook (accessed June 22, 2002).

(CMS Style 1, continued)

For an Article

Shepherdson, Charles. "History and the Real: Foucault with Lacan." *Postmodern Culture* 5.2. Jan. 1995. http://jefferson.village.virginia.edu/pmc/shepherd.195.html (accessed May 15, 1995).

INSTANT ACCESS

CMS STYLE 2

CITATIONS IN THE TEXT (AUTHOR/DATE)

Citing Printed Sources

Entry in the Text

Mussolini and Hitler were "natural bedfellows" because they opposed communism and thought alike about socialism (Flory and Jenike 1992).

Citing Electronic Sources

The reference in the text would be the same as for printed sources.

LIST OF REFERENCES

Citing Printed Sources

For a Book

Flory, Harriette, and Samuel Jenike. 1992. *The modern world*. White Plains, N.Y.: Longman.

For an Article

Jones, Clarence. 1992. Memories of a confidant. *Journal of Interdisciplinary History*. May.

(continued)

(CMS *Style 2, continued)*

Citing Electronic Sources

For a Book

Bureau of Labor Statistics. 1998. Writers and editors. In *1998-99 occupational outlook handbook.* http://stats.bls.gov/oco/ocos089.htm#outlook (accessed June 22, 2002).

For an Article

Shepherdson, Charles. 1995. History and the real: Foucault with Lacan. *Postmodern Culture* 5.2 (Jan.), http://jefferson.village.virginia.edu/pmc/shepherd.195.html (accessed May 15, 1995).

INSTANT ACCESS

COUNCIL OF SCIENCE EDITORS (CSE) STYLE <http://www.councilscienceeditors.org/>

The Council of Science Editors, formerly the Council of Biology Editors, is preparing the seventh edition of its style manual, *Scientific Style and Format,* for publication. The organization's Web site (<http://www.councilscienceeditors.org>) provides a substantial preview of the manual's forthcoming new edition, including guidelines for citing Internet sources.

CITATIONS IN THE TEXT

Print Sources

Document information within the text by introducing it with the name(s) of the author(s) and ending it with a superscript number that corresponds to a single numbered entry at the end of the text:

According to Kant and Murmu,[1] Indian patients require about four million units of blood per year; this figure is consistent with WHO's standard[2] of seven units per bed.

(CSE Style, continued)

Electronic Sources

World Wide Web documents are cited the same way as print documents; that is, each is assigned a number, and that number is used every time that document is referred to in the text.

FOR THE BIBLIOGRAPHY—ENTITLED "REFERENCES CITED"

The list of sources cited in the text appears at the end of the work, one entry per source, no matter how many times the source is cited in the text. The sources are numbered in order of their *first* appearance in the text. The list is titled "References Cited."

Book

2. Lapierre, D. The city of joy. New York: Warner; 1985. 221p.

Periodical Article

1. Kant S, Murmu LR. HIV-positive blood donors: Can India afford to inform? Lancet 1993; 12(8):342-79.

Electronic Sources

Although the *CBE Manual* does not require the Web address or date of access for electronic sources, adding this information creates a much more useful entry for readers:

1. Reisinger K, Haslinger C, Herger M, Hofbauer H. Biobib—A database for biofuels. Available from: WWW:http://edv1.vt.tuwien.ac.at/AG_HOFBA/Biobib/oxford.htm (Accessed 1999 June 22).

This Web document offers no date of "publication" or latest revision, so that information cannot be included in the entry.

3

MLA Documentation Style

The MLA format for referencing source materials was established by the Modern Language Association. It is used by scholars in English, foreign languages, and other fields of the humanities. The complete format can be found in the *MLA Handbook for Writers of Research Papers,* 6th ed. (New York: Modern Language Association, 2003). The MLA format requires short notes, or citations, put in parentheses within the text and a bibliography, called a "Works Cited" list.

INSTANT ACCESS

MLA DOCUMENTATION MODEL DIRECTORY

3A CITATIONS IN THE TEXT

1. Text Citation for a Paraphrase or Short Quotation from Prose (Five Lines or Fewer)
2. Text Citation for Prose Quotations of More than Four Lines
3. Text Citation for Paraphrases from Poetry and Verse Plays
4. Text Citation for Short Quotations from Poetry and Verse Plays (Three Lines or Fewer)
5. Text Citation for Longer Quotations from Poetry and Verse Plays
6. Text Citation for Nonprint or Electronic Sources

3B LIST OF WORKS CITED

Books

1. Book by One Author
2. Book by Two or Three Authors
3. Book by More than Three Authors
4. Edited Book

(MLA, continued)

5. Translated Book
6. Two or More Works by the Same Author
7. Book by a Corporate Author or Group
8. Book without an Author or Editor
9. Multivolume Work
10. Selection in an Anthology
11. Article in an Encyclopedia or Other Reference Book

Periodicals

12. Article in a Scholarly Journal Paginated by Year or Volume
13. Article in a Scholarly Journal Paginated by Issue
14. Popular Magazine Article
15. Newspaper Article

Electronic Sources

16. CD-ROMs and Other Unchangeable Databases
17. Personal or Professional Web Site
18. Information Database or Scholarly Project
19. Article in Online Periodical
20. Online Book
21. Online Posting

Other Sources

22. Personal Communication (Including E-Mail)
23. Lecture, Speech, Live Performance
24. Film or Television or Radio Program
25. Recording
26. Work of Art
27. Government Document
28. Pamphlet
29. Dissertation
30. Legal Case

3a Citations in the Text

1. TEXT CITATION FOR A PARAPHRASE OR SHORT QUOTATION FROM PROSE (FIVE LINES OR FEWER)

Identify paraphrases of any length or short quotations (no more than four typed lines) from prose by citing the *author's last name* and the *page number*, either in the text of your sentence or in parentheses at the end of the sentence or paragraph drawn from the source. Citations in parentheses are placed inside the period ending the sentence or paragraph.

▪ **If you mention the author's name in your sentence,** you need to provide only the page numbers—in parentheses at the end of the sentence within the period. For page numbers over 100, use only the last two digits of the second number when the two are within the same hundred: 97–98, 272–74, 299–301.

> Richard D. Robinson maintains that in Japan almost all executives began at the lowest positions in their companies: there is only one MBA program because employers do not seek outside applicants for the top jobs (132-33).

> Richard D. Robinson maintains that in Japan "the ratio of a top manager's salary to that of an entry-level blue-collar employee is only 5 or 6 to 1" (133).

▪ **If you do not mention the author's name in your sentence,** put the last name and page numbers in parentheses at the end of the sentence, with no comma between them.

> A survey found that 95% of the members of diet support groups are women (Chernin 196-97).

> Endless dieting is, for millions of American women, a "cause of unremitting pain and shame" (Chernin 204).

▪ **If you are discussing an entire work,** you do not have to cite page numbers.

> In his novel Bonfire of the Vanities, Tom Wolfe probed the emptiness of the highest levels of New York society.

▪ **If you are using more than one work by the same author,** include a shortened version of the title in your citation. Place quotation marks around the title of an article, a short story, or a poem; underline the title of a book or a play. If the citation also includes the author's name, follow it with a comma; there should be no comma between the title and the page numbers.

> Sensitivity training would improve the interview techniques of today's journalists (Clark, "The Underside" 139-40).

> Clark critiques the "journalism of body bags and stretchers, of funerals and sobbing mothers, of missing teen-age girls and bloodstains in car trunks" ("The Underside" 137).

- **If a work has two or three authors,** list them all either in your sentence or in the citation.

> According to Weitzman and Rizzo, only 39% of the people in elementary-school textbook illustrations are women or girls (301).

> Studies show that textbook illustrations still feature girls and women primarily in household scenes (Weitzman and Rizzo 300).

- **If a work has more than three authors,** either include all the last names or the first author's last name followed by *et al.* (from the Latin *et alii,* meaning "and the others"; there is no period after *et*).

> Salholz, Morgan, Greene, and Rosenfeld argue that feminists need to make child-care issues part of their agenda (88-89).

> Wordsworth's Prelude contains a "classic description of the intoxicating spirit of the early 1790s" (Abrams et al. 6).

- **If your citations include two authors with the same last name,** include their full names in the text or their first initials along with their last names in parenthetical documentation.

> Edward Hall believes the English person's reserve stems from the nursery: since English children usually share a room with their brothers and sisters, they develop an internalized "set of barriers" (177).

```
A careful study of child-raising practices in a
certain country can help explain adult behavior
there (E. Hall 176-78).
```

▪ **If a work has no author listed,** cite it by the title (or the first main word or two of a long title). For a journal article or an essay, use the title of the article (or a shortened version)—not the title of the journal or the book—and place these words in quotation marks. If you are citing a book without a named author, use the book title (or a shortened version) and underline it.

```
The new art museum addition combines 18,000-
pound concrete panels with reinforced steel
beams ("Campaign" 14-15).
```

[The complete article title is "Campaign 2000: Creating a Museum for the Future."]

▪ **When you use a quotation from an indirect source,** put the abbreviation *qtd. in* ("quoted in") in the parenthetical reference before the source. In the list of works cited, include only the work that you consulted (which would be Braudel in the following example).

```
According to Restif de La Bretonne, few people
in eighteenth-century France took baths "and
those who did confined them to once or twice per
summer" (qtd. in Braudel 330).
```

▪ **If a concept has two or more sources,** separate them with a semicolon in the parenthetical citation.

```
Critical opinion of Dorothy Parker is hardly
unanimous (Reynolds 317-22; Stoppard and Haynes
98-102; Tompkins 12-36).
```

2. TEXT CITATION FOR PROSE QUOTATIONS OF MORE THAN FOUR LINES

The longer prose quotation, more than four lines, is block-indented one inch (or ten spaces) from the left margin, without quotation marks. Indented quotations are generally introduced by a colon. The entire quotation should be double spaced. If you are quoting one paragraph, or part of one, do not indent the first line more than the rest. If you quote more than one paragraph, the beginning of every paragraph should be indented an additional quarter inch (or three spaces). The parenthetical citation occurs at the end of the quotation *outside* the final period. As with shorter quotations, the citation should include author and page number unless the author's name is mentioned in your text.

> Through his characterization of the Yahoos, Jonathan Swift criticizes the eating of meat:
>
> > I saw three of those detestable creatures, which I first met after my landing, feeding upon roots, and the flesh of some animals, which I afterwards found to be that of asses and dogs, and now and then a cow dead by accident or disease. They were all tied with strong withes, fastened to a beam; they held their food between the claws of their fore-feet, and tore it with their teeth. (275-76)

3. TEXT CITATION FOR PARAPHRASES FROM POETRY AND VERSE PLAYS

As with paraphrases from prose, identify paraphrases from poetry and verse plays by citing the author's last name. Instead of a page number, however, include the line number of the poem, either in your sentence or in parentheses at the end of a sentence or paragraph. For verse plays, include the act, scene, and line number. Hamlet 1.2.129, for example, refers to act 1, scene 2, line 129 of the play.

> In "The Eve of St. Agnes," Keats places humans in the natural world by comparing the bedesman to the owl, the rabbit, and the sheep (2-6).

> Ben Jonson's Volpone criticizes capitalism by naming gold as the modern saint and a money vault as the modern church (1.1.3).

4. TEXT CITATION FOR SHORT QUOTATIONS FROM POETRY AND VERSE PLAYS (THREE LINES OR FEWER)

If the quotation from a poem or a verse play is three lines or less, enclose it in quotation marks and include the lines within your text. If you quote more than one line, separate the lines with a slash (/), putting a space before and after it. Quotations from poetry are referred to by the line number (not by a page number). Quotations from verse plays are referenced by the act, scene, and line number.

> Wordsworth frequently states his faith in the power of the natural world: "To me the meanest flower that blows can give / Thoughts that do often lie too deep for tears" ("Ode: Intimations of Immortality" 203-04).

> In A Midsummer Night's Dream, Shakespeare characterizes the poet as one who creates meaning from "forms of things unknown" (5.1.15).

5. TEXT CITATION FOR LONGER QUOTATIONS FROM POETRY AND VERSE PLAYS

Unless they have unusual spacing, verse quotations of more than three lines should be indented one inch (or ten spaces) from the left margin, without quotation marks or slashes. Each line of poetry should appear on a separate line. The entire quotation should be double spaced. These quotations are generally introduced with a colon. Line numbers can be added in parentheses after the final punctuation of the quotation.

> In "Inventory," Vick Adams describes the regimentation and constant anxiety of modern life:
>
> > He calculates time and a half
> > while eating and watching the news.
> > Drinks minus calories per mile
> > deposits minus withdrawals—
> > computations compounded constantly. (5-9)

6. TEXT CITATION FOR NONPRINT OR ELECTRONIC SOURCES

Provide the author's name (or the title) to direct readers to the entry in the list of works cited. If an electronic source has numbered paragraphs or sections, cite them as you would page numbers for a print source but preceded by "par." or "sec." If there is no numbering, simply cite the source.

> "Sissyhood Is Powerful" is the title of one review of Kimmel's Manhood in America in a popular electronic journal (Garner). The reviewer says that . . . .

3b List of Works Cited

At the end of the paper, beginning on a new page, list all the sources that you cited—not everything that you read. For this list, entitled "Works Cited," use the formats given here for the various types of sources. The second and subsequent lines of each entry are indented half an inch (or five spaces); the entire reference list is double spaced and alphabetized.

BOOKS

1. Book by One Author

> Walker, Alice. The Temple of My Familiar. New York: Harcourt, 1989.

Begin the entry with, and alphabetize it by, the author's last name. If there is no author, the entry begins with the book title, which is underlined.

Provide only the city (and not the state name) for the place of publication unless it is a small city: thus you would use *New York, Detroit,* or *Paris,* but *Lafayette, LA.* If more than one city is listed on the book's title page, use the first one.

Provide a shortened form of the publisher's name. Omit the first name of a publisher (*Holt,* not *Henry Holt*) and *Company, Publisher,* or *Incorporated* at the end. *Macmillan Publishing Company* should be shown as *Macmillan,* and

Oxford University Press as *Oxford UP* (*UP* stands for *University Press*). End the entry with the year of publication.

2. Book by Two or Three Authors

Dreyfus, Hubert L., and Stuart E. Dreyfus. Mind over Machine: The Power of Human Intuition and Expertise in the Era of the Computer. New York: Free, 1986.

3. Book by More Than Three Authors

Belenky, Mary Field, et al. Women's Ways of Knowing: The Development of Self, Voice, and Mind. New York: Basic, 1986.

Instead of using *et al.*, you may give the full names of all the authors in the order in which they appear on the title page.

4. Edited Book

Tompkins, Jane P., ed. Reader-Response Criticism: From Formalism to Post-Structuralism. Baltimore: Johns Hopkins UP, 1980.

5. Translated Book

Barthes, Roland. The Pleasure of the Text. Trans. Richard Miller. New York: Hill, 1975.

6. Two or More Works by the Same Author

Fitz, Earl. Clarice Lispector. Boston: Hall, 1985.

---. "Freedom and Self-Realization: Feminist Characterization in the Fiction of Clarice Lispector." Modern Language Studies 10.3 (1983): 51-56.

7. Book by a Corporate Author or Group

Commission on the Humanities. The Humanities in American Life: Report of the Commission on the Humanities. Berkeley: U of California P, 1980.

8. Book without an Author or Editor

The Chicago Manual of Style. 14th ed. Chicago: U of Chicago P, 1993.

When alphabetizing an entry beginning with a title, ignore an initial *A, An,* or *The.*

9. Multivolume Work

The Entire Set

Neather, Carl A., and George Francis Richardson. A Course in English for Engineers. 2 vols. Boston: Ginn, 1930.

One Volume

Battle, Kemp P. History of the University of North Carolina. Vol. 2. Raleigh, NC: Edwards, 1912.

10. Selection in an Anthology

Vance, John A. "Johnson's Historical Reviews." Fresh Reflections on Samuel Johnson: Essays in Criticism. Ed. Prem Nath. Troy, NY: Whitston, 1987. 63-84.

Place the name of the selection in quotation marks. Place its page numbers at the end of the entry, after a period. Use only the last two digits of the second number when the two page numbers are in the same hundred: 31–89, 212–43, 271–301.

11. Article in an Encyclopedia or Other Reference Book

Signed Article

Harmon, William. "T. S. Eliot." The World Book Encyclopedia. 1992 ed.

With familiar reference books, such as encyclopedia sets, full publication information is not required. With less familiar reference books, provide the full publication information.

Unsigned Article

"The 'Anusim.'" Encyclopedia of Jewish History. Ed. Ilana Shamir and Shlomo Shavit. New York: Facts on File, 1986.

PERIODICALS

12. Article in a Scholarly Journal Paginated by Year or Volume

The entire year's issues are paginated as a unit.

Murphy, Lawrence W. "Professional and Nonprofessional Teaching of Journalism." Journalism Quarterly 9 (1932): 46-59.

Put the title of the article in quotation marks; underline the journal title. After the journal title, provide the volume number and then the year in parentheses. A colon separates the year and the page numbers of the complete article.

13. Article in a Scholarly Journal Paginated by Issue

Each issue begins with page 1.

Cole, Richard R. "Much Better Than Yesterday, and Still Brighter Tomorrow." Journalism Educator 40.3 (1985): 4-8.

Place the title of the article in quotation marks; underline the journal title. Follow the volume number with a period, and give the issue number before the year in parentheses. Put the page numbers of the complete article after a colon.

14. Popular Magazine Article

Weekly Magazine

Borger, Gloria. "Can Term Limits Do the Job?" U.S. News and World Report 11 Nov. 1991: 34-36.

Show the date in day-month-year order after the magazine title, and abbreviate the name of the month. Place the page numbers of the complete article at the end of the entry after a colon. If the article is on discontinuous pages, put a plus sign after the first page of the article rather than listing all the pages: 25+.

Monthly Magazine

Richardson, John H. "Mother from Another Planet." Premiere May 1992: 62-70.

15. Newspaper Article

"Combat Stress in Women to Be Studied for the First Time." Times-Picayune [New Orleans] 11 Jan. 1993: A7.

If the article is signed, the writer's name should be the first item in the entry. If the city's name is not part of the title of a locally published newspaper, add it in brackets after the title.

ELECTRONIC SOURCES

The basic principle for citing electronic sources is that the documentation must be sufficient to allow the reader to retrieve the material; if the database is revisable or temporary, like much that appears on the Internet, the documentation must show both when the material was published and when it was accessed. The documentation guidelines here are from the *MLA Handbook for Writers of Research Papers,* 6th ed. (2003) and the MLA Web page <http://www.mla.org/www_mla_org/publications/style/style_faq>.

16. CD-ROMs and Other Unchangeable Databases

Provide the same publication information that you would for a printed source. In addition, provide the title of the database (underlined), the publication medium (*CD-ROM, Diskette,* or *Magnetic tape*), the name of the vendor (if available), and the electronic publication date.

Hills, Charles. "Ascending the Mountain of Words." New Statesman 16 Oct. 1998: 58. InfoTrac: General Periodical Index. CD-ROM. Information Access. Aug. 1998.

17. Personal or Professional Web Site

Wedemeyer, Bill. The One-Room School Homepage. 21 Mar. 2000 <http://www.msc.cornell.edu/~weeds/SchoolPages/welcome.html>.

Include the name of the site's creator (if given), the title of the site (or a description, such as *Home page,* if it has no title), the name of any institution or organization associated with the site (if relevant), the date of access, and the URL.

18. Information Database or Scholarly Project

Literature, Arts, and Medicine Database. Ed. Dr. Felicia Aull. 38th ed. Jan. 2000. NYU School of Medicine. 21 Mar. 2000 <http://mchip00.med.nyu.edu/lit-med/lit-med-db/topview.html>.

Include the title of the database or project, the name of the editor (if given), the version or edition number (if given), the date of electronic publication or latest update, the name of any sponsoring institution, the date of access, and the URL.

Antin, Mary. The Promised Land. Boston: Houghton Mifflin, 1912. A Celebration of Women Writers. Ed. Mary Mark Ockerbloom. 1999. U of Pennsylvania. 21 Mar. 2000 <http://digital.library.upenn.edu/women/antin/land/land.html>.

To cite a document in an information database or scholarly project, begin with the author's name, the title of the document, and any publication facts given about the print version, if there is one, and the URL.

19. Article in an Online Periodical

Sauer, Geoffrey. "Wireless Eavesdropper." Bad Subjects: Political Education for Everyday Life 48 (Mar. 2000). 21 Mar. 2000 <http://eserver.org/bs/48/sauer.html>.

For articles in online journals, magazines, and newspapers, include the author's name, the title of the article, the name of the periodical, the volume and issue numbers (if given), the date of publication, the page or paragraph numbers (if given), the date of access, and the URL.

20. Online Book

Cather, Willa. O Pioneers! 1913. Alex Catalogue of Electronic Texts. 1992. U of California at Berkeley. 21 Mar. 2000. <http://sunsite.berkeley.edu/~emorgan/texts/literature/american/1900-/cather-o-366.txt>.

Include the author's name, the title of the work, publication information about the printed version (if given), the name of the editor or translator (if there is one), the date of electronic publication (if given), the date of access, and the URL.

To cite a part of an online book (such as a short story or poem), add the name of the part after the author's name.

21. Online Posting

Lachance, François. "Phoenician Disputations." Online posting. 4 Nov. 1999. Humanist Discussion Group. 21 Mar. 2000 <http://lists.village.virginia.edu/lists_archive/Humanist/v13/0251.html>.

To cite a posting to an e-mail discussion list, include the writer's name, the title of the posting, the description *Online posting,* the date the message was posted, the name of the forum (if known), the date of access, and the URL or the e-mail address of the list's moderator.

OTHER SOURCES

22. Personal Communication (Including E-Mail)

Neville, Kate. "Re: A Creole Translation." E-mail to the author. 7 Mar. 2002.

Calabria, Frank. Letter to Mary Calabria. 7 Feb. 1999.

To cite unpublished documents such as e-mail messages and letters, provide the name of the writer, a description of the document that includes the recipient, and the date. For e-mail messages, also include the subject line in quotation marks.

23. Lecture, Speech, Live Performance

Kinstoli, Luigi. "Exploration South." Travel South Convention. Birmingham. 22 Oct. 2002.

If there is no title, use a descriptive label, such as *Lecture* or *Keynote speech,* without quotation marks.

Empyrean Dances. Chor. Edward Stierle. Joffrey Ballet. Opera House, San Francisco. 2 July 1992.

The entry needs to include the site and date of the event, as well as any other pertinent information about originators and performers.

24. Film or Television or Radio Program

Zemeckis, Robert, dir. Forrest Gump. Perf. Tom Hanks, Sally Field, Robin Wright. Paramount, 1994.

TV Nation: Year in Review. Dir. Michael Moore. NBC, 28 Dec. 1994.

Pertinent information, such as performers, writers, and names of series episodes, can be included in an entry; underline the name of a series, and put quotation marks around the title of an episode. If the work of a particular person is the reason for the reference, the entry can begin with that person's name, last name first. Use a comma to separate the person's first name from the rest of the entry.

25. Recording

Verdi, Giuseppe. "Triumphal March." Aïda. Perf. National Philharmonic Orchestra. Cond. James Levine. RCA Red Seal, 1978.

If you are citing an element of a longer work, such as one piece on a CD or in an opera, place its name in quotation marks and underline the name of the longer work.

26. Work of Art

da Vinci, Leonardo. The Last Supper. 1495-1498. Santa Maria delle Grazie, Milan.

The date of creation of the artwork, between its title and the site or owner, is optional.

Shen Chou. Landscape in the Manner of Ni Tsan. 1484. Nelson Gallery-Atkins Museum, Kansas City, MO. The Arts of China. 3rd ed. By Michael Sullivan. Berkeley: U of California P, 1984. 207.

To cite a photograph or slide of a work of art, add the full publication information, including page or slide number, to the artwork information.

27. Government Document

United States. Internal Revenue Service. 1981 Statistics of Income: Corporate Income Tax Returns. Washington: GPO, 1984.

Give the name of the government first (such as United States or New York State), followed by a period, and then the name of the agency. *GPO* stands for *Government Printing Office.*

28. Pamphlet

Careers for the Writing Major. New Orleans: Writing Krewe, 2002.

29. Dissertation

Valenti, Jeanette Y. "Delmira Augustini: A Reinterpretation of Her Poetry." Diss. Cornell, 1975.

The example shows an unpublished dissertation. A published dissertation is cited like a book: the title is underlined, and the publication data appear at the end of the entry, after the year of the dissertation.

30. Legal Case

Loving v. Virginia. No. 388. US1. 12 June, 1967.

Underline, or italicize, the name of the case in the text but not in the list of works cited.

The example here is for a U.S. Supreme Court decision. If your paper cites many kinds of legal documents, consult *A Uniform System of Citation* (Cambridge, MA: Harvard Law Review Assn.) or *The Chicago Manual of Style* (Chicago: U of Chicago P).

3c Preparing Papers in MLA Style

1. Set one-inch margins on the top, bottom, and sides of each page.
2. Number each page, in the upper right corner, one inch from the right and one-half inch from the top. Type your

last name before the number. On a computer, your name and the page number can be placed in the header.

3. You do not need a title page. (If your teacher requires a title page, follow his or her instructions for format). On the first page of the paper, type your name, your instructor's name, the course number, and the date on separate lines beginning at the left margin one inch from the top. Double-space between each line. Then double-space again and type the title—centered—without underlining it or placing it in quotation marks. Then double-space again and begin typing the text.
4. Indent the first word of each paragraph half an inch (or five spaces) from the left; indent block quotations one inch (or ten spaces).
5. Double-space the entire text, including indented quotations and the list of works cited.
6. Use a separate page, at the end of the paper, for your references. Center the words *Works Cited* at the top of the page. Type the first line of each entry an inch from the left margin; each subsequent line should be indented half an inch (or five spaces). Double-space within and between all entries.

Figure 4 shows samples of MLA style for a first page, subsequent pages, and a "Works Cited" page.

Sanchez 3

Works Cited

Abreu, Elinor. "Let a Hundred Search Engines Bloom." The Standard.com. 23 July 2002. 21 Aug. 2002 <http://biz.yahoo.com/st/00723/16775.html>.

Lawrence, Steve, and C. Lee Giles. "Searching the Web: General and Scientific Information Access." IEEE Communications 37.1 (1998):116–22.

Sanchez 2

football fans. The first page of such a search engine is, in computer talk, a "vertically integrated portal"—a *vortal*. *Internet.Com Webopedia* defines *vortal* this way:

> *Vertical Industry Portal* is a portal Web site that provides information and resources for a particular industry. Vortals are the Internet's way of catering to consumers' focused-environment preferences.

Sanchez 1

Ramon Sanchez

Professor North

English 102

25 August 2002

From Portal to Vortal:

Are General Search Engines Putting Themselves out of Business?

One of the dreams of every college freshman is to go to "the big game." Here at State College that means football, with one hundred thousand screaming fans in the stadium, for every home game. As a

FIGURE 4 Sample MLA Pages

4

APA Documentation Style

The APA format for referencing source materials was established by the American Psychological Association. It is used by psychologists, sociologists, and other social scientists. The complete format can be found in the *Publication Manual of the American Psychological Association,* 5th ed. (Washington, DC: APA, 2001). The APA format requires short notes, or citations, put in parentheses within the text instead of footnotes or endnotes. The following section will show you how to create these citations, prepare a bibliography page, entitled "References," and type your paper in APA format.

INSTANT ACCESS

APA DOCUMENTATION MODEL DIRECTORY

4A CITATIONS IN THE TEXT

1. Text Citation for a Paraphrase
2. Text Citation for Quotations of Fewer Than Forty Words
3. Text Citation for Quotations of More Than Forty Words

4B REFERENCE LIST

Books

1. Book by One Author
2. Book by Two or More Authors
3. Edited Book
4. Translated Book
5. Edition Other Than the First
6. Book by a Corporate Author or Group
7. Book without an Author or Editor

(APA, continued)

8. Multivolume Work
9. Essay or Article in a Book
10. Article in an Encyclopedia or Other Reference Book
11. Article in a Scholarly Journal Paginated by Year or Volume
12. Article in a Scholarly Journal Paginated by Issue
13. Popular Magazine Article
14. Newspaper Article
15. Review of Book, Film, or Video

Electronic Sources

16. Internet Articles Based on a Print Source
17. Daily Newspaper Article, Electronic Version Available by Search
18. Article in an Internet-only Journal
19. Report from an Organization, Available on Organization Web Site, No Publication Date Included
20. U.S. Government Report Available on Government Agency Web Site, No Publication Date Indicated
21. Message Posted to Online Forum or Discussion Group

Other Sources

22. Paper Presented at a Meeting
23. Audiovisual Sources
24. Government Document, Research Report, Monograph
25. Material from an Information Service
26. Dissertation
27. Legal Case

4a Citations in the Text

1. TEXT CITATION FOR A PARAPHRASE

In this system, identify source materials that you are paraphrasing by citing the *author's last name* and the *publication date,* either in your sentence or in parentheses. You do not have to cite page numbers for paraphrases. Citations in parentheses should appear immediately after you mention the source or information.

▪ **If you mention the author's name and the publication date in your sentence,** you will not need any additional citation within the text.

```
In a 1983 study, Deborah Mayo began questioning
the scientific validity of experiments involving
laboratory animals.
```

▪ **If you mention the author's last name in your sentence,** place the date of publication in parentheses right after the name.

```
Mayo (1983) questioned the scientific validity of
experiments involving laboratory animals.
```

▪ **If you do not mention the author's name or the publication date in your sentence,** put both in parentheses, with a comma between them.

```
An early study (Mayo, 1983) questioned the
scientific validity of experiments involving
laboratory animals.
```

▪ **If you cite two works by one author published in the same year,** distinguish them by placing an *a* and a *b* after the date within the parentheses. To assign the *a* or *b,* alphabetize the works by title in the list of references.

```
Franklin and Hayes (1992a)
```

▪ **If you cite two authors with the same last name,** use their first and middle initials within the parentheses.

```
(D. G. Mayo, 1983)
```

▪ **If a work has two authors,** combine the names with *and* in your sentence. Use an ampersand (&) instead of *and* in a parenthetical citation.

```
Franklin and Hayes (2001) criticized animal
testing practices in the cosmetics industry.
```

```
One recent study (Franklin & Hayes, 2001)
criticized the cosmetics industry for its
inaccurate and inhumane testing procedures.
```

▪ **If a work has more than two authors,** cite all of them, if there are not more than five, the first time, either in your sentence or in the parenthetical citation. In subsequent references in either location, include only the last name of the first author followed by *et al.* (Latin meaning "and the others"; there is no period after *et*). If a work has six or more authors, use *et al.* after the first author's last name in all references in the text.

First Reference

```
Heinrich, Smith, and Blaine (2002) concluded
that driver-education programs are woefully
ineffective.
```

Subsequent Reference

```
The ineffectiveness of current driver-education
programs concerns insurance companies (Heinrich
et al., 2002).
```

▪ **If a work has no author,** cite it by the first two or three words of the title, starting with the first important word. For a journal article or an essay, use a shortened version of its title—not the title of the journal or the book—and place these two or three words in quotation marks. If you are citing a book, supply a shortened version of its title, italicized.

```
To secure good research assistantships, graduate
students should learn everything they can about
the university's privately funded grant projects
("Getting the First," 2001).
```

[The complete title of the article is "Getting the First Job: Try for a Research Assistantship."]

In *Jobs for Biologists* (1990), students can find tips on landing a job at a zoo or museum.

[The complete title is *Jobs for Biologists in a Changing World.*]

▪ **If you use a quotation from an indirect source,** precede the source information in the parenthetical citation with the words *as cited in.* In the reference list, include an entry only for the secondary source.

▪ **If you cite two or more works by the same author in one parenthetical citation,** give the author's name, followed by the years in chronological order, separated by commas.

```
(Stiles, 1991, 1994)
```

▪ **If you cite two or more works by different authors in one parenthetical citation,** give the works in alphabetical order and separate them with semicolons.

> Several researchers have confirmed Erikson's theory of an adolescent identity crisis (Bryson, 1963; Drummond, 1970; Oliphant, 1968).

▪ **If you cite a personal communication,** such as a letter, an e-mail message, or a telephone conversation, you do not need to include a reference list entry because the information is not accessible to your readers. Cite the communication in the text, giving the initials as well as the last name of your source and as exact a date as possible.

> According to museum official F. Calabria (personal communication, May 22, 2002), the renovations will be completed by 2004.

2. TEXT CITATION FOR QUOTATIONS OF FEWER THAN FORTY WORDS

Shorter quotations should be incorporated within your paragraphs: they should not be indented separately. To document them, include the author's name and the date of publication as you would for a paraphrase, either within your sentence or in parentheses. You should also cite the page number(s), using the abbreviation *p.* or *pp.,* in parentheses immediately after the quotation. If the citation also includes the name or the date, these items are separated by commas.

> Combrinck-Graham (1991) asks the essential question for revamping current counseling techniques: "How can there be family therapy without children?" (pp. 373-374).

> When "Brutus is making his rounds" (Rosenkoetter & Bowes, 1991, p. 277), nursing home patients exercise, converse, and relax with a well-trained dog.

3. TEXT CITATION FOR QUOTATIONS OF MORE THAN FORTY WORDS

The longer quotation, over forty words, is block-indented five spaces from the left margin and typed without quotation marks. The quotation should be double spaced. If you are quoting an entire paragraph, or part of one, do not indent the first line more than the rest. The first line of any subsequent paragraphs within the quotation should be indented an additional five spaces. The page reference (and the author and date, if they are not mentioned in the text) appears in parentheses at the end of the quotation, *outside* the final period. Long quotations are generally introduced by a colon.

```
British researchers began experiments concerning
a gene that may actually determine maleness:
    Tests in mice show that after the gene is
    switched on, a cascade of genetic events
    takes place, and the testes begin to form.
    The testes go on to pump out testosterone,
    which in humans subsequently provokes the
    sprouting of beards, the deepening of
    voices, and the other masculine traits that
    cause anxiety in adolescent boys.
    (Kinoshita, 1991, p. 47)
```

```
Beard (1969) explains the consequences of the
young child's egocentric thinking:
    He attributes life and feeling, in the first
    place, to all objects, though later only to
    those which move; he believes that natural
    objects are man-made and that they can be
    influenced by his wishes or by actions at a
    distance. (pp. 24-25)
```

4b Reference List

At the end of the paper, on a new page, list all the sources that you have cited—not everything that you read. For the entries in this list, entitled "References," use the formats given here for the various types of sources. The second and subsequent lines of each entry are indented half an inch (or five spaces); the entire reference list is double spaced.

Alphabetize the entries by the authors' last names or by the first important word of the title of works that have no author. If two or more works by an author are cited, arrange them chronologically, from the oldest to the most recent. If two or more works by an author were written in the same year, arrange them alphabetically by title and differentiate them by adding a letter after the year (for example, 1989a and 1989b).

BOOKS

1. Book by One Author

> Markel, M. H. (1992). *Technical writing: Situations and strategies* (3rd ed.). New York: St. Martin's.

Begin the entry with, and alphabetize it by, the author's last name. Use initials for the author's first and middle names. If there is no author, the entry begins with the book title.

Place the date of publication in parentheses after the author's name.

Capitalize only the first word of the title, proper names, and the first word after a colon. Italicize the title.

Provide only the city (and not the state or country name) for the place of publication unless it is a small city: thus you would use *Chicago, Detroit,* or *Paris,* but *Monterey, CA.* If more than one city is listed on the title page, use the first one.

Provide a shortened form of the publisher's name, omitting the first name of the publisher (*Morrow,* not *William Morrow*) and *Company, Publisher,* or *Incorporated* at the end (but retain essential words, such as *Books* or *Press*). For example, *W. W. Norton & Company* should appear as *Norton; Harcourt Brace, Publishers* should appear as *Harcourt Brace.* Give the full names of associations and university presses.

2. Book by Two or More Authors

> Holmes, E. R., & Holmes, L. D. (1995). *Other cultures, elder years.* Thousand Oaks, CA: Sage.

3. Edited Book

> DeGenova, M. K. (Ed.). (1997). *Families in cultural context: Strength and challenges in diversity.* Mountain View, CA: Mayfield.

4. Translated Book

Veyne, P. (Ed.). (1987). *A history of private life: Vol. 1. From pagan Rome to Byzantium* (A. Goldhammer, Trans.). Cambridge, MA: Harvard University Press. (Original work published 1985)

5. Edition Other Than the First

Bennett, L., Jr. (1984). *Before the Mayflower: A history of Black America* (5th ed.). Harmondsworth, England: Penguin Books.

If the book is not the first edition, place the edition number in parentheses after the title. For a revised edition, use *Rev. ed.*

6. Book by a Corporate Author or Group

U.S. Bureau of the Census. (1999). *Statistical abstract of the United States, 1999* (118th ed.). Washington, DC: U.S. Government Printing Office.

7. Book without an Author or Editor

The control of the campus: A report on the governance of higher education. (1982). Lawrenceville, NJ: Princeton University Press.

8. Multivolume Work

The Entire Set

Neather, C. A., & Richardson, G. F. (1930). *A course in English for engineers* (Vols. 1-2). Boston: Ginn.

One Volume

Battle, K. P. (1912). *History of the University of North Carolina: Vol. 2.* Raleigh, NC: Edwards and Broughton.

If the volume has its own title, include it after the volume number. (See the earlier entry for Translated Book for an example.) If an individual volume has a different editor or author than the series, give the series editor's name first and then that of the volume editor. Identify the two with the abbreviations *Series Ed.* and *Vol. Ed.* in parentheses after the names.

9. Essay or Article in a Book

Wilkinson, D. (1997). American families of African descent. In M. K. DeGenova (Ed.), *Families in cultural context* (pp. 35-51). Mountain View, CA: Mayfield.

The selection title is written without quotation marks and with lowercase letters (except for the first letter of the title, of proper names, and of a subtitle after a colon). The book title is in the same lowercase format but is italicized. Place the page numbers for the complete essay or article in parentheses, preceded by *p.* or *pp.*, after the book title.

10. Article in an Encyclopedia or Other Reference Book

Signed Article

Ives, S. (1990). Parts of speech. In *Collier's encyclopedia* (Vol. 18, pp. 487-490). New York: Macmillan.

Unsigned Article

Gypsies. (1978). In L. Shepard (Ed.), *Encyclopedia of occultism and parapsychology* (Vol. 1, pp. 400-401). Detroit: Gale Research.

PERIODICALS

11. Article in a Scholarly Journal Paginated by Year or Volume

The entire year's issues are paginated as a unit.

Battaglia, D. M., Datteri, D., & Lord, C. (1998). Breaking up is (relatively) easy to do: A script for the dissolution of close relationships. *Journal of Social and Personal Relationships, 15,* 829-845.

Do not italicize the title of the article, and do not capitalize it (except for the first word, proper names, and the first word after a colon).

Capitalize and italicize the title of the journal.

Italicize the volume number. It is followed by a comma and the complete page numbers of the article.

12. Article in a Scholarly Journal Paginated by Issue

Each issue begins with page 1.

Blanton, J. S. (2000). Why consultants don't apply psychological research. *Consulting Psychology Journal: Practice and Research, 52* (4), 235-247.

Italicize the volume number. It is followed by the issue number in parentheses (not underlined), a comma, and the complete page numbers of the article.

13. Popular Magazine Article

Weekly Magazine

Wolk, D. (2000, October 16). Comics: Not just for specialty stores anymore. *Publishers Weekly, 247* (42), 36-43.

Monthly Magazine

Stewart, D. (2000, October). Kudzu: Love it—or run. *Smithsonian Magazine, 31,* 64-70.

In citations for popular magazines, the volume number follows the magazine title.

14. Newspaper Article

Zernike, K. (2000, June 29). Caps, gowns, diplomas: On to kindergarten! *New York Times,* pp. A-1, B-6.

Give all page numbers, separated by commas, for articles that appear on discontinuous pages. Use *p.* or *pp.* before the page numbers. For an *unsigned article,* start the entry with the title, and alphabetize it by the first significant word. In the parenthetical citation in the text, use a shortened version of the title that starts with that word; enclose the title in quotation marks, and capitalize the first letter of all important words: ("Caps, Gowns, Diplomas," 2000).

15. Review of Book, Film, or Video

Mackey, M. (1995, February 12). Don't know much about history [Review of the book *Lies my teacher told me: Everything your American history textbook got wrong*]. *San Francisco Sunday Examiner/Chronicle Book Review*, pp. 3, 8.

Identify the type of medium (book, film, video, or television program) in brackets.

ELECTRONIC SOURCES

There are two goals for references to electronic sources of information:

- to give the author credit
- to make it possible for the reader to find the material

16. Internet Articles Based on a Print Source

O'Barr, W., & Conley, J. (2000). When cultures collide: Social security and the market [Electronic version]. *Journal of Psychology and Financial Markets*, 1, 92–100.

In this example, you are simply indicating that you viewed a print article in electronic form. If you think that the article was changed (its format is different, there are no page numbers, or commentaries have been added), you will need to add the date you retrieved the document and the URL.

O'Barr, W., & Conley, J. (2000). When cultures collide: Social security and the market. *Journal of Psychology and Financial Markets*,

1, 92–100. Retrieved November 20, 2001, from http://jbr.org/articles.html

17. Daily Newspaper Article, Electronic Version Available by Search

Blakeslee, S. (2001, September 25). Watching how the brain works as it weighs a moral dilemma. *New York Times.* Retrieved March 15, 2002, from http://www.nytimes.com

18. Article in an Internet-only Journal

Wagner, L. (2001). Virtual advising: Delivering student services. *Online Journal of Distance Learning Administration,* 4(3), Retrieved June 1, 2002, from http://www.westga.edu/~distance/main11.html

19. Report from an Organization, Available on Organization Web Site, No Publication Date Indicated

International Society for Mental Health Online. (n.d.) *Children and Trauma: Reflections on the World Trade Center Disaster.* Retrieved October 15, 2001, from http://www.ismho.org

20. U.S. Government Report Available on Government Agency Web Site, No Publication Date Indicated

United States Census Bureau. (n.d.) *Census Participation.* Retrieved December 10, 2001, from http://census.gov/dmd/www/refroom.html

21. Message Posted to Online Forum or Discussion Group

Carruthers, J. (2002, January 20). The role of effort in student success. Message posted to http://www.teachers.net/chat/

OTHER SOURCES

22. Paper Presented at a Meeting

Hendrix, M. (2000, January). *Can we get there from here?* Paper presented at the annual meeting of the Society for an Architectural Future, Chicago.

23. Audiovisual Sources

Film, Videotape, Work of Art

Zemeckis, R. (Director). (1994). *Forrest Gump* [Film]. Hollywood, CA: Paramount Pictures.

Give the name and, in parentheses, the function of the originator of or primary contributors to the work. Identify the medium in brackets after the title. For works of art and for films and videos with limited distribution, give the location of the work or the address of the distributor in parentheses at the end.

Television Broadcast

Bikel, O. (Director). (1995, April 4). Divided memories. *Frontline.* New York: Public Broadcasting Service.

24. Government Document, Research Report, Monograph

U.S. Census Bureau. (1999, September). Money income in the United States. *Current population reports* (P60-206). Washington, DC: GPO.

Kreshner, L., Addams, B., & Winestein, C. (2001). *Use of manipulatives in teaching mathematics in grades four through six* (Report No. 6). New Orleans: State Mathematics Service.

A report or document number, if there is one, should appear in parentheses immediately after the title.

25. Material from an Information Service

Kurth, R. J., & Stromberg, L. J. (1984). *Using word processing in composition instruction.* Paper presented at the meeting of the American Reading Forum, Sarasota, FL. (ERIC Document Reproduction Service No. ED 251 850)

Give the document number in parentheses at the end of the entry; do not use a period after the number.

26. Dissertation

Fredericks, C. (1999). HIV testers and non-testers at a university student health center: A study of college student sexual risk-taking (Doctoral dissertation, University of Southern California, 1999). *Dissertation Abstracts International, 60* (02A), 0346.

27. Legal Case

Loving v. Virginia, 388 U.S. 1 (1967).

This is a citation for a decision rendered by the U.S. Supreme Court in 1967. It was recorded in Volume 388, on page 1, of the *United States Reports,* which is abbreviated as *U.S.*

In the text, the names are underlined or italicized: *Loving v. Virginia* (1967).

If your paper cites many kinds of legal documents, consult the *Publication Manual of the American Psychological Association,* 5th ed.; *The Chicago Manual of Style,* 15th ed.; or *A Uniform System of Citation.*

4c Preparing Papers in APA Style

1. Leave uniform margins of at least one inch on the top, bottom, and sides of each page.
2. Number all pages, including the title page, consecutively, with the numbers appearing at least one inch from the

right-hand edge of the page in the space between the top edge of the paper and the first line of text. A shortened version of the title should appear five spaces to the left of the page number or a double space above the page number, ending even with the number. On a computer, use the header to set up the shortened title and page number so that they will print on each page.

3. The title page, like all other pages, should have the shortened title and page number (which is 1) within the top margin. Immediately below the top margin on the left side, type *Running head* followed by a colon and your shortened title typed in capital letters. Then double-space twice and, with a double space between each line, type the paper's title, your name, and the name of your university in uppercase and lowercase letters centered on the page.
4. If your professor requires an abstract or summary of the paper, provide one on the second page. Below the top margin, type the word *Abstract* centered on the page. Then double-space and type the abstract itself as a single paragraph that is not indented.
5. On a computer, do not justify lines; leave the right-hand margin uneven.
6. Double-space the entire text, including indented quotations and the reference list. Indented quotations should be printed five spaces from the left margin.
7. Indent the first line of each paragraph five to seven spaces.
8. End each line of text with a complete word—do not hyphenate to divide words.
9. On the reference page, center the label *References* at the top. Start the first line of each entry at the left margin; each subsequent line should be indented five spaces. Double-space within and between all entries.

Note: We show APA references here with "hanging" indents; some teachers may prefer paragraph-style indents (first line indented, subsequent lines at the margin). APA recommends the hanging indent for papers in their final form.

Figure 5 shows samples of APA style for a title page, a first page, subsequent pages, and references.

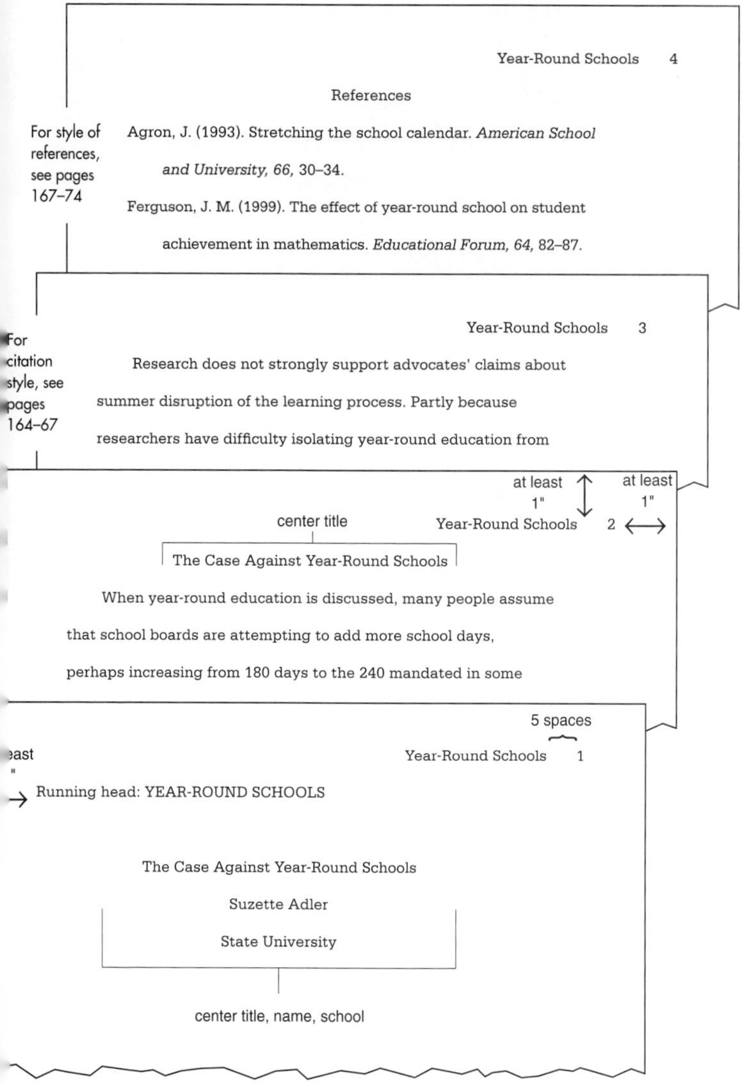
Year-Round Schools 4
References
For style of references, see pages 167–74
Agron, J. (1993). Stretching the school calendar. *American School and University, 66,* 30–34.
Ferguson, J. M. (1999). The effect of year-round school on student achievement in mathematics. *Educational Forum, 64,* 82–87.
Year-Round Schools 3
For citation style, see pages 164–67
Research does not strongly support advocates' claims about summer disruption of the learning process. Partly because researchers have difficulty isolating year-round education from
at least 1"
at least 1"
center title
Year-Round Schools 2
The Case Against Year-Round Schools
When year-round education is discussed, many people assume that school boards are attempting to add more school days, perhaps increasing from 180 days to the 240 mandated in some
5 spaces
Year-Round Schools 1
Running head: YEAR-ROUND SCHOOLS
The Case Against Year-Round Schools
Suzette Adler
State University
center title, name, school

FIGURE 5 Sample APA Pages

5

Chicago Manual of Style (*CMS*) Documentation Styles

Two documentation styles are presented in *The Chicago Manual of Style,* 15th ed. (2003). *CMS* Documentation 1 employs superscript numbers, numbered endnotes or footnotes, and (if the document is long) a bibliography at the end. Documentation 2 employs author/date parenthetical references within the text ("Smith 1990" for example) and a list of references at the end. This chapter illustrates both *CMS* styles.

INSTANT ACCESS

CMS DOCUMENTATION MODEL DIRECTORY

(CMS *Style 1, continued)*

(continued)

(CMS Style 2, continued)

37. A Book with an Unknown Author
38. A Book with a Corporate Author
39. An Edited Work
40. A Translated Work
41. An Edition Other Than the First
42. A Work in an Anthology
43. One Volume in a Multivolume Work
44. A Work in a Series
45. A Biblical Reference

Articles

46. In a Scholarly Journal Paginated by Whole Year's Volume
47. In a Scholarly Journal Paginated by Each Separate Issue
48. In a Popular Magazine
49. In a Newspaper

Electronic Sources

50. CD-ROMs and Other Unchangeable Sources
51. World Wide Web Sites
52. A Book Online
53. A Scholarly Project
54. An Article in an Electronic Journal or Magazine
55. A Newspaper Article
56. A Review
57. A Government Publication
58. An E-Mail Message
59. A Web Discussion Forum Posting
60. A Newsgroup or Listserv Message

Other Sources

61. Government Documents
62. Personal Communication
63. Interview
64. Book Review
65. Film or Videotape
66. Sound Recording
67. Source Quoted in Another Source

5F. PREPARING PAPERS IN *CHICAGO* Style

CMS DOCUMENTATION STYLE 1

Documentation style 1 (sometimes called "note-bibliography" or "humanities" style) uses raised numbers within the text. The numbers lead either to notes at the bottom of the page (footnotes) or to notes at the end of the document (endnotes). These notes may or may not be accompanied by a bibliography (generally, the bibliography becomes more necessary as the work becomes longer).

5a Citations in the Text

Information documented within the text is signaled with a superscript number. The note number should normally go at the end of the sentence, following the final punctuation. If you use a direct quotation in the text, the note number appears after the closing quotation mark. A direct quotation that is eight lines or more should be set off, single spaced, and indented four spaces from the left margin. Again the number appears right after the quotation's final punctuation. The note numbers run consecutively through the text.

5b Notes List

Each entry in the Notes list (or each footnote) should correspond to a superscript number in the text, and there is an entry for every numbered reference in the text. The entries are arranged numerically, with the numbers on the line followed by a period and two spaces. The entire Notes page (or each footnote) should be double spaced, with the first line of each entry indented one half an inch. (Some instructors may prefer that footnotes be single spaced.)

The first entry for each source generally has four elements—author, title, publication information, and page numbers—with these elements separated by commas. The authors' names are listed in normal order (first name then last name). The full title is given, followed by publication information. Here is a basic entry for a book:

Entry in the Text	Another good style manual is the one originally written by Kate Turabian.[1]
Footnote or Endnote	1. Kate L. Turabian, *A Manual for Writers of Term Papers, Theses, and Dissertations*, 6th edition (Chicago: University of Chicago Press, 1996).

The first footnote or endnote entry for an item should carry full information on the source (unless the presence of a Bibliography has caused the Notes entries to be shortened). Subsequent references to the same source may be shortened. Thus if note number 2 were to the same source cited above (Turabian), just to a different page, the entry would read either

2. Ibid., 159

or

2. Turabian, *A Manual*, 159.

The entry for an electronic source would be the same as the print source's entry, with the addition of the URL and the date accessed (see *Electronic Sources,* page 95).

BOOKS

The *basic format* for citing a book is author, title (plus subtitle if any), publisher's city and name, publication date, and page number:

1. Philip Simmons, *Learning to Fall: The Blessings of an Imperfect Life* (New York: Bantam Doubleday, 2002), 122.

1. A Book with Two or Three Authors

2. David Crystal and Ben Crystal, *Shakespeare's Words: A Glossary & Language Companion* (New York: Penguin Putnam, 2002), 16.

2. A Book with Four or More Authors

3. Mary Field Belenky et al., *Women's Ways of Knowing: The Development of Self, Voice, and Mind* (New York: Basic Books, 1986), 227.

3. A Book with an Unknown Author

4. *The Diamond Sutra* (China, 868).

4. A Book with a Corporate Author

5. Commission on the Humanities, *The Humanities in American Life: Report of the Commission on the Humanities* (Berkeley: University of California Press, 1980), 210.

5. An Edited Work

6. G. Reid Lyon, ed., *Frames of Reference for the Assessment of Learning Disabilities: New Views on Measurement Issues* (Baltimore: Paul H. Brookes, 1994), 52.

6. A Translated Work

7. Roland Barthes, *The Pleasure of the Text,* trans. Richard Miller (New York: Hill, 1975), 54.

7. An Edition Other Than the First

8. John Frederick Nims, ed., *Western Wind: An Introduction to Poetry,* 2nd ed. (New York: Random House, 1983), 110.

8. A Work in an Anthology

9. John A. Vance, "Johnson's Historical Reviews," in *Fresh Reflection on Samuel Johnson: Essays in Criticism,* ed. Prem Nath (Troy, NY: Whitston, 1987), 63-84.

9. One Volume in a Multivolume Work

10. Kemp P. Battle, *History of the University of North Carolina* (Raleigh, NC: Edwards, 1912), 1:17-23.

10. A Work in a Series

11. Edwin C. Broome, *A Historical and Critical Discussion of College Admission Requirements*, Columbia Univ. Contributions to Philosophy, Psychology and Education, vol. 11 (New York: Columbia University Press, 1903), 49.

11. An Encyclopedia or Dictionary

12. *Encyclopedia Britannica*, 15th ed., s.v. "Nestorius."

The "s.v." in front of "Nestorius" is the Latin abbreviation for *sub verbo* ("under the word").

12. A Biblical Reference

13. John 3:8 (Revised Standard Version).

PERIODICALS

13. In a Scholarly Journal Paginated by Whole Year's Volume

14. Lawrence W. Murphy, "Professional and Nonprofessional Teaching of Journalism," *Journalism Quarterly* 9 (1932): 46-59.

14. In a Scholarly Journal Paginated by Each Separate Issue

15. Richard R. Cole, "Much Better Than Yesterday, and Still Brighter Tomorrow," *Journalism Educator* 40, no. 3 (1985): 4-8.

15. In a Popular Magazine

16. John H. Richardson, "Mother from Another Planet," *Premiere*, May 1992, 62-70.

16. In a Newspaper

17. "Combat Stress in Women To Be Studied for the First Time," *Times-Picayune* (New Orleans), Jan. 11, 1993, sec. A7.

If the article is signed, the writer's name should go first. If the city's name is not included in the newspaper's title, include it in parentheses.

ELECTRONIC SOURCES

CMS style for online electronic sources closely follows the style for print sources: author, title, date, publication information, and (optional, but required by many teachers for changeable sources) date of access.

We show first a line of text with a footnote number, then a sample footnote (actually a shortened form of the Bibliography entry), and then the Bibliography entry (if there were going to be no Bibliography, the URL would be included in the note):

Text	According to the *Occupational Outlook Handbook*, employment opportunities will be good for technical writers at least through the year 2006.[1] Therefore students who....
Footnote or Endnote	1. Bureau of Labor Statistics, "Writers and Editors," in *1998-99 Occupational Outlook Handbook*.
Bibliography	Bureau of Labor Statistics. "Writers and Editors." In *1998-99 Occupational Outlook Handbook*, 1998. http://stats.bls.gov/oco/ocos089.htm#outlook (accessed June 22, 1999).

Note that here we show the entry for the Notes shortened because the eventual report will include a Bibliography that gives full information for each source.

17. CD-ROMs and Other Unchangeable Sources

1. Frank Morring, Jr., "Russian hardware allows earlier station experiments," *Aviation Week & Space Technology*, May 16, 1994, 57. InfoTrac General Periodicals Index-A, Abstract 15482317.

18. World Wide Web Sites

A Personal Web Site

The entry would include the author's name, title of the document, title of any larger work that document is a part of, date of publication or most recent revision, the URL, and the date of access:

1. Russel Hirst, "Homepage," July 8, 2002, http://web.utk.edu/~hirst (accessed July 9, 2002).

A Professional Site

2. Joy Brown, "Real Estate in Oak Ridge," http://ilead.realtor.com/display/?id=12516147& (accessed May 15, 2002).

Notice that this site, like many Web sites, shows no date of creation or revision, so the entry for it lacks that item (the date shown is the access date). If the Web site has a *corporate author,* the citation looks like this:

3. Bankrate, Inc., "Bankrate.com," July 9, 2002, http://www.bankrate.com/brm (accessed July 9, 2002).

19. A Book Online

4. Willa Cather, *O Pioneers!* (1913; Alex Catalogue of Electronic Texts, 1992), http://sunsite.berkeley.edu/~emorgan/texts/literature/american/1900-/cather-o-366.txt (accessed Mar. 21, 2000).

20. A Scholarly Project

5. Amelia R. Fry, *Conversations with Alice Paul: Woman Suffrage and the Equal Rights Amendment*, Suffragists Oral History Project, http://sunsite.berkeley.edu:2020/dynaweb/teiproj/oh/suffragists/paul (accessed May 3, 2002).

21. An Article in an Electronic Journal or Magazine

6. Peter Howe, "Exposure to Light: The Photographer's Eye in a Digital World," *Columbia*

Journalism Review, July/August 2002, http://www.cjr.org/year/02/4/howe.asp (accessed July 10, 2002).

22. A Newspaper Article

7. Henry Petroski, "We've Got More Risk Than Our Brains Can Handle," *WashingtonPost.Com*, June 30, 2002, page B02, http://www.washingtonpost.com/ac2/wp-dyn/A64827-2002Jun29? (accessed July 9, 2002).

23. A Review

8. Brendan Bernhard, "Bolshie Ballet: Martin Amis takes on Christopher Hitchens and Comrades," *LAWeekly*, July 5-11, 2002, http://www.laweekly.com/ink/02/33/books-bernhard.php (accessed July 10, 2002).

24. A Government Publication

9. American Folklife Center, Library of Congress, "Veterans History Project," August 27, 2001, http://www.loc.gov/folklife/vets (accessed July 8, 2002).

25: An E-Mail Message

10. Ralph Voss, "Kansas Travelogue," May 25, 2002, personal e-mail message to author, July 7, 2002.

Note that for e-mail it's wise to add a phrase specifying whether this was personal communication, professional communication, a note off a listserv, etc.

26. A Web Discussion Forum Posting

11. François Lachance, "Phoenician Disputations," Humanist Discussion Group, Nov. 4, 1999, http://lists.village.virginia.edu/lists_archive/Humanist/v13/0251.html (accessed Mar. 21, 2000).

If the author's name is not given, the owner of the site takes its place:

12. DIY Chat Boards, "stone birdhouse how-to?" June 21, 2002, http://diynet.com/DIY/post/1,2021,1_102461,FF.html (accessed July 9, 2002).

27. A Newsgroup or Listserv Message

13. Susan W. Gallagher, "User-centered design," Feb. 8, 1999, techwr-l@listserv.okstate.edu (accessed Feb. 10, 1999).

OTHER SOURCES

28. Government Documents

14. Internal Revenue Service, United States, *1981 Statistics of Income: Corporate Income Tax Returns* (Washington, D.C.: GPO, 1984), 327.

29. Personal Communication

15. Frank Calabria, letter to Mary Calabria, Feb. 7, 1999.

30. An Interview

16. Louise Erdrich, "An Emissary of the Between-World," interview by Katie Bacon, *Atlantic Unbound*, Jan. 17, 2001, http://www.theatlantic.com/unbound/interviews/int2001-01-17.htm (accessed July 10, 2002).

31. A Book Review

17. Mary Mackey, "Don't Know Much about History," review of *Lies My Teacher Told Me: Everything Your American History Textbook Got Wrong*, by James W. Louwen, *San Francisco Sunday Examiner/Chronicle*, Feb. 12, 1995: 3-4.

32. A Film or Videotape

18. *Forrest Gump*, dir. Robert Zemeckis. (Paramount, 1994).

33. A Sound Recording

19. Giuseppe Verdi, "Triumphal March," *Aïda,* National Philharmonic Orchestra, James Levine, RCA Red Seal 1978.

34. Source Quoted in Another Source

20. John Trimbur, "Comments on 'Consensus and Difference'," *College English* 52 (1990): 699-700, quoted in Sidney Dobrin, *Constructing Knowledges: The Politics of Theory-Building and Pedagogy in Composition* (Albany: SUNY Press, 1997), 19.

5c Bibliography

Under *CMS* Documentation Style 1, shorter works may only have a list of Notes at the end of the document. As the document becomes longer, use of a Bibliography (also called a "Select Bibliography" or "References") becomes more necessary. The bibliography is a list of references used in your report, arranged alphabetically by author's last name. Each entry in general includes the author's name (last name first), the full title of the work being cited, and the publication information (the place of publication, publisher's name, and date of publication), with those elements separated by periods. If they are relevant, particular page numbers (or a section of a document) may also be named. Thus a typical bibliographical entry looks like this:

Gitler, Ira. *Swing to Bop: An Oral History of the Transition in Jazz in the 1940's.* New York: Oxford University Press, 1985.

The first line of each entry begins at the left margin; subsequent lines are indented half an inch. The specific details of each bibliographic entry will vary somewhat depending on what kind of a document (book, article, Web page, etc.) is being cited, as explained above.

DIFFERENCES BETWEEN BIBLIOGRAPHY ENTRIES AND (FIRST) NOTE ENTRIES

1. In the bibliography, an author's names appear last name first ("Smith, Jane" instead of "Jane Smith").

2. Instead of commas, periods are used to separate the elements of the entries.

Compare the following first note entry with the corresponding bibliographic entry.

Entry for first note on this source	1. Robert J. Connors, "A Note from Robert Connors about Rhetoric and English Departments," WPA-L, June 21, 1996, http://www.niu.edu/acad/english/wac/connors.html (accessed May 15, 2000).
Entry for Bibliography	Connors, Robert J. "A Note from Robert Connors about Rhetoric and English Departments." WPA-L. June 21, 1996. http://www.niu.edu/acad/english/wac/connors.html (accessed May 15, 2000).

CMS DOCUMENTATION STYLE 2

Chicago recommends Style 2 for publications in the natural sciences and the social sciences. Its two parts are the citation in the text and the reference list. The citation in the text is usually enclosed in parentheses, and it gives the cited author's name and the date of the publication, for example (Smith 1995). The corresponding entry in the reference list gives full bibliographic information on each source cited in the text. The advantage of this system over Style 1 lies in its elimination of the redundancy inherent in Style 1. That is, if an author using Style 1 adds a Bibliography to the footnotes or list of endnotes, there will be lots of repeated information. Style 2 eliminates that repetition.

5d Citations in the Text

Information is documented within the text by parentheses; within the parentheses are the author's name and the date of the publication. The parentheses usually occur at the end of a sentence or clause, just before the punctuation mark. In the case of a source having two or three authors, both names are used, joined by "and": (Smith and Jones 1990) or

(Smith, Jones, and Adams 1990). For more than three authors, list the first author's name, followed by "et al." or "and others": (Smith, et al. 1997). If you need to cite a specific page or section of a document, add that into the parenthetical reference following a comma: (Smith 1997, 345).

5e List of References

The second part of the author-date system is a complete list of the sources referred to parenthetically within the text. The list is alphabetized by author's last name (or corporate author, if no person is listed), and the elements within it are separated by periods. An unusual feature of this list (called References, Works Cited, or Literature Cited) is that the year of publication immediately follows the author's name, so that the beginning of the entry in the References corresponds more closely to the parenthetical entry within the text. While some publications allow an author's given names to be abbreviated ("Smith, R. J." instead of "Smith, Robert John"), *Chicago* recommends the names be listed as they are on the the title page of the work being cited. Titles of works cited only use capital letters for first words. As in Style 1, multiple works by the same author use a long dash (———) for subsequent occurrences of the same name.

Here is a sample entry within text, followed by the corresponding reference entry:

Entry in the text Another good style manual is *A Manual for Writers of Term Papers, Theses, and Dissertations* (Turabian 1996)....

Reference entry Turabian, Kate. 1996. *A manual for writers of term papers, theses, and dissertations.* Chicago: University of Chicago Press.

BOOKS

The *basic format* for citing a book is author, date, title, and publication information.

Simmons, Philip. 2002. *Learning to fall: the blessings of an imperfect life.* New York: Bantam Doubleday.

35. A Book with Two or Three Authors

Crystal, David, and Ben Crystal. 2002. *Shakespeare's words: A glossary & language companion.* New York: Penguin Putnam.

36. A Book with Four or More Authors

Belenky, Mary Field, Blythe Clinchy, Nancy Goldberger, and Jill Tarule. 1986. *Women's ways of knowing: The development of self, voice, and mind.* New York: Basic Books.

37. A Book with an Unknown Author

The diamond sutra. 868. China.

Here neither author nor publisher is known.

38. A Book with a Corporate Author

Commission on the Humanities. 1980. *The humanities in American life: Report of the commission on the humanities.* Berkeley: University of California Press.

39. An Edited Work

Lyon, G. Reid, ed. 1994. *Frames of reference for the assessment of learning disabilities: New views on measurement issues.* Baltimore: Paul H. Brookes.

40. A Translated Work

Barthes, Roland. 1975. *The pleasure of the text.* Translated by Richard Miller. New York: Hill.

41. An Edition Other Than the First

Nims, John Frederick Nims, ed. 1983. *Western wind: An introduction to poetry.* 2nd ed. New York: Random House.

42. A Work in an Anthology

Vance, John A. 1987. Johnson's historical reviews. In *Fresh reflection on Samuel Johnson: Essays in criticism,* edited by Prem Nath. Troy, N.Y.: Whitston.

43. One Volume in a Multivolume Work

Battle, Kemp P. 1912. *History of the University of North Carolina.* Vol. 1. Raleigh, No. Car.: Edwards.

44. A Work in a Series

Broome, Edwin C. 1903. *A historical and critical discussion of college admission requirements.* Columbia Univ. Contributions to Philosophy, Psychology and Education, vol. 11. New York: Columbia University Press.

45. A Biblical Reference

John 3:8. (Revised Standard Version).

ARTICLES

46. In a Scholarly Journal Paginated by Whole Year's Volume

Murphy, Lawrence W. 1932. Professional and nonprofessional teaching of journalism. *Journalism Quarterly* 9: 46-59.

47. In a Scholarly Journal Paginated by Each Separate Issue

Cole, Richard R. 1985. Much better than yesterday, and still brighter tomorrow. *Journalism Educator* 40, no. 3: 4-8.

48. In a Popular Magazine

Richardson, John H. 1992. Mother from another planet. *Premiere,* May, 62-70.

49. In a Newspaper

> Combat stress in women to be studied for the first time. 1993. *Times-Picayune* (New Orleans), Jan. 11, sec. A7.

If the article is signed, the writer's name should go first. If the city's name is not included in the newspaper's title, include it in parentheses.

ELECTRONIC SOURCES

CMS 2 style for online electronic sources follows the regular guidelines for printed works, with the addition of the URL. For changeable sources such as World Wide Web sites, most teachers would also prefer the addition of the date the page was accessed.

We show first a line of text with a parenthetical reference, and then the References entry:

Text According to the *Occupational Outlook Handbook*, employment opportunities will be good for technical writers at least through the year 2006 (Bureau of Labor Statistics 1998). Therefore students who....

References Bureau of Labor Statistics. 1998. Writers and editors. In *1998-99 occupational outlook handbook.* http://stats.bls.gov/oco/ocos089.htm#outlook (accessed June 22, 1999).

50. CD-ROMS and Other Unchangeable Sources

> Morring, Frank, Jr. 1994. Russian hardware allows earlier station experiments. *Aviation Week & Space Technology* (May 16): 57. InfoTrac General Periodicals Index-A. Abstract 15482317.

51. World Wide Web Sites

A Personal Web Site

The entry would include the author's name, title of the document, title of any larger work that document is a part of, date of publication or most recent revision, the URL, and the date of access:

Hirst, Russel. 2002. Homepage, July 8. http://web.utk.edu/~hirst (accessed July 9, 2002).

A Professional Site

Brown, Joy. Real estate in Oak Ridge. http://ilead.realtor.com/display/?id=12516147& (accessed May 15, 2002).

Notice that this site, like many Web sites, shows no date of creation or revision, so the entry for it lacks that item (the date shown is the access date). If the Web site has a *corporate author,* the citation looks like this:

Bankrate, Inc. 2002. Bankrate.com, July 9. http://www.bankrate.com/brm (accessed July 9, 2002).

52. A Book Online

Cather, Willa. 1913. *O Pioneers!* Alex Catalogue of Electronic Texts, 1992. http://sunsite.berkeley.edu/~emorgan/texts/literature/american/1900-/cather-o-366.txt (accessed Mar. 21, 2000).

53. A Scholarly Project

Fry, Amelia R. *Conversations with Alice Paul: Woman suffrage and the equal rights amendment.* Suffragists Oral History Project. http://sunsite.berkeley.edu:2020/dynaweb/teiproj/oh/suffragists/paul (accessed May 3, 2002).

54. An Article in an Electronic Journal or Magazine

Howe, Peter. 2002. Exposure to light: The photographer's eye in a digital world. *Columbia Journalism Review,* July/August. http://www.cjr.org/year/02/4/howe.asp (accessed July 10, 2002).

55. A Newspaper Article

Petroski, Henry. 2002. We've got more risk than our brains can handle. *WashingtonPost.Com,*

June 30, B02. http://www.washingtonpost.com/ac2/wp-dyn/A64827-2002Jun29? (accessed July 9, 2002).

56. A Review

Brendan Bernhard. 2002. Bolshie ballet: Martin Amis takes on Christopher Hitchens and comrades. Review of *Koba the Dread,* by Martin Amis. *LAWeekly,* July 5-11. http://www.laweekly.com/ink/02/33/books-bernhard.php (accessed July 10, 2002).

57. A Government Publication

American Folklife Center, Library of Congress. 2001. Veterans history project, Aug. 27. http://www.loc.gov/folklife/vets (accessed July 8, 2002).

58. An E-Mail Message

Voss, Ralph. 2002. Kansas travelogue, May 25. Personal e-mail message to author July 7, 2002.

Note that for e-mail it's wise to add a phrase specifying whether this was personal communication, professional communication, a note off a listserv, etc.

59. A Web Discussion Forum Posting

Lachance, François. 1999. Phoenician disputations. Humanist Discussion Group, Nov. 4. http://lists.village.virginia.edu/lists_archive/Humanist/v13/0251.html (accessed Mar. 21, 2000).

If the author's name is not given, the owner of the site takes its place:

DIY Chat/Boards. 2002. Stone birdhouse how-to? June 21. http://diynet.com/DIY/post/1,2021,1_102461,FF.html (accessed July 9, 2002).

60. A Newsgroup or Listserv Message

Gallagher, Susan W. 1999. User-centered design, Feb. 8. techwr-l@listserv.okstate.edu (accessed Feb. 10, 1999).

OTHER SOURCES

61. Government Documents

Internal Revenue Service, United States. 1984. *1981 Statistics of income: Corporate income tax returns.* Washington, D.C.

62. Personal Communication

Calabria, Frank. 1999. Letter to Mary Calabria, Feb 7.

63. Interview

Erdrich, Louise. 2001. An emissary of the between-world. Interview by Katie Bacon. *Atlantic Unbound,* Jan. 17. http://www.theatlantic.com/unbound/interviews/int2001-01-17.htm (accessed July 10, 2002).

64. Book Review

Mackey, Mary. 1995. Don't know much about history. Review of *Lies My Teacher Told Me: Everything Your American History Textbook Got Wrong,* by James W. Louwen. *San Francisco Sunday Examiner/Chronicle,* Feb. 12: 3-4.

65. Film or Videotape

Forrest Gump. 1994. Dir. Robert Zemeckis. Paramount.

66. Sound Recording

Verdi, Giuseppe. 1998. Triumphal March. *Aïda.* Perf. National Philharmonic Orchestra, cond. James Levine. RCA Red Seal.

67. Source Quoted in Another Source

Trimbur, John. 1990. Comments on 'Consensus and difference.' *College English* 52: 699-700. Quoted in Sidney Dobrin, *Constructing knowledges: The politics of theory-building and pedagogy in composition* (Albany: SUNY Press, 1997).

5f Preparing Manuscripts in *Chicago* Style

1. Your title page should include the full title of your paper and your name. Your instructor may require other information as well. Do not place a page number on the title page, but do count it in the page numbering.
2. Leave margins of at least one inch on the top, bottom, and sides of each page.
3. Number all pages except the title page (thus the first number shown will be a 2) in the upper right corner. *Chicago* does not require you to put either a short version of the paper's title or your last name with the page number, but your instructor may well add such a requirement.
4. Double space the entire manuscript, including any long quotations that are set off from the rest of the text, as well as any footnotes, endnotes, and references.
5. If you are using Documentation Style 1 and your instructor wants a bibliography in addition to the footnotes or the endnotes page, that bibliography should begin on a new page, with "Bibliography" centered at the top of the page. Entries are alphabetized and doublespaced, with the first line of each entry at the left margin and all other lines indented one-half an inch. If you have several entries in a row by the same author, use a long dash to begin the second and subsequent entries.
6. If you are using Documentation Style 2, the references list should begin on a new page, with "References" (or "Works Cited") centered at the top of the page. Entries are alphabetized and doublespaced, with the first line of each entry at the left margin and all other lines indented one-half an inch. If you have several entries in a row by the same author, use a long dash for the second and subsequent entries.

Note: Figure 6 shows relevant parts of sample pages for *CMS* Documentation Style 1 references. Because this sample paper has both endnotes and a bibliography, the content of the endnotes has been shortened. If there were to be no bibliography, the content of each endnote that makes the first reference to a source would be complete, not shortened.

Page numbering and doublespacing continue on bibliography page.

12

Bibliography

Erenberg, Lewis A. "Things to Come: Swing Bands, Bebop, and the Rise of the Postwar Jazz Scene." *Recasting America: Culture and Politics in the Age of the Cold War.* Edited by Larry May. Chicago: University of Chicago Press, 1989.

Feather, Leonard. *Inside Jazz.* New York: Da Capo Press, 1977.

Gillespie, Dizzie, with Al Fraser. *To Be or Not . . . To Bop.* Garden City, N. J.: Doubleday, 1979.

Gitler, Ira. *Swing to Bop: An Oral History of the Transition in Jazz in the 1940's.* New York: Oxford University Press, 1985.

Page numbering continues on Notes page. Double spacing continues.

11

Notes

1. Grover Sales, *Jazz: America's Classic Music,* 127.

2. Leonard Feather, *Inside Jazz,* 32.

3. Ibid.

4. Ira Gitler, *Swing to Bop,* 95.

These are shortened entries; full entries are found in the bibliography.

First page of text; starts with page 2.

2

In two sentences, Thelonius Monk sets forth the gospel of bebop: "For years they were telling me, 'play commercial, be commercial.' I say play your own way. You play what you want, and let the public pick up on what you are doing—even if it does take them fifteen, twenty years."[1] The fact that Monk's music is now generally viewed as being outside the mainstream of bebop only emphasizes this point. Of course, during the formative years of

SIDESTEPPING THE MAINSTREAM:

BEBOPPERS SAY NO TO "HI-DE-HO"

enter title, name,
urse number, date.

Title page: Page is counted, but carries no number. Margins of at least 1" all around, throughout paper.

BY

RICHARD VOGEL

English 102

May 15, 2002

FIGURE 6. Sample CMS Pages

6

Document Design

6a Document Design Principles

INSTANT ACCESS

KEY DESIGN PRINCIPLES

- The document should be *professional in appearance.*
- The document should be *consistent* in the ways it uses important design elements, such as page layout, color, and white space.
- The document should be *easy for readers to use.*

CREATING A PROFESSIONAL APPEARANCE

Two key factors in giving your report a professional appearance are the binding and the typography. By following the guidelines below, you will ensure that your paper meets the goals of document design.

Binding

The easiest way to create a professional binding is to take your manuscript pages to a local copying service and ask for a *plastic comb binding*. You will need a cover, which the copying service will be happy to sell you. Students often choose a clear plastic cover, which can be followed by their title page or by a color photocopy of an illustration appropriate to the report's subject (with its source duly acknowledged); in the latter case, the title page follows the illustration. The cost of the whole package is usually only a few dollars.

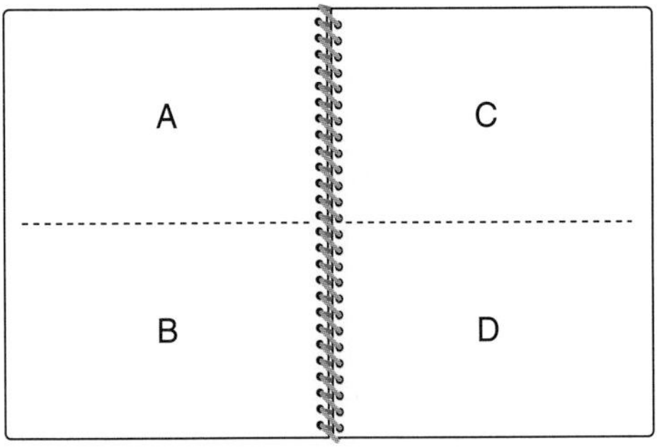

FIGURE 7. Design of Two-Page Spreads

Typography

Today's word processors offer a wide range of choices, but for most projects you're better off using *no more than two fonts*—one a font with serifs (the short cross-lines at the ends of the main strokes of the letters), such as Times, for the text, and the other a font without serifs (a *sans-serif font*), such as Arial or Univers, for the headings. For academic projects, 12-point type and double-spacing are standard.

USING DESIGN ELEMENTS CONSISTENTLY

Establish a consistent "look" to your report by treating the design of all its pages similarly. If you have had your report copied front-and-back, so that your reader always sees two-page spreads, you need to envision each pair of pages as shown in Figure 7: two pages give you four blocks of space with which to work.

On one pair of pages you might have text in block A, a sketch in block B, and text in both blocks C and D (with no interruption between blocks). On another pair of pages you might have a graph in block A, text in block B, text in block C, and art in block D. (Note that you wouldn't want text in A and C and art in B and D, or text in B and D and art in A and C—such pages look top- or bottom-heavy.) Of course, on many pages you might want all text, or on some all art.

Size each visual appropriately, and make sure the accompanying text is on the page facing the visual. Each visual element also needs a caption—at the minimum, a number and a title (and if necessary an acknowledgment of the visual's source)—and it needs to be surrounded by at least one inch of white space.

MAKING YOUR DOCUMENT EASY FOR READERS TO USE

One final key element is the use of headings and subheadings to indicate the outline of your report. In a twenty-page report it's appropriate to use perhaps three or four levels.

INSTANT ACCESS

GUIDELINES FOR VISUALS

- **Are you using the *right kind* of visual for this situation?** For example, pie charts show one kind of thing (proportional relationships) well but other kinds of things (such as changes over time) poorly. Make sure you are building on each kind of visual's natural strengths, not fighting its natural weaknesses.
- **Do the text and the visual *work well together*?**

1. The text needs to stress one or two key points about what is in the visual.
2. Each visual needs to be mentioned in the text.
3. Each visual should appear as soon after its text reference as possible.

- **Have you *adapted* the visual—both its *type* and amount of *detail*—to this setting and to this audience?** Strive for an appropriate level of *simplicity* rather than complexity.
- **Does the visual, as the reader will see it, have *good production qualities*?** Are its lines crisp and clear? Is it neatly done?
- **Is each visual bordered generously by *white space*?** Use one inch of white space on all sides (on an 8½- by 11-inch page).
- **Does each visual have an *appropriate caption*?** At a minimum, a visual should have a number and a title.
- **Have you *cited the source* of each visual?** Unless you took the picture yourself or did the drawing yourself, you must give credit to its source (even if only with an "adapted from . . ." acknowledgment).

REPORT TITLE
Level 1 Heading
Level 2 Heading
Level 3 heading. This lowest level of heading is run into the text paragraph. The other levels of headings are on separate lines.

A NOTE ON PAGE NUMBERING: Be sure to number *every* page. Unless you have specific instructions to the contrary, once you place an Arabic number 1 on a page, every page after that should be numbered sequentially.

6b Designing Web Pages

Before addressing the design of a Web page, you should consider these two questions: What is the *purpose* of this page? What kind of *audience* is this page intended for? Combined into one, the question becomes: *What type of Web page are you designing?*

TYPES OF WEB PAGES

Two clues to a Web page's type are its purpose and its audience. In the box below are some possible types.

INSTANT ACCESS

TYPES OF WEB PAGES

Personal: A page that represents one person (sometimes a family).

Entertainment: A page that hopes to make viewers laugh, cry, enjoy.

Informational (including news): A page that, at least on the surface, wants only to transmit information.

Advocacy: A page that openly tries to change its viewers' minds.

Commercial/Marketing/Business: A page that serves as a company's presence on the Web.

INSTANT ACCESS

OPTIONS FOR SITE DESIGN

Ladder: In a ladder design, page A leads only to page B, which leads only to page C, which leads only to page D, and so on. A simple personal home page could easily use this kind of design.

Grid: A grid design has a number of pages arranged as if in rows and columns. Viewers can move to the head of any column, then down the pages in that column, switching to any other column at any time (depending on the navigational aids present). A college or university's home page might use this structure. The departments in the College of Arts and Sciences could be the columns, with categories like faculty, courses, administration, and special programs being the rows.

Tree: In a tree design, page A leads to perhaps two options, B and C. Page B may lead to D and E, while C leads to F and G. Page D may lead to two others, E to two others, and so on. Thus a company's home page might start with one "front" page, which leads to divisions of marketing, management, and research. Then each of those pages might lead to other options within each division.

Web: In a true web design, any page can lead to any other page. This design requires the most navigation aids because readers can easily get lost within it. More people have the technical capability to create this kind of site than have the design ability to make all the parts easily accessible to the user.

ELEMENTS OF WEB DESIGN

Once you know the type of Web page you want—its purpose and its audience—you can make good decisions about the important design options: *site design, navigation aids, page design* (also known as *screen structures*), and *content.*

Site Design

Site design refers to the organization of all the individual screens on your Web site. When you consider the relationship one page of your site has to the next, you are worrying about site design. The box "Options for Site Design" (above) describes various types of Web site organization.

Navigation Aids

Navigation aids are elements of Web page design that help readers find their way from screen to screen within a site.

The more complicated the site design, the more important it is to provide plenty of navigational aids for your readers.

INSTANT ACCESS

OPTIONS FOR NAVIGATION AIDS

Menu: A list of all the main parts of a site. Menus can appear anywhere on the page, often in a separate "frame" from the rest of the page.

Search: Helps readers find what they want quickly. The Search option uses a text box into which users type what they are looking for.

Index: An alphabetically organized search function especially useful for readers who do not know how to spell what they are searching for.

Map: A visual representation of the structure of a Web site.

Breadcrumb trail: Reminds you where you have been on a site and shows options for where you can go next. The simplest form of this aid, or "trail," is two arrows, one labeled Back and the other labeled Next.

Page Design

Page design includes all the elements a viewer sees when looking at an individual screen. The critical factor in page design is that people do not *read* Web pages; they look at them, they *browse* them. Everything you do in page design should be aimed at a viewer who needs to know *at a glance* what your site has to say.

INSTANT ACCESS

OPTIONS FOR PAGE DESIGN

Number and arrangement of visual elements: Simplicity is the key. If your page has one menu, one graphic, four or five lines of text, maybe a bulleted list, and a search box, that's five things already ("five *chunks,*" some designers would say)—and probably enough. Five chunks per screen is good; seven is a maximum; nine may well be too many.

Paragraph length: If your paragraph fills an entire screen, few people will read it. Keep paragraphs short and to the point, more like business-letter paragraphs than term-paper paragraphs.

(continued)

(Options for Page Design, continued)

Sentence length: Once again, shorter is better. On the Web, a twenty-word sentence is almost always too long. Remember, your viewer is *looking at* the site, not really reading it.

Use of headings and lists: The more you break up the appearance of your Web page, especially with visual elements such as headings and subheadings that help your viewer see its organization, the better the response your site will get. And because key information often is placed in lists, setting lists off from the rest of the text helps make the page easy for your viewer to use.

WRITING FOR THE WEB

The content of a Web page is its most important element. If the other elements—site design, navigation, or page design—get in the way of the writing, the page's priorities are upside down.

INSTANT ACCESS

KEY PRINCIPLES OF WRITING FOR THE WEB

Use "chunking": In writing for the Web it is especially important to keep similar elements together, whether that means all the words and pictures relevant to one thing, or just all the words.

Write "inverted-pyramid" paragraphs: Journalism students learn to write their paragraphs so that the most important information is in the first sentence, the next most important in the second sentence, and so on. Because people looking at text on the Web are typically just browsing, literally skimming the text, this technique is especially important.

Write one-idea paragraphs: On the Web, your paragraphs cannot sprawl from one thing to the next, to the next, to the next. Short, tightly focused paragraphs are best.

Revise your text for conciseness: If you can say the same thing shorter, you should. To achieve economy, you have to revise your writing on the sentence level. (See pages 22–26 in **1d, Revising.**)

Highlight key words: Because your viewers' eyes are moving so fast across the screens you create, it's a good idea to highlight the key words. Of course, if the report you are putting on the Web has a glossary, you can make those highlighted words hypertext links to the glossary.

7

Professional Communication

The following pages present patterns for three types of professional transactions as well as suggestions for pursuing jobs online.

- **The job- or internship-application letter plus résumé:** Someone has advertised an opening, and you want to be the one to fill it.
- **Direct-request letters:** You are asking for something.
- **Persuasive letters:** You want to change the reader's beliefs or actions.

7a Job- or Internship-Application Letters

A job- or internship-application letter is a specialized form of persuasion: your letter should persuade the employer to consider you for the position. In it, you want to appear serious, well organized, and qualified, to indicate that you want to work at the company and will do the job well. A sample job-application letter is shown in Figure 8.

7b Résumés

When you send a letter of application, you should include a brief résumé with it. This one- or two-page document should summarize your education and work experience. You can also post your résumé with online job-search services, such as those described on the following pages. A simple résumé is shown in Figure 9.

1413 State Street
Gainesville, FL 32301
February 15, 2003

J. D. Abercrombie, Senior Biologist
Thompson Biological Systems Research Center
Columbia, FL 32442

Dear Dr. Abercrombie:

I would like to apply for one of the summer internships in wildlife biology your company has advertised in the biology department at State Tech University. I will be graduating this May with a B.S. in biology and am looking for worthwhile practical field experience prior to entering graduate school this fall.

As a biology major at State Tech, I took primarily wildlife- and ecosystems-oriented classes within the wildlife and fisheries option. I also had a strong minor in math, 21 hours instead of the usual 15. My long-term career interest is to earn an M.S. in Ecology and to secure employment as a career professional with the U.S. Fish and Wildlife Service.

In addition to the usual variety of part-time and summer jobs, my work experience includes a part-time lab assistantship in the raptors unit at State Tech's Veterinary Teaching Hospital. For the last year, I have been the primary person in charge of the care and feeding of many injured hawks, eagles, and other raptors brought in by the public for eventual return to the wild or placement in captive breeding programs.

With my academic and work backgrounds and my career interest in this area, I can bring a fair amount of knowledge and experience to the position. I am available any time at your convenience for an interview, and I look forward to hearing from you soon.

Sincerely,

Mary Washington
(555) 555-5555 (after 5 p.m.)
mwashington@sttech.edu

FIGURE 8. Sample Job-Application Letter. Here is a sample job-application letter from a student applying for a summer internship position in her major field. Notice how her letter clearly applies for the job, explains her credentials, and suggests the next step—while stressing what she can contribute to this research center.

MARY WASHINGTON
1413 State Street
Gainesville, FL 32301
(555) 555-5555
email: mwashington@sttech.edu

Computer Skills
Word, PowerPoint,
Statistical Analysis,
MatLab

EDUCATION
B.S. in Biology, Wildlife and Fisheries Science Option, State Tech University, expected May 10, 2003. Math Minor. GPA 3.5 (on a 4.0 scale).

Important Coursework

Basic Biology, 9 hours	Biocalculus, 6 hours
Chemistry, 9 hours	Models in Biology, 6 hours
Botany, 3 hours	Calculus, 6 hours
Zoology, 6 hours	Statistics, 3 hours
Wildlife & Fisheries, 6 hours	Technical Writing, 3 hours

EXTRACURRICULAR ACTIVITIES
Treasurer, Biology Club. Collected annual dues, kept budget, helped create brochure describing club to attract new members. 2001–2002.
Volunteer, Humane Society of Gainesville. Staffed intake desk 5 hours a week during school, 10 hours a week on holidays. Interacted with public, assisted in handling of animals.

EMPLOYMENT
Part-time laboratory assistant, raptors unit, State University Veterinary Teaching Hospital. Fed and cared for 35 birds in various stages of health. Supervised high-school interns. 2002–2003.
Part-time groundskeeper, State University Veterinary Teaching Hospital. Maintained shrubs and other plants. Monitored supplies. Prepared budgets for new planting projects. 2001–2002.
Desk clerk, Somerset Hilton Hotel, Somerset, New Jersey. Helped guests with check-in and check-out. Monitored all cash and charge transactions. Trained new workers. Full time, 1999–2000.

REFERENCES
Upon request from the State University Placement Service, letters are available from Dean Melanie Lucas (Dean of Student Life), Professor Bob Smith (Biology Dept.), and Suzanne Cramer (veterinary hospital lab supervisor).

FIGURE 9. Sample Résumé. Here is an example of one of the many acceptable formats for a one-page résumé. (Some software programs also provide templates for résumés.) Note how Mary used bold print and italics to set off headings and her jobs.

Possible Résumé Categories

Education
Relevant Coursework
Work Experience (you might divide it into Professional Work Experience and Other Work Experience)
Skills
Computer (or Technical) Skills
Specialized Training (for additional training courses or workshops)
Hobbies
Extracurricular Activities
Academic Honors
Honors and Awards

7c Online Job Searches

Depending on the kind of job or internship you are looking for, you can search by type of job; by keyword; by your skills; or by the city, state, or country where you want to find employment.

CAUTION: If you search for one of these services and do not find it, simply type "jobs" or "employment" into the text box of any large search engine, such as Yahoo! or AltaVista, and the most recent sites and their URLs will pop up. Do *not* use the services of any site that requires payment; there are too many good free services available.

SITES TO SEARCH FOR JOBS

This is only a partial listing of some of the most popular job-related sites. You should explore all of these and more, and you certainly should use more than one of them.

Career Search Launch Pad <http://www.pantos.org/cslp/>: You can search several major job search engines from this one site.
Career Mosaic <http://www.careermosaic.com/>
CareerMagazine <http://www.careermag.com/>
Monster.com <http://www.monster.com/>
NationJob <http://www.nationjob.com/>
Net-Temps <http://www.net-temps.com/>

INSTANT ACCESS

ONLINE RÉSUMÉS

Many of the job-finding services allow you to post your own résumé in their databanks, which can make it easier for employers who are looking for someone with your unique blend of education and experiences. Usually, for you to post your résumé you will need to have a version written in hypertext markup language (HTML). Most word-processing packages now have utilities that will do that for you.

7d Direct-Request Letters

A letter of request might ask for information on products or services, a company, or a program. Figure 10 shows a sample direct-request letter.

[inside heading]

[inside address]

Dear Professor Watson:

I will be graduating next May with a B.A. in Accounting from Tonapaw College and would like to continue my studies by getting an M.A., also in accounting. Will you please send me the relevant information and application forms for your university's M.A. program in accounting?

I am especially interested in your statistics course requirements, financial aid packages, and internship programs. I would also like to have any information you can send about your former students' job placement.

Once I receive this information, I hope to arrange interviews with the directors of the graduate programs at the schools that look the best suited to me. I look forward to hearing from you soon, and I look forward to the possibility of meeting you in person in the near future.

Sincerely,

[signature block]

FIGURE 10. Sample Direct-Request Letter. Because this type of letter or memo asks for something the reader provides routinely, it does not need to be long or involved. If you feel that persuasion is necessary, you should consider using the persuasive form.

7e Persuasive Letters

When you want to use a letter or a memo to change someone's actions, use a persuasive pattern. Figure 11 shows a sample persuasive letter. Because of the difficulty of these types of situations, you will need to plan carefully. First consider these three questions:

- What is the claim you are trying to make? (For example, that your teacher should accept the course substitution you propose in your college curriculum.)
- What is the evidence in support of this claim? (For example, that the proposed substitute course's requirements are more demanding than those of the course the curriculum specifies.)
- What opinions will your readers have about your claims? How resistant will they be? What values or needs can you tap into to convince them? (Perhaps your readers will be more likely to approve the course substitution if you provide syllabi for both of the courses in question.)

To be effective, an argument needs to reach readers' values, attitudes, or beliefs. You might follow this pattern for a persuasive letter or memo:

1. Begin with a reference or an appeal to the shared value, belief, or attitude. Then state your claim, connecting it to that value.
2. In the next paragraphs, state any other evidence in support of your claim.
3. In the final paragraph, more fully explain the benefits that will follow from your reader's adopting this changed belief or course of action.

7f Oral Presentations

KEY PRINCIPLES FOR DOING ORAL PRESENTATIONS

Plan Your Talk Carefully—Write Out Answers to These Questions

1. What, exactly, have you been asked to do?
2. Why are you doing it? (a) What is *your* purpose? (b) What is the purpose of the people who invited you?
3. Who is your audience?
4. What is the setting?

[inside heading]

[inside address]

Dear Professor Smith:

As you may recall, I was a student in your History 355, Contemporary Issues in Foreign Affairs, course last spring. I remember your interest in the Persian Gulf and the comment you made several times that it would be nice to have a course just on the history and politics of that region. Because it becomes more apparent every day that the politics of that region will be an important factor in the twenty-first century, I am requesting your approval of a three-hour independent study course next fall, on the topic of the Persian Gulf's history and politics, with particular attention to the circumstances surrounding the 1991 Persian Gulf War.

My own interest in the Persian Gulf was triggered by having spent five months there on active duty with the 577th Combat Engineers. As I came to know the people and the region better, I became more convinced that any understanding of the current political situation there that was not shaped by a thorough knowledge of the region's history was bound to be erroneous.

Completion of this independent study will bring benefits to both of us. I will fulfill another three hours of study toward my B.A. and learn more about a subject that not only interests me greatly but also is important to all of us. For you, directing the independent study will provide an opportunity to test the availability of texts and other appropriate course materials that you could use if you ever do teach this as a regular course.

I will stop by during your office hours next week to discuss this request in more detail. I hope you will agree with me that such a course is well worth doing.

Sincerely,

[signature block]

FIGURE 11. Sample Persuasive Letter. Here is an example of a persuasive letter. This student had earlier mentioned the possibility of an independent study course to her professor. He had replied, "Well, you will have to convince me."

INSTANT ACCESS

GUIDELINES FOR VISUALS IN SHORT PRESENTATIONS

- **Limit yourself to one idea per visual.** You cannot explain the "faster, better, and cheaper" philosophy of all of NASA's Mars missions in one visual. You *can* compare Pathfinder's costs with those of earlier and later missions.
- **Limit the number of words you put on each visual.** You cannot write a three-paragraph narrative history of the Pathfinder mission, put it on a poster board, and expect anyone to read it that way. You *can* do a timeline, listing five or seven key dates in the mission.
- **Make sure the letters you use can be read from the back of the room.** Titles should be in letters at least an inch high, headings three-quarters of an inch, and text at least a half inch.
- **Use color or boldface type to accentuate key points.** A nice touch is to add the highlighting as you speak. If you use a pen, make sure that it's a pen that works on the kind of visual you're using and that people in the back of the room can see the marks you make. If you add highlights with a cursor and the click of the mouse, make sure you do not lose focus on your audience as you do it.
- **Practice your talk with the visual aids, and if at all possible do so in the room where you'll be delivering the talk.** Of course, practice is important, but practicing "under game conditions" is even more important. Find a time when the room you'll be speaking in is unused, and deliver your presentation there exactly as you intend it to happen before your live audience. And while you're practicing, remember one final point: *Look at your audience, not at your visuals!*

Prepare Your Talk As a *Talk,* Not As a Written Report

1. Reinforce your talk's *structure.* For example, distribute or display an outline of your talk, so people can remember where you've been and anticipate where you're going.
2. Simplify your talk's *content.* It's better to give a slow, tightly focused talk that people will understand and appreciate than to give a fast, scattered talk people will have difficulty following.

INSTANT ACCESS

CHECKLIST FOR ORAL PRESENTATIONS

- Double-check that you are going to the right room at the right time on the right day. Write down all the key details; do not trust your memory.
- If at all possible, visit the room before you give your talk, and try a few lines from the position where you will be standing when you speak.
- Make sure the room contains the technology you need for your talk—and that it is working smoothly. Make sure that if the technology fails, you will be able to use your backup plan: a blackboard needs chalk; a flipchart needs marking pens.
- If you are using technology (such as a laptop and a digital projector), get it set up and ready to go before other people come into the room. Having to stop at the very beginning of your talk to fiddle with the technology will not help your nerves.
- Keep your focus: in a five- to seven-minute presentation, you can make three key points. Keep paring down your presentation (and especially your graphics) to make those key points stand out.
- Dress at a level appropriate for the setting and audience. If you are "dressing up" for the talk, make sure you're comfortable in that suit.
- Remember that the way to deal with nerves is to over-prepare. Turn your nervous energy into practice time.
- Before the presentation, be sure you have put your name and the date on any handouts or visuals you are using.
- Bring copies of your business cards (or make other provisions) so that people can get in touch with you later if they wish to.

Choose Visuals and Props Carefully

All visuals must meet several strict criteria (see *Guidelines for Visuals* for more).

1. Easy to see.
2. Sufficiently foolproof.
3. Adapted to *this* audience, *this* setting.

Practice Your Talk

Practice your talk under "game conditions," with at least one of those practices being in the room where you will actually deliver it.

Deliver Your Talk Effectively

1. Look at your audience.
2. Slow way down.
3. Talk it, don't read it.
4. Stand comfortably.
5. Pause before you start, arrange your notes, say "Hello, my name is . . . ."

Be Sure to Answer Questions Thoughtfully

You *must* end by saying "Any Questions?"

1. Be sure you listen to the whole question before you start answering it.
2. Do not try to bluff your way through answers you don't know. It's always better to say something like "Let me answer as much of that as I can, and for the rest I'll get back to you."

8

Sentence Fragments

8A INSTANT ACCESS OVERVIEW

A sentence fragment is a *part* of a sentence that begins with a capital letter and ends with a period, making it look like a complete sentence. But a complete sentence must meet *all three* of these conditions:

- It must contain a *subject.*
- It must contain a *complete verb.*
- It must not begin with a *subordinating word or words.*

To revise a sentence fragment, you can turn it into a complete sentence or make it part of another sentence—often the one just before or after the fragment.

Sentence Fragment

➤ **I suddenly saw my sister. *Buried up to her head in the neighbor's sandbox.***

Revised

➤ **I suddenly saw my sister/, ~~B~~uried up to her head in the neighbor's sandbox.** (b)

8b Testing for Fragments

1. What is the subject? If a group of words lacks a subject, it is a fragment. The subject names the "doer" of the verb. (The only exception is sentences in the *passive voice,* in which the subject receives the verb's action, as in "The book was borrowed by Henry." Here, *book* is the subject, receiving the action of *was borrowed,* and *Henry,* the object of the preposition *by,* is the doer.) 216–17

➤ **Jack played all his favorite songs/ ~~A~~**a**nd took requests.**

[The fragment "And took requests" lacks a subject.]

➤ **The play, ~~was~~ an enormous hit/, ~~W~~**w**as performed on Broadway more than five hundred times.**

2. What is the verb? Is it complete? A group of words without a complete verb cannot be a sentence. Testing for a complete verb has two steps:

a. Make sure there is some form of a verb in the sentence.

b. Make sure the verb form you have found is not a *verbal.* Verbals include infinitives (the *to* + *verb* form), participles (the *-ed, -ing,* and *-en* forms of verbs used as modifiers), and gerunds (the *-ed, -ing,* and *-en* forms used as nouns). 214–16

➤ **Throwing down the newspaper/, Suzi declared that she was sick of boring comic strips.**

[*Throwing* is a verbal, not a complete verb.]

3. Is there an independent clause? Even if both a subject and a complete verb are present, they must be part of an independent clause. (An *independent clause* is a group of words that contains a subject and a complete verb and can stand on its own as a sentence.) Make sure the clause you are testing does not begin with a subordinating word or phrase (*after, because, unless,* and the others listed on page 237). These words introduce *dependent clauses.* If the sentence does begin with a dependent clause, be sure that clause is connected to an independent clause. 216–20

➤ **Because the room was too smoky/, She left the party early.** (handwritten correction: "s" above "She")

[*Because* introduces a dependent clause.]

8c Revising Fragments

You can revise a sentence fragment in many ways. Here are two of the most common:

- Attach the fragment to the sentence right before it or right after it (depending on where it seems to work better).
- Make whatever changes are required within the fragment itself to make it a separate sentence.

These examples illustrate both methods. Notice how the meaning of each sentence in the resulting pairs is slightly different, depending on how the fragment has been revised.

Sentence Fragment

➤ **Sarah took out her own hand axe. *Her razor-sharp Estwing.***

["Her razor-sharp Estwing" is a fragment; it lacks a verb.]

Fragment Revised to Make One Sentence

➤ **Sarah took out her own hand axe/, Her razor-sharp Estwing.** (handwritten correction: "h" above "Her")

Fragment Revised to Make Two Sentences

➤ **Sarah took out her own hand axe. Her razor-sharp. ~~Estwing.~~** (handwritten insertions: "Estwing" after "Her", "was honed" after "razor-sharp")

9

Comma Splices

9A INSTANT ACCESS OVERVIEW

A comma splice occurs when two or more independent clauses are connected with only a comma. Sometimes the comma is accompanied by a *conjunctive adverb* (such as *however* or *therefore*) or a transitional word or phrase (such as *in other words*), but the result is still a comma splice.

Comma Splice

➤ **He left the house, his wallet was still on the table.**

[To connect these two independent clauses correctly, you could use either a comma *plus* a coordinating conjunction or a semicolon.]

Revised

➤ **He left the house, ^but his wallet was still on the table.**

➤ **He left the house; his wallet was still on the table.**

[A semicolon rather than a comma needs to precede *his wallet.*]

9b Testing for Comma Splices

1. Check to see if the sentence contains two or more independent clauses. An independent clause contains a subject and a complete verb and can stand on its own as a sentence, such as "The music stopped." A dependent clause begins with a subordinating word such as *after, when,* or *if* and can never stand alone as a sentence—for example, "when the music stopped."

2. Next, check the way the clauses are joined. There are two acceptable ways to connect independent clauses:

- a comma plus a coordinating conjunction (*and, but, or, nor, for, so,* and *yet*)
- a semicolon (or, in special circumstances, a colon)

Two independent clauses joined any other way make a comma splice.

3. You can also check for comma splices by underlining the clauses. If you are not sure whether what you have underlined is an independent clause, circle its subject and double-underline its verb; then make sure it does not begin with a subordinating word or phrase.

Comma Splice

➤ **A small person still can compete at the very highest levels of soccer, that person has to be fast and tough.**

[The two independent clauses are joined only by a comma.]

9c Revising Comma Splices

There are four revision techniques for eliminating comma splices:

- Use a period and create two sentences.
- Use a comma and a coordinating conjunction to create a *compound sentence.*
- Use a semicolon (or, in special conditions, a colon) to create a compound sentence.
- Use a subordinating conjunction and a dependent clause to create a *complex sentence.*

USE A PERIOD AND CREATE TWO SENTENCES

One simple way to correct a comma splice is to place a period between the independent clauses, thus making two separate sentences:

➤ **Eventually I want to go to graduate school in St. Louis~~,~~. ~~my~~ My goals are to study journalism and get a job at a small-town paper.**

CREATE A COMPOUND SENTENCE

You can also correct a comma splice by using a coordinating conjunction (*and, but, or, nor, for, so,* and *yet*) preceded by a comma to join the two clauses. Your choice of the right coordinating conjunction can help your readers understand the relationship between the independent clauses more exactly. The result is a compound sentence: a sentence with two or more independent clauses.

➤ **At midnight my roommate couldn't find anything to eat in the room, so she went to the convenience store for a dozen doughnuts.**

➤ **Sherlock Holmes never said "Elementary, my dear Watson" in any of Arthur Conan Doyle's stories, but he did use the word *elementary* to describe the deductions he made.**

One additional way to create a compound sentence is to use a pair of *correlative conjunctions (either . . . or; not only . . . but also)* to create a balance between the two clauses:

➤ ***Either* these negotiations will be successful, *or* fighting may once again break out.**

➤ ***Not only* are there many new players on the team this year, *but also* the league has been restructured.**

Punctuating Compound Sentences

Use a comma before the conjunction in compound sentences to separate the two independent clauses clearly:

> **William Cody's Wild West Shows began in the 1880s, *and* Annie Oakley's mock battles were his biggest draw.**

> **Jazz originated among black musicians in nineteenth-century New Orleans, *yet* their Dixieland music also gave birth to what we now call rock and roll.**

ANOTHER WAY TO CREATE A COMPOUND SENTENCE

If the ideas expressed in the two independent clauses are closely related, you may correct the comma splice with a semicolon or with a colon, thus creating a compound sentence.

Use a Semicolon

The semicolon is especially appropriate to connect independent clauses that are closely related and about equal in length. The semicolon can be used on its own or with a conjunctive adverb (listed on page 243). Each conjunctive adverb signals a slightly different relationship between the two clauses. Note that adding the conjunctive adverb does not change the need for a semicolon to join the independent clauses:

> **Microwave ovens can interfere with the electronic impulses sent out by pacemakers; *therefore,* stores and restaurants must post warnings wherever these ovens are in use.**

When you use a conjunctive adverb after the semicolon, a comma normally follows the adverb, as in the preceding example. Note also that the conjunctive adverb does not always have to follow immediately after the semicolon, as in this revision of the previous example:

> **Microwave ovens can interfere with the electronic impulses sent out by pacemakers; stores and restaurants, *therefore*, must post warnings wherever these ovens are in use.**

Use a Colon

A colon can be used to link independent clauses in one special situation: when the second clause explains or provides an example of the idea stated in the first clause.

➤ **Pepper is not very good as a hunting dog: he hates to get dirty.**

➤ **Being a hospital volunteer has taught me a crucial lesson: a caring family is as important as medicine itself.**

➤ **Researchers cannot guarantee that the new drug is safe: not enough tests have been done on it.**

CREATE A COMPLEX SENTENCE

You can also correct a comma splice by making one of the independent clauses a dependent clause, thus creating a *complex sentence*. To make a clause dependent, add a subordinating word or phrase, such as a subordinating conjunction or a relative pronoun. The subordinating conjunctions and relative pronouns that introduce all dependent clauses can indicate many different relationships among ideas. (For a listing, see page 243.)

When
➤ **^ Stephanie walked into the cafeteria, she didn't see anyone she knew.**

10

Run-On Sentences

10A INSTANT ACCESS OVERVIEW

Run-on sentences (sometimes called fused sentences) occur when two or more independent clauses have no punctuation separating them. (An *independent clause* has a subject and a complete verb and can stand on its own as a sentence.) Two independent clauses may properly be separated with a period, with a comma plus a coordinating conjunction (*and, but, or, nor, for, so,* or *yet*), with a semicolon (with or without a conjunctive adverb, such as *however*), or with a colon. Or one clause may be turned into a dependent clause with the addition of a subordinating conjunction or a relative pronoun.

- **Winter came early this year. ~~t~~ T the first snow fell before Halloween.**
- **The song was popular , and its tune was heard everywhere.**
- **Double-click on *Reload;* the image should come right back.**
- **~~Double~~ If you double-click on *Reload,* the image should come right back.**

10b Testing for Run-On Sentences

1. Check to see if the sentence contains two or more independent clauses. An independent clause contains a subject and a complete verb and can stand on its own as a sentence, such as "The rain came down in torrents." A dependent clause begins with a subordinating word, such as *after, when,* or *if,* and can never stand alone as a sentence—for example, "After the rain came down in torrents."

2. Next, check the way the clauses are joined. There are two acceptable ways to connect independent clauses:

- with a comma plus a coordinating conjunction (*and, but, or, nor, for, so,* and *yet*)
- with a semicolon (or, in special circumstances, a colon)

Two independent clauses joined with only a comma (and no coordinating conjunction) create a comma splice (discussed in the previous section); two independent clauses joined without any punctuation or connecting word create a run-on sentence.

10c Revising Run-On Sentences

There are four revision techniques for eliminating run-on sentences:

- Use a period to create two sentences.
- Use a comma and a coordinating conjunction to create a *compound sentence.*
- Use a semicolon (or, in special circumstances, a colon) to create a compound sentence. A conjunctive adverb (such as *however, nonetheless,* or *therefore*) may be used with the semicolon.
- Use a subordinating conjunction or a relative pronoun to make one of the clauses dependent and thus create a *complex sentence.*

USE A PERIOD TO CREATE TWO SENTENCES

You may choose to correct a run-on sentence by placing a period between the two independent clauses, thus creating two sentences. Use this revision technique when there is not a close relationship between the two ideas.

> **Jim Thorpe was the best performer in track and field at the 1912 Olympic Games** *. H* **~~he~~ was also a successful college football player.**

USE A COMMA AND A COORDINATING CONJUNCTION TO CREATE A COMPOUND SENTENCE

You can also correct a run-on sentence by inserting a coordinating conjunction (*and, but, or, nor, for, so,* and *yet*) preceded by a comma. The right coordinating conjunction will help your readers better understand the relationship between the clauses of the compound sentence:

> **Dad hid the presents in the attic** *, for* **he didn't want any of us children to find them.**

To indicate a balanced relationship between the two clauses, you may also choose to use a pair of *correlative conjunctions* (*either . . . or; not only . . . but also*):

> *Not only will the* **~~The~~ new registration procedures ~~will~~ work better for the registrar's office** *, but also* **the students will be happier ~~too~~.**

USE A SEMICOLON OR A COLON TO CREATE A COMPOUND SENTENCE

When the ideas in a compound sentence are closely related, you may join the two independent clauses with a semicolon:

> **Three planes were waiting for the same gate;** **two groups of passengers were going to be unhappy.**

To indicate the nature of the relationship between two independent clauses, you can use a conjunctive adverb (see the list on page 243) in addition to the semicolon:

; however,
➤ **The game was already hopelessly lost the band seemed determined to keep people cheering.**

When the second clause explains or provides an example of the idea stated in the first clause, you may use a colon rather than a semicolon to connect the two clauses:

➤ **Time was always running out on Jameer: today's test was but one more example.**

USE A SUBORDINATING CONJUNCTION OR A RELATIVE PRONOUN TO CREATE A COMPLEX SENTENCE

If you make one of the clauses in a run-on sentence a dependent clause, you have created a *complex sentence.* The subordinating conjunctions and relative pronouns (such as *after, because, if, since, until,* or *which*) create particular relationships between the two clauses (see the complete list of these words on page 237).

Because she
➤ **~~She~~ was hungry, she got into line right away.**

which
➤ **Carolyn and Mary hurried into the candy store, ~~it~~ sold rocky road and butter praline fudge.**

11

Verb Errors

11A INSTANT ACCESS OVERVIEW

The most common problems with verbs are subject-verb agreement, form, tense, and mood errors. The pages that follow explain these problems in more detail. (For a complete discussion of verbs, see **19v, Verbs,** in Part Three, pages 279–85.)

SUBJECT-VERB AGREEMENT ERRORS

Subjects and verbs must agree in *number*—both singular or both plural. The subject always determines whether the verb should be singular or plural.

➤ **The design of the new cars ~~help~~ helps their gas mileage.**

[A prepositional phrase (*of the new cars*) separating the subject (*design*) from the verb (*help*) has fooled the writer into making the verb agree with the plural object of the prepositional phrase (*cars*) instead of the singular subject (*design*).]

➤ **At the front of the procession ~~was~~ were the president of the college and the dean of students.**

[The inverted sentence order, in which the verb precedes the subject, has fooled the writer into using a singular verb, *was,* with a plural (compound) subject, the *president* of the college and the *dean* of students.]

FORM ERRORS

Verbs change form to indicate time (tense) and convey certain other information. *Regular verbs* change only their endings (*talk, talked*) whereas *irregular verbs* change internally (*sing, sang, sung; go, went, gone*). Most verb form errors involve the wrong forms of irregular verbs (especially *lie* and *lay* and *sit* and *set*) or dropped endings (*s, es, d, ed*). The most common irregular verbs are listed under **19v, Verbs,** in Part Three, pages 280–84. Beyond that, a dictionary is the best guide to verb forms.

➤ **Irina had never ~~swam~~ swum that fast before.**

➤ **He ~~laid~~ lay down to rest awhile.**

➤ **Why don't you ~~set~~ sit with her at church?**

INAPPROPRIATE SHIFTS IN TENSE

Tense shifts distort the sequence of actions being described:

> ➤ **When they received our gift, they ~~had~~ sent a thank-you note immediately.**

In this example, the simple past action of the first verb (*received*) seems to be preceded by the past perfect action of the second verb (*had sent*); that is, they seem to have sent the thank-you note before receiving the gift, a sequence of events contrary to the order in which the events actually happened. The solution to the problem is to put the two verbs in the same tense.

Inappropriate shifts in tense occur not only in single sentences but also in paragraphs and groups of paragraphs. (For a complete discussion of verb tenses, see **19v, Verbs,** in Part Three, pages 282–84.)

MOOD ERRORS

The mood of a verb tells whether the verb expresses

- a fact (*indicative mood*)
- a doubt, a condition wished for, or a condition contrary to fact (*subjunctive mood*)
- a command (*imperative mood*)

The most common mood error is use of the indicative rather than the subjunctive to express doubt or a wish or to describe something that is contrary to fact. (For a complete discussion of mood, see **19v, Verbs,** in Part Three, pages 284–85.)

➤ **I wish my refund check ~~was~~ were already here.**

As with verb tense, make shifts in mood only for good reasons. Especially, be careful not to slip accidentally into the imperative mood, the one used for instructions or commands.

➤ **We should all be grateful for the sacrifices of the people who fought in World War II. ~~Take~~ *Each of us should take* time to remember that freedom comes with a price.**

11b Subject-Verb Agreement Errors

Subjects and their verbs always need to agree in *number*—singular or plural. No matter where the subject appears in the sentence, the subject always determines whether the verb will be singular or plural.

SUBJECT AND VERB SEPARATED BY MODIFIERS

When other words come between the subject and the verb, be careful not to let the number of the verb be determined by the closest noun. The *subject*—which is not necessarily the closest noun to the verb—always controls the number of the verb.

➤ **Of all my video cassettes, the tape containing Eddie Murphy's collection of comedy routines ~~make~~ ^makes me laugh the loudest.**

[Although *comedy routines* is plural, the subject, *tape,* is singular.]

➤ **The new word processing programs that have every kind of option ~~is~~ ^are the best yet.**

[The subject, *programs,* is plural; the verb should be plural as well.]

➤ **Traditional country music played on acoustic instruments ~~are~~ ^is still popular in many places.**

[The subject, *music,* is singular; the verb should be singular as well.]

COMPOUND SUBJECTS JOINED BY THE CONJUNCTION *AND*

When the parts of a compound subject are joined by *and*, the verb is always plural. It doesn't matter whether the individual parts of that compound subject are singular or plural.

***Jack and Tom* are going with us.**

***Jack and the other boys* are going with us.**

***Jack and I* are going.**

***Both Jack and I* are going.**

Agreement Error Revised

➤ **My answering machine and my CD player ~~is~~ *are* two electrical appliances I cannot live without.**

COMPOUND SUBJECTS JOINED BY THE CONJUNCTIONS *OR* OR *NOR*

When the elements of a compound subject are joined by *or* or *nor,* the element closer to the verb determines whether the verb is singular or plural. If the element of the subject closer to the verb is singular, the verb is singular. If it is plural, the verb is plural.

***Either Karen or her daughter* <u>is</u> going to pick me up.**

***Either Karen or her daughters* <u>are</u> going to pick me up.**

***Neither the tires nor the alignment* <u>is</u> in good shape.**

***Neither the alignment nor the tires* <u>are</u> in good shape.**

Agreement Error Revised

➤ **Either a school bus or parents' cars ~~is~~ *are* going to be used to take the students on the field trip.**

SUBJECTS THAT ARE COLLECTIVE NOUNS

When the subject is a collective noun (such as *group* or *team*), the verb may be either singular or plural, depending on the context. Collective nouns are treated as *singular* when the individuals within the group are considered as a group, and as *plural* when the individuals within the group are considered as individuals. (For a list of common collective nouns, see **19n, Nouns,** in Part Three, page 255.)

Singular Uses of Collective Nouns

➤ **Our *band* of happy travelers <u>is</u> leaving now.**

➤ **The *majority* is always right.**

➤ **The *committee* is meeting tomorrow.**

Comparison of Singular and Plural

➤ **The class ~~are~~ *is* going on a field trip to the museum.**

➤ **The class of 2003 ~~is~~ *are* going their separate ways immediately after graduation.**

SUBJECTS THAT ARE INDEFINITE PRONOUNS

When the subject is an indefinite pronoun, the verb may be either singular or plural, depending on the pronoun and its context. Indefinite pronouns are those that do not specify a particular person or thing. (For a list of common indefinite pronouns, see **19p, Pronouns,** in Part Three, pages 263–64.)

Most indefinite pronouns are singular and take a singular verb:

***Nobody* is going to the game.**

***Someone* is going to pay for this damage.**

***Anyone* is better company than Gary.**

***Such* is life.**

***One* is all I want.**

***Everybody* is going.**

Some indefinite pronouns (such as *both, few, many, others,* and *several*) are plural and take a plural verb:

➤ ***Many* are volunteering, but *few* are actually showing up.**

A few indefinite pronouns (such as *all, some, none, more, most,* and *any*) can be either singular or plural, depending on their context:

Singular Use of Indefinite Pronoun

➤ ***All* of this book is as good as the first chapter.**

[*All* can be either singular or plural. Here its number is set by the object of the prepositional phrase that follows it.]

Plural Use of Indefinite Pronoun

➤ ***All* the books were by one author.**

Agreement Errors Revised

➤ **Some of the Kool-Aid ~~have~~ has been spilled.**

[Because *Kool-Aid,* the object of the prepositional phrase, is singular, the indefinite pronoun (*Some*) should be treated as singular also.]

➤ **Some of the passengers ~~is~~ are getting off here.**

[Because *passengers,* the object of the prepositional phrase, is plural, the indefinite pronoun (*Some*) should be treated as plural also.]

SUBJECTS THAT ARE RELATIVE PRONOUNS

When the subject of a dependent clause is a relative pronoun, such as *which, that,* or *who,* the verb should be singular or plural, depending on the number of the pronoun's antecedent:

➤ **The presiding officer suddenly had a great idea, *which* was to table the new motion and end the meeting.**

[Here *which* refers to *idea*—a singular noun—so *which* is considered singular and is followed by the singular form of the verb, *was.*]

➤ **I called up two of my friends *who* seem to understand my problem.**

[Because *who* refers to *friends*—a plural noun—*who* is considered to be plural here and is followed by the plural form of the verb, *seem.*]

11c Verb Form Errors

Common errors in verb form include errors in irregular verbs and errors in verb endings (*s, es, d, ed*).

REGULAR VERSUS IRREGULAR VERBS

Most English verbs form their past tense and past participles by adding *ed* or *d.* However, the irregular verbs form their past tense and past participles in irregular ways. The three most common irregular verbs are *be, have,* and *do.*

	Present		Past		Past Participle
	Singular	*Plural*	*Singular*	*Plural*	
to be	I am you are he, she, it is	we are you are they are	I was you were he, she, it was	we were you were they were	been
to have	I have you have he, she, it has	we have you have they have	I had you had he, she, it had	we had you had they had	had
to do	I do you do he, she, it does	we do you do they do	I did you did he, she, it did	we did you did they did	done

Other common irregular verbs are *lay, awake, choose, dive, spring,* and *swim.* (For a more extensive list, see **19v, Verbs,** in Part Three, pages 280–82.)

When you use an irregular verb, make sure you're using the correct form:

➤ **Gerald had ~~wrote~~ written a letter to his teacher explaining his absences.**

[This verb should be in past perfect tense, formed by *had* plus the past participle, *written.*]

If you are in doubt about the correct form of a verb, you can consult a dictionary. Dictionaries nearly always list all the forms of each verb. For example, the *American Heritage* entry for *write* lists *wrote, written, writing, writes;* those are (in order) the past tense, past participle, present participle, and third-person singular present tense of *write.*

VERB ENDINGS: *S, ES, D, ED*

Most regular verbs in English form the third-person singular (*he, she,* or *it* does something) by adding either *s* or *es.*

The teacher *requests* your presence in class tomorrow.

Ann *protests* her innocence.

Phish's music *takes* you away.

Susan always *tosses* her coat onto the bed.

Some spoken dialects of English regularly drop the ending *s* or *es* in informal settings.

Spoken Dialect Forms

"The teacher *request* your presence in class tomorrow."

"Ann *protest* her innocence."

"Phish's music *take* you away."

"Susan always *toss* her coat onto the bed."

In standard written English those dropped endings need to be restored: *requests, protests, takes,* and *tosses.*

Regular verbs in English form their past tense and past participles by adding *d* or *ed.* Some spoken dialects do not regularly add these endings.

Spoken Dialect Forms

"She *love* him until he *die.*"

"That book *change* my life."

"He *use* to be my friend."

In standard written English, *d* or *ed* needs to be restored.

Correct Written Forms

She *loved* him until he *died.*

That book *changed* my life.

He *used* to be my friend.

11d Shifts in Verb Tense

Readers expect verb tenses to change only when there are changes in the time of the action being described. Most verb tense errors involve shifting verb tenses in ways that violate the action sequence being described. Sequence-of-tense errors were discussed in the Instant Access Overview (**11a,** page 142); a similar error in longer passages involves consistency of tense—shifts in tense that are unnecessary and inconsistent.

Inappropriate Shifts in Tense: In 1895 Borglif *developed* the system of professional craft training that still *characterized* German factory development today. Under that system, young men *go* out to learn their

> **trades under the leadership of a mentor, who *was* a senior craftsperson and basically *ran* the shop. The young men's schooling thus *is divided* into assisting a master craftsperson and getting hands-on experience.**

If that passage were talking about something that occurred in 1895 but does not continue today, it should stay in the past tense (for completed past action). But the words *still* and *today* in the first sentence indicate that the passage is describing something that occurred in 1895 and continues today. In this situation, you can leave the first verb in the past tense (because it refers to 1895) but then switch immediately to the present for the rest.

> **Revised: In 1895 Borglif *developed* the system of professional craft training that still *characterizes* German factory development today. Under that system, young men *go* out to learn their trades under the leadership of a mentor, who *is* a senior craftsperson and basically *runs* the shop. The young men's schooling thus *is divided* into assisting a master craftsperson and getting hands-on experience.**

11e Mood Errors

The mood of a verb tells whether the verb expresses a fact (indicative mood); a doubt, a condition wished for, or a condition contrary to fact (subjunctive); or a command (imperative). (See **19v, Verbs,** pages 284–85). To avoid mood errors, remember to use the subjunctive for doubts, conditions wished for, or conditions contrary to fact.

> **If I ~~was~~ ^were ruler of the universe, I would give the moon and the stars to you.**

Additionally, avoid shifts in mood that will seem inconsistent or arbitrary.

> **To bring the bow of the boat across the wind, the skipper begins by hauling in the mainsail a little. Next, ~~shout,~~ ^the skipper shouts "Coming about!" and ~~push~~ ^pushes the tiller all the way over.**

[The second sentence should be in the indicative, like the first sentence, rather than in the imperative.]

12

Using Commas

12A INSTANT ACCESS OVERVIEW

Commas divide the words in a sentence into groups and thus clarify meaning. This overview shows where commas should be used and where they should not. The pages that follow explain these uses in more detail, grouping them into two categories: correct and incorrect uses.

CORRECT USES OF COMMAS

A comma is *necessary* in each of these ten situations:

1. To set off introductory elements

   ➤ ***With her long hair flowing free*, Marina caught everyone's eye.**

2. To set off nonessential (nonrestrictive) elements

   ➤ **Antonio called one man, *his father*, to share the good news.**

3. To separate the independent clauses of a compound sentence

   ➤ **The newest mountain bikes are durable, *and* the best of them are also lightweight.**

4. To separate coordinate adjectives

   ➤ **Hamed's computer is a *newer*, *faster* one than mine.**

5. To separate three or more items in a series

   ➤ **Sam never dreamed that a subject like Latin American history could be so *complex*, *challenging*, *and interesting*.**

6. To set off transitions, parenthetical elements, absolute phrases, and contrasts

   ➤ **Then, *his hopes dashed*, he ran for the bus without looking back.**

7. To set off nouns of direct address, tag questions, words such as *yes* and *no,* and interjections

   ➤ ***Yes*, *my friends*, we have had a fantastic time, *haven't we?***

8. To set off phrases of attribution, such as "she said," that identify the source of a quotation

   ➤ **"Let's head for the door," *Andre said* suddenly.**

9. To separate the parts of dates, addresses, and numbers

   ➤ **We will leave on *May 5*, *2002,* to visit *Jackson Hole*, *Wyoming,* and several national parks nearby.**

10. To prevent confusion

    ➤ **The members of the winning team marched *in*, *in* no hurry to end their victory parade.**

INCORRECT USES OF COMMAS

A comma is *not necessary* in these ten situations:

1. Between a verb and its subject or object

   ➤ **The bizarre exploits of the *Sopranos*~~,~~ seem to fascinate television viewers.**

2. After a coordinating conjunction (*and, but, or, nor, for, so, yet*)

   ➤ ***Harry Potter and the Goblet of Fire* has 734 pages, but~~,~~ young readers have not been intimidated by its length.**

3. Before and after essential (restrictive) elements

   ➤ **Mark forgot the key~~,~~ he needed~~,~~ to open the padlock.**

4. Before the first or after the last item in a series

   ➤ **A happy dog will have~~,~~ a shiny coat, bright eyes, and a healthy appetite~~,~~ nearly all the time.**

5. Between two compound elements

   ➤ **Both the door~~,~~ and its frame need repainting.**

6. Between cumulative adjectives or adverbs

   ➤ **Latonya still uses an old~~,~~ manual typewriter.**

7. Between an adjective and a noun or between an adverb and an adjective

   ➤ **"Beanie babies" were one of those suddenly~~,~~ popular toys.**

8. After *such as* or *like* or before *than*

 ➤ **His tests required more studying, than I was used to.**

9. Before an indirect quotation

 ➤ **Was it Milton's character Satan who said, he would rather rule in Hell than serve in Heaven?**

10. With question marks, exclamation points, parentheses, and dashes

 ➤ **Leon is like his father, (who played for the Dodgers).**

12b Correct Uses of Commas

Many errors in comma usage involve the failure to use commas where they should be used. The following pages discuss the ten most common uses of commas.

1. TO SET OFF INTRODUCTORY ELEMENTS

A comma follows any introductory word, phrase, or clause unless there would be no chance of misreading. The comma separates the introductory information from the rest of the sentence. Here are examples showing different kinds of introductory elements that are followed by a comma:

> Adverb: ***Suddenly*, steam erupted from the boiler in the basement.**
>
> Prepositional Phrase: ***On the other hand*, you may find it easier just to walk to the party.**
>
> Participial Phrase: ***Entering the bank*, she was astonished by the ten-foot Calder mobile hanging between the two rows of elevators.**
>
> Absolute Phrase: ***Her eyes blindfolded*, Stacy waited for the children to make the shout that would begin the game.**
>
> Infinitive Phrase: ***To do well in college*, he would have to find tutors who could meet with him regularly.**
>
> Dependent Clause: ***After she had worked at a day-care center for two years*, she decided against having children.**

If the sentence has two (or more) such introductory elements, each one is normally followed by a comma:

➤ ***At the beginning of the season*, *after the starting quarterback had been benched for disciplinary reasons*, the team fell apart.**

Some writers omit the comma after a short introductory element when the omission would not cause even temporary uncertainty: "*Next week* they leave for England." However, using a comma with such introductory phrases is never incorrect.

CAUTION: Sometimes an opening phrase based on a participle or an infinitive may be the subject of the sentence, so to follow it with a comma would create an error:

➤ **Wearing infrared sunglasses can prevent damage to your eyes.**

➤ **To beat the school shot-put record was her only goal.**

Similarly, if the introductory words begin a sentence that is in *inverted order* (the verb comes before the subject), no comma follows them:

➤ **At the left of the stage stood the security guards, waiting to escort the candidate back to her car.**

2. TO SET OFF NONESSENTIAL (NONRESTRICTIVE) ELEMENTS

When you insert additional information about someone or something into a sentence—information that is nonrestrictive, or not essential to the meaning—set it off with commas. Be sure in such cases to use a *pair* of commas, unless the nonrestrictive material is at the beginning or the end of the sentence.

You can check to see if an element is nonessential by deciding whether the sentence makes sense without it. In the first example below, the words "Tiger Woods was the first man since 1953 to win three major golf tournaments in a year" convey the writer's meaning quite clearly; the clause set off by commas, "as his official Web site notes," just adds detail.

➤ **Tiger Woods, *as his official Web site notes*, was the first man since 1953 to win three major golf tournaments in a year.**

➤ **Lieutenant Worf, *growling and muttering under his breath*, escorted the visitor to the guest-of-honor seat.**

➤ **The sunset was framed with bright red clouds, *the most beautiful I've ever seen.***

➤ **All the kids immediately got in line to ride on the Tilt-a-Whirl, *which is the most popular ride at the fair this year.***

CAUTION: As you revise your writing to set nonessential elements off with commas, be careful to distinguish between nonessential elements and essential elements. If the added phrase or clause is essential for the reader's understanding of the sentence, then it is *restrictive* and should not be set off with commas:

➤ **Behavioral modification programs are the best method that adults can use to lose weight.**

➤ **We punish people who commit crimes by sending them to prison.**

To review the distinction between essential and nonessential, consider the second example above: without the restrictive clause, the meaning seems to be that we punish all people by sending them to prison. But as the restrictive clause makes clear, the intended meaning is that only those who commit crimes are punished by being sent to prison. Because the clause provides an essential shaping of the sentence's meaning, it is not set off by commas. (For additional examples of the distinction between essential and nonessential elements, see **19r, Restrictive and Nonrestrictive Clauses,** in Part Three, pages 268–69.)

3. TO SEPARATE THE INDEPENDENT CLAUSES OF A COMPOUND SENTENCE

Compound sentences have two or more independent clauses. When these clauses are joined by a coordinating conjunction (*and, but, or, nor, for, so,* and *yet*), a comma is needed before the conjunction to separate the clauses clearly. Without the comma, the intended division in the sentence might not be apparent:

➤ **Pablo tried to phone Luis, and Julia ran across the street to see if the child was still at home.**

[If the beginning of the sentence is misread as "Pablo tried to phone Luis and Julia," the rest of the sentence—"ran across the street . . ."—makes no sense.]

➤ **Mr. Combs didn't find his jade ring in the treehouse, for the children had hidden it in the bushes.**

(For more on independent versus dependent clauses, see **19c, Clauses,** in Part Three, page 237.)

CAUTION: Writers often have difficulty distinguishing between a compound sentence (two independent clauses) and a sentence with a *compound predicate* (two verbs but only one subject). Be careful that you do not erroneously insert a comma between the two parts of a compound predicate:

➤ **Mary flew home, and drove her car back later.**

➤ **The students in the residence hall must decide this issue for themselves, or give up any hope of self-governance.**

4. TO SEPARATE COORDINATE ADJECTIVES

When two or more adjectives relate equally to the noun they modify, they are called *coordinate adjectives,* and they are separated by commas. If you can put *and* between the adjectives and not change the meaning, they are working individually and are thus coordinate:

➤ **The *dark, gaping* hole quickly filled with water.**

➤ **His *bitter, dry, shriveled, chewy* fruitcake was not a family favorite.**

If *and* does not make sense between the adjectives, you are using cumulative adjectives, which function as a unit, and no comma is needed:

➤ **This printer has *three popular operating* features.**

NOTE: Often, a noun or an adjective is placed before a noun to create a single concept from the two words: *table leg, rearview mirror, kitchen sink, light bulb, easy chair.* No comma should separate the essential modifier from the noun.

5. TO SEPARATE THREE OR MORE ITEMS IN A SERIES

You need to use commas to separate three or more items in a series—words, phrases, or clauses:

➤ **Try to remember to *feed the dog, bring in the mail, and take out the trash.***

Be sure to insert a comma before the *and* to keep the units separate and to prevent any possibility of misreading:

➤ **On the visit to our old summer camp, we enjoyed talks with old friends, nights under the stars, and sailboats on the lake.**

[Without the comma before *and,* this sentence could seem to mean that the nights were spent under sailboats.]

EXCEPTION: If there are commas within the items in a series, the punctuation mark that separates the series should be a ***semicolon:***

➤ **Marty set his table with plates that were red, white, and blue; napkins that were yellow, green, and brown; and a tablecloth that was gold, green, and black.**

CAUTION: When only two items are combined with a conjunction, such as *and,* no comma is needed.

➤ **His favorite food is a sandwich made with salmon and watercress.**

6. TO SET OFF TRANSITIONS, PARENTHETICAL ELEMENTS, ABSOLUTE PHRASES, AND CONTRASTS

You can add many types of explanatory phrases to your sentences to provide more information for your readers. These elements should be set off from the rest of the sentence with commas.

Transitions

Such transitions as *therefore, however, furthermore, indeed, then, in fact, to the contrary,* and *for instance* may be used to begin sentences or to connect parts of sentences. Use a comma to separate the transitional word or phrase from the rest of the sentence; if the transition occurs in the middle of the sentence, place a comma before and after it:

➤ ***Therefore*, I am ready to leave now.**

➤ **John, *on the other hand*, walked away uninjured.**

➤ **The book I read, *for example*, was much longer.**

When a conjunctive adverb, such as *however* or *nonetheless,* is used to begin the second of two independent clauses joined by a semicolon, the adverb is followed by a comma:

➤ **The ball bounced right off the edge of the backboard; *therefore*, the referee stopped the play.**

➤ **Debbie took the subway across town; *in fact*, she rode it to the end of the line.**

(See **19c, Conjunctive Adverbs,** in Part Three, page 243, for a list of conjunctive adverbs and further discussion of their use.)

Parenthetical Elements or Interrupters

A parenthetical element is a word or a group of words that offers an aside—something that is clearly not necessary in the sentence, breaks up the flow of words, or seems like an afterthought. Such elements are usually set off with commas (although dashes or parentheses may be used instead):

➤ **The biggest waves, *I think*, are yet to come.**

➤ **Your first chemistry course, *most people say*, is the hardest one.**

➤ **The contemporary novel, *according to my English teacher*, is not a very high form of art.**

Absolute Phrases

An absolute phrase is a phrase that modifies the entire sentence; a comma separates such a phrase from the sentence it modifies. These phrases usually consist of a noun and a participle, as in the following examples:

➤ ***The race having been postponed*, the boats were towed back into San Diego harbor.**

➤ ***Their bus no longer functioning*, the team members decided to run the final mile to the game.**

➤ ***His pride shattered*, the lawyer had to admit that he hadn't planned his presentation very carefully.**

(For more examples of absolute phrases, see **19p, Phrases,** in Part Three, page 260.)

Contrasting Elements

A word or a phrase that marks a sharp contrast with the rest of the sentence is usually set off with a comma or commas:

➤ **The officers, *unlike the rest of the crew*, wanted the fleet kept together under one command.**

➤ **The casino, *not known for its high standards of entertainment anyway*, sank to a new low with that fan dancing act.**

7. TO SET OFF NOUNS OF DIRECT ADDRESS, TAG QUESTIONS, WORDS SUCH AS *YES* AND *NO*, AND INTERJECTIONS

Several kinds of short elements allow you to address readers directly but are not essential to the meaning of the sentence. These elements should be set off by commas.

Nouns of Direct Address

➤ **The problem, *friends and acquaintances*, is one of character, not intelligence.**

➤ **Always remember, *future voters*, that your vote is worth nothing if you don't use it.**

Tag Questions

➤ **Luigi looks better after taking a vacation, *don't you think?***

➤ **We're leaving right after the encore, *aren't we?***

Words Such As *Yes* and *No* and Interjections

➤ ***Yes,*** **I would agree with his point in general.**

➤ **You ask if I agree with her; *no,* I don't.**

➤ ***Well,*** **that's your opinion.**

➤ ***Oh,*** **I suppose I'll go along with it this time.**

[Mild interjections such as *oh* are usually followed by a comma instead of an exclamation point.]

8. TO SET OFF PHRASES SUCH AS "SHE SAID" THAT IDENTIFY THE SOURCE OF A QUOTATION

Use commas to set off a quotation from the phrase that introduces it or identifies its source:

➤ ***Mae West declared,*** **"When choosing between two evils, I always like to try the one I've never tried before."**

Place a comma following a quotation *within* the closing quotation mark:

➤ **"Golf is a good walk spoiled,"** ***said Mark Twain.***

9. TO SEPARATE THE PARTS OF DATES, ADDRESSES, AND NUMBERS

The elements of dates or addresses are set off by commas when they appear as part of a sentence:

➤ **Georgia O'Keeffe kept a house in *Abiquiu, New Mexico,* for her guests, but she often lived up the road, at Ghost Ranch.**

➤ ***December 7, 1941,*** **Pearl Harbor Day, is called "the day that will live in infamy."**

EXCEPTION: No comma separates the zip code from the name of a state or the month from the year:

➤ **Please send the package to 5522 Iroquois Drive, St. Paul, Minnesota 55106.**

➤ **He left town in April 2003.**

Use the comma to separate the digits of long numbers into groups of three, counting from the right. The comma with numbers of four digits is optional (except in years, street numbers, and page numbers, where a comma is never used):

➤ **On the new riverboat gambling ship, Carolyn made $*1,921* [*or* $1921] the first night, but she had been hoping for the $*1,234,999* grand prize.**

10. TO PREVENT CONFUSION

Sometimes you need to insert a comma into a sentence just to prevent misreading:

➤ **The police found the murderer, murdered.**

➤ **Those who can, do.**

A comma can also clarify a sentence by replacing a word or words that have been omitted:

➤ **My goal was to live more slowly; my method, to get lots of sleep.**

[The comma replaces the missing word, *was*.]

12c Incorrect Uses of Commas

In the following ten situations, including a comma would be incorrect.

1. BETWEEN A VERB AND ITS SUBJECT OR OBJECT

Especially when several words appear between a subject and its verb, a writer may insert an unnecessary comma between them:

➤ **The gray brick building that looked like a fortress in the rain, turned out to be a campus library.**

➤ **Droves of teenagers of every shape, size, and kind of dress, swarmed into the streets.**

Similarly, a writer may mistakenly insert a comma between the verb and its object when several words are between them:

➤ **After leaving the small town where she was born, La Shondra found in the city, a satisfaction that she had never known.**

2. AFTER A COORDINATING CONJUNCTION

Although compound sentences joined by coordinating conjunctions (*and, but, or, nor, for, so, yet*) require a comma before the coordinating conjunction, some writers regularly insert an unnecessary comma after the conjunction as well:

➤ **Kara liked being able to download music online, but~~,~~ she felt bad for the bands that were losing money because of this new option.**

➤ **Terri took all her books home for the weekend, but~~,~~ she did not get any work done.**

3. BEFORE AND AFTER ESSENTIAL (RESTRICTIVE) ELEMENTS

Words, phrases, and clauses that are necessary to the meaning of a sentence should not be set off by commas:

➤ **A majority of students~~,~~ whom we polled~~,~~ felt their classes were too big.**

➤ **All the university administrators~~,~~ who returned our questionnaires~~,~~ thought the class size was just about right.**

(For more examples, see **19r, Restrictive and Nonrestrictive Clauses,** in Part Three, pages 268–69.)

4. BEFORE THE FIRST OR AFTER THE LAST ITEM IN A SERIES

Do not put a comma either before a series or after the last item:

➤ **Jen's strengths in~~,~~ running, jumping, and throwing~~,~~ made her a natural for the basketball team.**

➤ **The biologists selected four trees for their studies of acid rain, soil erosion, and insect damage~~,~~ in the southern Rockies.**

➤ **Bayfield, Superior, and Grand Portage~~,~~ make the points of a Lake Superior triangle that is rich in history for many different races and nationalities of people.**

5. BETWEEN TWO COMPOUND ELEMENTS

Writers often mistake a compound predicate (a predicate containing two verbs and their modifiers) for a compound sentence (a sentence with two independent clauses). Having made this mistake, they then insert a comma between the two parts of the compound predicate:

➤ **Our directions told us to stay on the path for two miles, and then to turn right onto High Bridge Trail.**

➤ **These particles can become highly charged with negative ions under the right conditions, and can create an increase in the whole field's electrical activity.**

Check to see whether your sentence contains a compound verb (or a compound subject) or is a compound sentence; the only one that merits a comma by virtue of its being *compound* is the compound sentence.

6. BETWEEN CUMULATIVE ADJECTIVES OR ADVERBS

If a group of adjectives or adverbs lean on each other and work together to modify the noun or the verb, they are *cumulative,* and they are not separated by commas:

➤ **He wouldn't part with his faded, Yankees, baseball cap.**

NOTE: If two or more adjectives modify a noun separately, or if two or more adverbs modify a verb separately, they are called *coordinate adjectives* or adverbs and should be separated by commas:

➤ **The Nacra is a *fast, dependable* catamaran.**

➤ **The North Fork of the Little Pigeon River flows *clean, clear, and cold* through the Smokies.**

7. BETWEEN AN ADJECTIVE AND A NOUN OR BETWEEN AN ADVERB AND AN ADJECTIVE

If a series of adjectives modifies a noun, there should be commas between the adjectives but not between the last adjective and the noun:

➤ **Jack chose to attend the school with the biggest, most current, and most accessible, library collection.**

Sometimes the adjective that modifies a noun will itself be modified by an adverb. Do not separate the adverb from the adjective with a comma:

➤ **Our school has a barely~~,~~ adequate library.**

8. AFTER *SUCH AS* OR *LIKE* OR BEFORE *THAN*

The phrases *such as* and *like* should not be separated by a comma from the words following them:

➤ **A real expert, such as~~,~~ Professor French, would disagree with you.**

➤ **The Colorado Rockies, like~~,~~ their northern counterparts, provide recreation for millions of skiers.**

In a comparison, do not put a comma in front of *than:*

➤ **The long way to the top is a more scenic path~~,~~ than this one.**

➤ **Marcelle plays drums better~~,~~ than Frank does.**

9. BEFORE AN INDIRECT QUOTATION

Although direct quotations are usually set off by commas, indirect quotations (reported speech as opposed to quoted speech) are not:

➤ **Bob Dylan once wrote~~,~~ that it takes a lot to laugh but a freight train to cry.**

➤ **Princess Diana maintained~~,~~ that one of the worst things in life was to feel unloved.**

10. WITH QUESTION MARKS, EXCLAMATION POINTS, PARENTHESES, AND DASHES

If a direct quotation ends with a question mark or an exclamation point, do not also include a comma:

➤ **"Prepare to jibe!"~~,~~ called the skipper.**

➤ **"Are you ready now?"~~,~~ asked the doctor.**

When material is enclosed in parentheses or set off with dashes, there should be no commas:

➤ **My mother's quilt~~,~~ (a family heirloom)~~,~~ has four generations of work in it.**

➤ **Several national parks~~,~~—including my favorite, Yosemite—~~,~~ are now requiring visitors to leave their cars at the entrance and ride tour buses in the park.**

13

Pronoun Errors

13A INSTANT ACCESS OVERVIEW

VAGUE OR AMBIGUOUS PRONOUN REFERENCE

The reference of each pronoun should be immediately clear. Unclear pronoun reference usually is caused either by lack of specificity or by too much distance between pronoun and antecedent.

➤ **He took out his gear to begin rappelling down the mountain. He knew that ~~it~~** *the gear* **was the key to his success.**

LACK OF AGREEMENT BETWEEN PRONOUN AND ANTECEDENT

Most pronoun mistakes involve disagreement in *number*—singular or plural—between pronouns and their antecedents (the nouns to which they refer). Disagreement occurs mainly in four situations.

1. Nouns joined with *and* usually take a plural pronoun:

➤ **After hunting all morning for my hammer and chisel, I decided I would never find ~~it~~** *them.*

2. When two or more nouns are joined with *or* or *nor,* the pronoun that refers to them should agree with the closest noun:

➤ **Neither the challenging boats nor the defending champion returned to ~~their~~** *its* **dock unharmed.**

3. Most indefinite pronouns (words such as *each, one, anybody, somebody, no one,* and *everybody*) are treated as singular:

➤ **Each of the boys must accept ~~their~~ his own share of responsibility.**

(For a list of indefinite pronouns that are always singular, are always plural, or may be either, depending on the context, see **19p, Pronouns,** in Part Three, pages 263–64.)

4. Pronouns that refer to collective nouns (words such as *team* and *group*) are singular or plural, depending on whether the noun emphasizes the group or the members individually:

➤ **The group realized the waiter had mixed up ~~its~~ their orders.**

INAPPROPRIATE SHIFTS IN PERSON

Needless shifts between first (or third) person and second person can cause confusion. (*Person* is the point of view: first person, *I* or *we;* second person, *you;* or third person, *he, she, it,* or *they.*)

➤ **Good teachers listen closely to each question. ~~You~~ They know that the answer may help many students.**

BIASED USES OF PRONOUNS

Pronoun choices must be inclusive to reflect the diverse human population. Use masculine pronouns only when indicating only males.

➤ **~~Every student~~ All students will have ~~his~~ their own e-mail account**s **next year.**

➤ **Every student will have his** or her **own e-mail account next year.**

13b Vague or Ambiguous Pronoun Reference

The reference of each pronoun should always be immediately clear to readers. Two kinds of problems are common here—problems with the *specificity* of the reference and problems with the *nearness* of the reference.

PROBLEMS WITH SPECIFICITY OF REFERENCE

To make sure each pronoun has a specific antecedent, you need to rewrite sentences that contain *ambiguous pronoun references.* In the sentence shown here, the problem is that the reader cannot be sure which person the pronoun refers to:

➤ **When Dr. Thomas made the first incision on Mr. Innis, ~~his~~** *Dr. Thomas's* **heart began to beat faster.**

[The sentence needs to make clear *whose* heart began to beat faster.]

Avoid using a pronoun to refer to an entire clause or sentence instead of to one specific noun:

➤ **When my mother got a job and was no longer home to cook on weeknights, I wasn't pleased ~~with it.~~** *that she had stopped cooking.*

[Does "it" refer to the mother's getting a job or to the mother's not being home to cook?]

➤ **The ~~cook is new and doesn't know how~~** *new cook's inability* **to operate this boiler/ ~~which~~ could cause a problem.**

[Is the problem the cook's newness, the cook's ignorance of the boiler, or the boiler itself?]

➤ **~~When you apply for a job, you should~~** *If you don't* **learn about the company/ ~~It may not work out if you don't.~~** *when you apply for a job, you may not be hired.*

[*What* may not work out—your being hired or the job?]

Special Problems with *It*

You should avoid using the pronoun *it* to refer to a noun if the sentence also contains another type of *it* structure:

➤ **Although ~~it~~ *eating at the cafeteria* usually doesn't make Charles happy, ~~to have to eat at the cafeteria,~~ he will do it every time rather than miss a meal.**

Special Problems with *This*

Like other pronouns, *this* should not be used to refer to an entire sentence or clause. At the beginning of a sentence, *this* is most effectively used *with a noun* to indicate the exact meaning. (For more examples of using *this* with a noun, see **1d, Revising,** page 25.)

➤ **My little brother refuses to get up and get dressed before the bus comes. This *stubbornness* has made him late to school many times.**

PROBLEMS WITH NEARNESS OF REFERENCE

Sometimes, as shown in the preceding examples, a pronoun is not clear because too many nouns are nearby that it might refer to. In other cases, a pronoun's reference is not clear because the noun it refers to is too far away. Unless you are sure that the reference is clear, a pronoun should not refer to a noun that appears much earlier in a long sentence (or in a previous sentence).

We realized the first-aid kit in one of our four vans was empty about five minutes after the health inspectors finished checking all our vehicles. We were lucky that the inspectors overlooked ~~it.~~ *that kit.*

[Will readers remember, so many words later, what *it* refers to?]

There are many ways to rewrite such sentences to make the pronoun reference clearer.

13c Lack of Agreement with Antecedent

The pronoun you use to refer to a noun must be singular if the noun is singular and plural if the noun is plural.

➤ **_Mr. James_ decided that _he_ wanted to go on to graduate school for further training in _his_ chosen field.**

➤ **If these _tables_ were refinished, _they_ would regain _their_ original luster.**

AGREEMENT WITH NOUNS JOINED BY *AND*

When two or more nouns are joined by *and,* the pronoun that refers to them must be plural.

➤ **When _Bob and Jaime_ left the dorm to take the test, _they_ left Bob's calculator behind.**

➤ **After a _dove and a canary_ came out of the hat, _they_ immediately flew out over the auditorium.**

The only exception occurs when the two nouns describe the same person or form a single unit:

➤ **My best _friend and confidante_ stood waiting by _her_ car when I came out of the airport terminal.**

➤ **In this new budget, _research and development_ has lost _its_ supremacy in our company.**

AGREEMENT WITH NOUNS JOINED BY *OR, NOR, EITHER . . . OR,* OR *NEITHER . . . NOR*

When two or more nouns are joined by *or, nor, either . . . or,* or *neither . . . nor,* the pronoun is singular if both nouns are singular, and it is plural if both nouns are plural.

Singular Nouns: **If the state doesn't increase the education budget next year, _either the junior college or the technical school_ will lose _its_ accreditation.**

Plural Nouns: **_Neither the symphony members nor the conductors_ were willing to give up _their_ plans for next year's schedule.**

If one noun is singular and the other is plural, the pronoun agrees with the noun that is nearer to it.

Singular and Plural Nouns

➤ ***Either your floppy disks or your computer's hard drive* has a virus infecting *its* files.**

➤ ***Either your computer's hard drive or your floppy disks* have a virus infecting *their* files.**

INDEFINITE PRONOUNS

Many indefinite pronouns (*each, everyone, everybody, everything, anybody, anyone, either, neither, no one, someone,* and *something*) always take singular verbs, and singular personal pronouns are used to refer to them:

➤ **As the ballerinas come back on stage, *each bows her* head to the roaring crowd.**

➤ **The two young men were surprised to learn that *neither was his* father's sole heir.**

A few indefinite pronouns (*both, few, many, others, ones,* and *several*) are always plural:

➤ **Having slept through their alarms, *both were* late for *their* eight o'clock classes.**

➤ ***Others are* coming with us to see the play.**

A few indefinite pronouns (*all, any, enough, more, most, none,* and *some*) may be either singular or plural, depending on their context. Compare:

➤ ***Some* of the leaves *were* brown and wrinkled.**

➤ ***Some* of the leaf *was* brown and wrinkled.**

COLLECTIVE NOUNS

When a collective noun (such as *team, group,* or *chorus*) applies to the group as a whole, use a singular pronoun to refer to that noun. When a collective noun refers to members acting individually, choose a plural pronoun.

Singular	Plural
Our *team* won *its* first conference championship this year.	**The *team* ran out of the locker room to tell the coach that *their* uniforms had not arrived.**

13d Inappropriate Shifts in Person

Avoid shifts between first person (*I, we*), second person (*you*), and third person (*he, she, it, they*) while you are still referring to the same people or things.

➤ **~~The student~~** *Students* **should realize that in college ~~you~~** *they* **are responsible for setting ~~your~~** *their* **own schedule***s***.**

➤ **~~The student~~** *You* **should realize that in college you are responsible for setting your own schedule.**

➤ **When ~~one~~** *you* **first enter~~s~~ the Lincoln Memorial, you are struck by a feeling that Lincoln is really there.**

➤ **When ~~one~~** *visitors* **first enter~~s~~ the Lincoln Memorial, ~~you~~** *they* **are struck by a feeling that Lincoln is really there.**

13e Biased Uses of Pronouns

When you use a singular pronoun or noun, such as *everyone* or *each student,* choose a singular pronoun to refer to it. If you are talking about a male student, *he* is appropriate, as is *she* for a female student. But if you mean to include both males and females, do not use *he,* because it excludes women. To be inclusive, you have three options:

- Use *he or she* (*him or her, his or hers*).

  ➤ **Every contestant should bring three copies of his** *or her* **winning essay to the grand prize luncheon.**

- Change the antecedent to the plural so that you can use *they* (or *them* or *theirs*).

> All ^ / s ^ / their ^ / s ^
>
> ➤ **~~Every~~ contestant should bring three copies of ~~his~~ winning essay to the grand prize luncheon.**

- Rewrite the sentence without the pronoun.

> Each ^ / whose essay won a prize ^
>
> ➤ **~~Every~~ contestant should bring three copies ~~of his winning essay~~ to the grand prize luncheon.**

Overusing *he or she* can make your writing awkward ("He or she should bring his or her books to his or her classes"). To incorporate unbiased language without interrupting the flow of your writing, choose carefully among the three options for pronouns.

Remember also not to stereotype certain roles for certain genders: for instance, if you are writing about a secretary or a pilot, you should carefully consider the three options instead of assuming that a secretary would be female or a pilot male. (For more discussion about avoiding bias in your writing, see **19b, Biased Uses of Language,** in Part Three, pages 230–33.)

14

Using Apostrophes

14A INSTANT ACCESS OVERVIEW

This Instant Access Overview shows the four most common kinds of errors with apostrophes: in possessive case, in contractions, in some plurals, and in pronoun homonyms.

APOSTROPHES IN THE POSSESSIVE CASE

Nouns

Nouns show possession with an apostrophe and an *s;* if the plural form already ends in an *s,* the apostrophe is placed after this *s:*

the *book'*s conclusion	**his *boss'*s car**
all the *girls'* keys	**the *linemen'*s shoes**

Whether both parts of a pair of nouns show possession depends on whether both share possession:

➤ **Jon and Annie's tapes**

[They jointly own the tapes.]

➤ **Jon's and Annie's tapes**

[They each own some of the tapes.]

Pronouns

Two types of pronouns—*personal* pronouns and *indefinite* pronouns—form their possessives in very different ways:

- **Personal pronouns,** such as *I, you,* and *they,* form their possessives by switching to a different form (*I* becomes *my* or *mine*) or by adding an *s* (*it* becomes *its,* and *their* becomes *theirs*).

➤ **Everything I have is *yours.***

➤ **This tarp is *hers;* that one is *ours.***

▪ **Indefinite pronouns,** such as *one* or *anyone,* form their possessives by adding an apostrophe and an *s* (*one's* or *anyone's*):

➤ **Are you *anybody's* lab partner?**

➤ **Denise is *everyone's* friend.**

APOSTROPHES IN CONTRACTIONS

Contractions are shortened forms of two words combined into one, such as *don't* for *do not, weren't* for *were not,* or *can't* for *can not.* The apostrophe in a contraction replaces the missing letters:

➤ **I *can't* understand why you *didn't* like it.**

➤ **Samantha *wouldn't* have entered the race if her roommates *hadn't* dared her.**

APOSTROPHES TO FORM PLURALS

Apostrophes also appear in the plurals of letters, numerals, and words referred to as words:

➤ **Remember to remove some of those *and's* from your sentences and cross your *t's.***

➤ **Europeans draw a line through their 7's so that they won't look like *1's.***

ITS VERSUS *IT'S* AND OTHER PRONOUN HOMONYMS

The word *it* is a personal pronoun and, like other personal pronouns, forms its possessive simply by adding an *s,* with no apostrophe:

➤ **The lion shook *its* head and roared.**

When you add an apostrophe and an *s* to *it,* you create the contraction for *it is:*

➤ **Tell me when *it's* safe to come out.**

14b Apostrophes in the Possessive Case

NOUNS

Use the apostrophe to indicate the possessive case of nouns. The apostrophe is equivalent to the preposition *of,* another marker of possession:

the friend of my brother → **my brother's friend**

the problem of the children → **the children's problem**

the end of the day → **the day's end**

the dog of the boys → **the boys' dog**

In these cases of possession, the placement of the apostrophe also shows whether the noun (the owner) is singular or plural.

With Singular Nouns

For singular nouns, add the apostrophe and then *s:*

the author's creativity [one author]

a week's pay [one week]

the valley's residents [one valley]

NOTE: When a singular proper noun ends in *s,* the possessive form may be written with just an apostrophe or with an apostrophe and *s.* Most authorities prefer adding the apostrophe and *s:*

James's calendar [*or* James' calendar]

With Plural Nouns

For nouns with *regular plurals,* add the apostrophe after the *s:*

the teachers' decision [more than one teacher]

the carpenters' tools [more than one carpenter]

the heroes' parade [more than one hero]

the colonies' concerns [more than one colony]

the Kennedys' ambitions [more than one Kennedy]

the buses' fumes [more than one bus]

For nouns with *irregular plurals,* use that plural form and then add an apostrophe and *s:*

➤ **women's rights**

➤ **children's toys**

➤ **alumni's phone-a-thon**

➤ **two deer's hides**

For Compounds and Word Groups

For compounds and word groups, add the apostrophe and *s* only to the final word:

➤ **her sister-in-law's party**

➤ **the attorney general's office**

➤ **Ken Griffey, Jr's batting average**

For Pairs of Nouns

To indicate *individual ownership* for pairs of nouns, add the apostrophe and *s* to each noun:

➤ **Carmela's and Juana's coats** [two separate coats]

➤ **the judge's and the defense attorney's opinions** [two separate opinions]

To indicate *joint ownership* for pairs of nouns, add the apostrophe and *s* to the final noun:

➤ **Jaime and Sarah's house** [a house owned jointly]

➤ **the father and mother's preferences** [shared preferences]

PRONOUNS

Not all pronouns are made possessive by adding an apostrophe and an *s*. How a pronoun indicates possession depends on the type of pronoun it is.

Personal pronouns do not use apostrophes to show possession. Personal pronouns show possession by either switching to a different form (*him* or *he* becomes *his*) or simply adding an *s* (*their* becomes *theirs; your* becomes *yours*).

Personal Pronoun	Possessive Form
I	**my, mine**
you	**your, yours**
he, she, it	**his, her, hers, its**

we	**our, ours**
you	**your, yours**
they	**their, theirs**

Indefinite pronouns show possession by adding an apostrophe and an *s:*

one's friends	**anyone's remarks**
somebody's mother	**another's livelihood**
everybody's happiness	

(For more on the types of pronouns, see **19p, Pronouns,** in Part Three, pages 263–64.)

14c Apostrophes in Contractions

A contraction is a shortened form of two words combined into one. When you form a contraction, you must show that some letters are missing. Signal the missing letter or letters with an apostrophe:

can + not → can't	**I + am → I'm**
will + not → won't	**I + will → I'll**
does + not → doesn't	**we + are → we're**
did + not → didn't	**you + are → you're**
would + not → wouldn't	**they + are → they're**
should + not → shouldn't	

CAUTION: When you use contractions, the tone of your writing becomes informal—almost conversational. Contractions are not recommended in academic and professional writing. If you are in doubt about how your reader will respond to a contraction, do not use it.

14d Apostrophes to Form Plurals of Letters and Numerals

To form the plural of a letter or a numeral or of a word considered as a word, add an apostrophe and *s*. These words and numbers—but not the apostrophe and *s*—are generally placed in italics:

Watch your *p*'s and *q*'s.

We cannot distinguish his *3*'s from his *8*'s.

We said our *thank you*'s and left quickly.

To form the plural of an abbreviation followed by a period, use the apostrophe and *s:*

two Ph.D.'s **two V.P.'s**

When an abbreviation or acronym is written without periods, its plural does not contain an apostrophe:

MIAs **IOUs** **UFOs** **VCRs**

With decades, do not include an apostrophe:

the 1990s

14e *Its* versus *It's* and Other Pronoun Homonyms

Remember that *it,* like other personal pronouns, forms its possessive without an apostrophe. But you need to use an apostrophe when you are forming the contraction of *it is: it's.* Three other pairs of *pronoun homonyms* can also cause confusion for writers.

Pronoun Homonyms

Contraction	*Possessive*
***It's* hot today.**	***Its* heat slows me down.**
***Who's* driving today?**	***Whose* keys are these?**
***You're* my one chance.**	***Your* chance will come.**
***They're* coming soon.**	***Their* turn will come soon.**

Because *its, whose, your,* and *their* are the possessive forms of personal pronouns (also called *possessive adjectives*), they do not use apostrophes to form possessives. The only pronouns that form possessives with apostrophes are *indefinite pronouns* (such as *one* or *someone*).

15

Problems with Modifiers

15A INSTANT ACCESS OVERVIEW

Correct use of modifiers helps make written English more precise.

MISPLACED MODIFIERS

Misplaced modifiers are words, phrases, or clauses placed too far away from the words they modify:

➤ W ***With a temperature of 500 degrees,*** **Darren could see that the engine, was running much too hot.**

[The original makes it sound as if Darren were running quite a temperature!]

DANGLING MODIFIERS

Dangling phrases or clauses have no word to modify:

we could see

➤ ***Pouring the brown, soapy water through a filter,*** **the first real indications of the pollution.** ~~**could be seen.**~~

[There is no word in the original sentence for the introductory phrase to modify; the person doing the pouring is not mentioned.]

SQUINTING MODIFIERS

Squinting modifiers are words, phrases, or clauses that could modify either what comes before or what comes after:

➤ **Chayyal said *definitely* she would be here.**

➤ **Chayyal said *definitely* she would be here.**

[Did she definitely make the statement, or will she definitely be somewhere?]

OVERSTACKED MODIFIERS

Overstacked modifiers are so numerous that they obscure the meaning:

Overstacked: **This *much-debated, incredibly expensive, multinationally constructed, limited use, too small, excessively fragile, dangerously unsafe* space station should not be built.**

Revised: **This *much-debated* and *incredibly expensive* space station should not be built. Even though it is *multinationally constructed,* it will be of *limited use* because it is *too small, excessively fragile,* and *dangerously unsafe.***

IMPROPER ADVERB OR ADJECTIVE FORMS

To add *ly* or not to add *ly*? What is the *comparative* form of *round*? This chapter's final section discusses modifiers' suffixes:

➤ **Although he did not agree with the ruling, the defendant did his community service as ~~cheerful~~ cheerfully as possible.**

➤ **Captain Janeway found the universe to be ~~more infinite~~ bigger than she had thought.**

15b Misplaced Modifiers

Modifiers must be placed as close as possible to the word(s) they modify. *Misplaced modifiers* are words, phrases, or clauses that are located closer to words they don't modify than to the words they do modify:

➤ **Pat showed the new pool ~~to~~ her guests *that had just been filled with water.***

[The sentence needs to be revised to make it clear that the pool, not the guests, had just been filled.]

If you find a modifier that has drifted away from its object, change the sentence to get them back together.

➤ **Thirty-two trout were caught by fishermen. *that had been banded.***

➤ h **~~*H*~~*anging over the fireplace.* Jack was showing off his new painting.**

As we were flying
➤ ***~~Flying~~* *over Chicago,* the Sears tower looked even more impressive. ~~to us.~~**

15c Dangling Modifiers

Whatever modifiers refer to must be named in the sentence. *Dangling modifiers* are usually phrases that begin with the *-ed, -ing,* or *to + verb* form of a verb (*verbal phrases*) and that do not clearly refer to any other word or phrase in the sentence. These modifiers can confuse readers:

you can easily see
➤ ***Driving through downtown,* the effects of the fire. ~~are easy to see.~~**

[The sentence needs to be revised so that *driving* has something to modify.]

If the object that a modifying clause or phrase is intended to describe is not named in the sentence, rewrite the sentence to include the object.

➤ ***With ice one inch thick on its wings,*** [the plane was bound to have] **an accident.** ~~**was inevitable.**~~

➤ ***To take the tournament championship,*** [the students on the team had to cut corners] ~~**corners had to be cut**~~ **when it came to schoolwork.**

➤ [Because I was] ~~***Being***~~ ***a high school senior,*** **my parents didn't want to move until the school year ended.**

EXCEPTION: One construction looks like a dangling modifier, but it is in fact acceptable. An *absolute modifier,* consisting of a subject and a participle, modifies a whole sentence:

➤ ***Her arms shaking uncontrollably,*** **Lisa left the cold water.**

➤ ***The day finally coming to an end,*** **she closed her briefcase and headed for the door.**

➤ ***His savings depleted,*** **Rufus wearily phoned his grandmother.**

(For more on absolute phrases, see **19p, Phrases,** in Part Three, page 260.)

15d Squinting Modifiers

A *squinting modifier* is unclear because it could modify more than one thing in the sentence—usually the word or phrase before it as well as the word or phrase after it:

➤ **Tom told the bank** ***with great difficulty,*** **he could get the money.**

➤ **Tom told the bank** ***with great difficulty,*** **he could get the money.**

[Was it hard for Tom to tell the bank, or hard to get the money?]

If you find you have written a sentence with a squinting modifier in it, rewrite the sentence to make clear exactly what the modifier refers to:

➤ **The otters in Abrams Creek *only* are affected by the presence of humans in the campgrounds.**

➤ **The otters in Abrams Creek *only* are affected by the presence of humans in the campgrounds.**

[Are the Abrams Creek otters the only animals affected, or is the presence of humans the only thing that affects the Abrams Creek otters?]

15e Overstacked Modifiers

In government, military, scientific, and technical writing, modifiers are often stacked one on top of the other until no one knows what goes with what. The modifiers in such stacks could be nouns, adjectives, or prepositional phrases. These *overstacked modifiers* are one of the main reasons that the jargon of the Pentagon and other bureaucracies is so difficult to understand:

Overstacked: **The *insufficiently correlated atmospherically disturbed nitrogen-binding negative-charge ionized* molecules glow.**

Revised: **A few of the molecules glow. Although the data about these glowing molecules are *insufficiently correlated* right now, the particles seem to be *nitrogen-binding* molecules that are *negatively charged* and *ionized.* Apparently, they glow when they are *atmospherically disturbed.***

Unstack overstacked modifiers to make the sentence clear, even if you have to use a few more words (or sentences) to do so.

Overstacked: **The purpose of this research is to determine the feasibility of the finite-element method as a predictor for actual laboratory testing using a *three-dimensional, nonlinear, transient, dynamic, stress-and-strain finite-element* code developed at Livermore National Laboratory for analyzing average tibias and fibulas under varying conditions of impact loading.**

Revised: **The purpose of this research is to determine the feasibility of the finite-element method as a predictor for actual laboratory testing. The research will analyze average tibias and fibulas under varying conditions of impact loading, using a *finite-element* code**

developed at Livermore National Laboratory. The code is *three-dimensional* and *nonlinear,* allowing representation of *transient* and *dynamic stresses* and *strains.*

15f Improper Adverb or Adjective Forms

The two most common problems with adverbs and adjectives are confusion about whether to add an *ly* and confusion about the correct *comparative* and *superlative* forms.

TO ADD *LY* OR NOT?

Most adverbs are formed by adding *ly* to an adjective. Although conversational English often ignores this distinction, written English always observes it.

Spoken	Written
The coach told us to play the next five minutes as *slow* as possible.	**The coach told us to play the next five minutes as *slowly* as possible.**

The absence of an *ly* ending generally means that the modifier is an *adjective*—but the words that modify verbs, adjectives, or adverbs need to be *adverbs:*

Adjective	Adverb
Paul walked with a *heavy* step out the door.	**Paul walked *heavily* out the door.**

COMPARATIVES AND SUPERLATIVES

Many adjectives and adverbs change form as they move from the *positive* form (*big*), to the *comparative* (*bigger*), and to the *superlative* (*biggest*). *Big,* like most one-syllable adjectives and like two-syllable adjectives that are accented on the first syllable, forms its comparative or superlative by adding *er* or *est.* (For a word that ends in *y,* the *y* changes to *i* when *er* or *est* is added.)

For adjectives that are longer than two syllables and for most adverbs, *more* and *less* are used to form comparatives and *most* and *least* are used to form superlatives. A few common modifiers have irregular forms, such as *good-better-best, bad-worse-worst,* and *some-more-most.*

There are no degrees of comparison for words that describe absolute concepts. It is illogical to speak of something being "more perfect," "less round," or "most (or very) unique."

➤ **Our universe is ~~the most~~ infinite in size.**

It is ungrammatical to use double comparative or superlative forms, such as "more prettier" or "most prettiest."

➤ **Shanelle was ~~more~~ happier than I had ever seen her before.**

(For sample lists of positive, comparative, and superlative forms of common adjectives and adverbs, see **19a, Adjectives** and **Adverbs,** in Part Three, pages 227–28. For words not covered in those lists, consult a good dictionary.)

16

Faulty Parallelism

16A INSTANT ACCESS OVERVIEW

Parallelism is a similarity of form in words, phrases, or clauses that have similar functions in a sentence or a paragraph. *Faulty parallelism* is the lack of parallel structure:

➤ **Lucinda likes *swimming, skating,* and ~~to ski~~ skiing.**

➤ **In that dormitory, all the students have to tell the counselors where they are going and ~~their study schedule.~~ when they will be studying.**

Readers expect parallel word structures, especially when there is some underlying parallelism of meaning. In particular, the following four situations generally signal a need for parallelism.

ITEMS IN LISTS

Words, phrases, or clauses in a list or series should all have the same grammatical structure:

➤ **You can find information on authors in three ways: *ask* a librarian, type the author's name into the online catalogue, or ~~by looking~~ look in *Contemporary Authors.***

ITEMS JOINED BY COORDINATING CONJUNCTIONS

Words or phrases joined by coordinating conjunctions should have the same structure:

➤ **They went *to a party* and to the *movies.***

PARTS OF A SENTENCE JOINED BY CORRELATIVE CONJUNCTIONS

Elements joined by correlative conjunctions, such as *either . . . or* and *not only . . . but also,* should be parallel:

➤ **Domingo is not only *a great striker* but also ~~plays~~ a *great* ~~at~~ *goalie.***

COMPARISONS OR CONTRASTS

Two elements that are compared or contrasted should be expressed in parallel structures:

➤ **Some politicians would rather ~~*be talking*~~ talk about government waste and mismanagement than *try* to do anything about them.**

16b Items in Lists

Items in a list, such as "swimming, skating, and skiing," need to have the same grammatical structure. For example, the first sentence below has been corrected so that each item appears in the *-ing* form, and the second one has been corrected so that each item appears in the same order:

➤ **From the park, we could hear *the banging of drums, the wailing of* guitars, and ~~cymbals crashing.~~** the crashing of cymbals.

➤ **We read and discussed *Love Medicine* by Louise Erdrich, *Beloved* by Toni Morrison, *Woman Warrior* by Maxine Hong Kingston, and ~~Gretel Ehrlich's~~ *Heart Mountain*.** by Gretel Ehrlich.

16c Items Joined by Coordinating Conjunctions

Words or phrases linked by a *coordinating conjunction* (*and, but, or, nor, for, so,* and *yet*) must have parallel structure. For example, repeat any preposition (such as *in, on,* or *for*) used in the first phrase; repeat the *to* if the first phrase is an infinitive:

➤ **Her concern was not *for a high-paying job* but** for **a *learning experience*.**

➤ **She decided *to cut* the old permanent out of her hair and ~~try changing~~** to change **her hair color.**

16d Parts of a Sentence Joined by Correlative Conjunctions

You also need to use parallel structures for parts of a sentence connected by *correlative conjunctions* (*both . . . and, either . . . or, neither . . . nor, not only . . . but also, whether . . . or*). To make the meaning clear, use the same structure after each of the two parts of the conjunction.

➤ **I knew that either I had to study more or ~~the course should be dropped.~~** *I had to drop* **the course.**

➤ **Whether we win or ~~a loss results,~~** *lose,* **we will know that we did our best.**

16e Comparisons or Contrasts

Parallel structures are also needed to clarify the meaning of comparisons or contrasts, which are usually signaled by the word *than:*

➤ **Stephen thought finding a girlfriend was more important than** *getting* **good grades.**

➤ **Saving all the bibliographic information in a computer file is easier than ~~to write~~** *writing* **it all down on paper.**

17

Mixed Constructions

17A INSTANT ACCESS OVERVIEW

A *mixed construction* is a sentence whose parts do not fit together well.

MISMATCHED SUBJECT AND PREDICATE

Walden, by

➤ **One book we read in high school was ^ Thoreau.**

[Thoreau is the name of the author, not of the book.]

MISMATCHED CLAUSES

, the delay

➤ **When planes take off late ^ causes airlines to lose passengers.**

➤ **When planes take off late, ^ ~~causes~~ airlines ~~to~~ lose passengers.**

["When planes take off late" is a dependent clause, not a subject.]

MISMATCHES WITH *IS WHEN, IS WHERE,* OR *THE REASON . . . IS BECAUSE*

finding

➤ **Being really alone is ~~when you find~~ ^ nothing in your mailbox, not even junk mail.**

You know you are

➤ **^ ~~Being~~ really alone ~~is~~ when you find nothing in your mailbox, not even junk mail.**

[Words or phrases linked by *is* should be parallel in structure.]

17b Mismatched Subject and Predicate

The subject and the predicate (the verb plus its object or other complements) of a sentence should make sense together. If they do not, the result is one type of *mixed construction.* (A more specific name for this version of the error is *faulty predication.*)

➤ ***Building*** **a new little league park would** ~~***be***~~ ^create **a great** ***place*** **for the boys and girls to have fun.**

➤ ~~***Building***~~ ~~**a**~~ ^A **new little league park would** ***be*** **a great** ***place*** **for the boys and girls to have fun.**

[It is the *park* that would be a great place, not *building* it.]

17c Mismatched Clauses

Sometimes a writer will begin a sentence with one type of structure and end it with another, thus creating a confusing combination:

➤ **Not only does her head ache/** ^since **the accident** ~~**caused**~~ ^, but she is also experiencing **neck pain.**

[Pairing *not only* with *but also* helps to logically relate the clauses.]

➤ **After running ten miles,** ~~**was the reason**~~ ^ **Sandra became dehydrated.**

["Running" can be a reason for becoming dehydrated; "after running" cannot be.]

17d Mismatches with *Is When, Is Where,* or *The Reason . . . Is Because*

In sentences stating definitions, constructions such as *is when, is where, is why,* and *the reason . . . is because* can cause confusion and awkwardness. Using *reason* with *because* is repetitive, *where* should be used only for locations, and *when* should be used only for time.

the imposition of ... by one nation

➤ **A sanction *is* ~~*when* one nation imposes~~ a penalty on another for misconduct.**

one party's failure

➤ **A breach of contract *is* ~~*where* one party fails~~ to live up to the terms of the contract.**

18

For Multilingual/ ESL Writers

18A INSTANT ACCESS OVERVIEW

This Instant Access Overview provides a list, with short examples, of the most common writing problems encountered by students whose native language is not English. The pages that follow explain these problems in more detail. Many of the discussions are also touched on in other places in this book, where they have been marked with a globe icon.

ARTICLES AND NOUNS (PAGES 198–204)

- **Indefinite and definite articles:** a, an, and the
- **Proper nouns and articles:** *Asia, September, the Atlantic Ocean*
- **Common nouns and articles:** *The three friends* who study *chemistry* work together on *a supercomputer.*

ADJECTIVES (PAGES 204–06)

- **Order of cumulative adjectives:** the small, square, wooden card table
- ***-Ing* and -ed verbs used as adjectives:** The *bored* tourist thought it was the most *boring* museum of the trip.

ADVERBS (PAGES 206–07)

- **Placement of adverbs:** Quickly, he began running toward the bus. He had never been so late before.

PREPOSITIONS (PAGES 207–09)

- **Prepositions of time and place:** *At noon,* when I arrived *on campus,* I went *in the administration building* located *by the large fountain.*

- **Phrasal prepositions:** according to, across from, out of
- **Phrasal constructions:** preferable to, thankful for

VERBS (PAGES 209–16)

- **Two-word verbs:** admit to, agree on, agree with
- **Helping verbs:** He *can* win. He *has* eaten. He *could be* playing.
- **Verbs in conditional sentences:** If the store *closes* early, she *will come* by our house.
- **Verbs followed by gerunds and infinitives:** They *finished dancing.* They *offered to help* her. They *expect* him *to stay.*

SENTENCE STRUCTURE (PAGES 216–20)

- ***It* and *there* structures:** *There were* clouds earlier. Now *it is* raining.
- **Direct and indirect questions and quotations:** The clerk asked, "Would you like to charge your purchase?" I said I would pay in cash.

If you speak English as a second—or third or fourth—language, this entire book is intended to help you with the writing you will do in college, which you can enrich by drawing on your own life experiences and cultural traditions.

Part One may be especially helpful for working with the differences between the language(s) you know and academic English:

Thesis statements and topic sentences: In some languages, a thesis is only implied, not stated directly, to show respect for the reader's ability to consider ideas independently. Most American college assignments, however, require a thesis statement to convey the main idea of the entire essay and topic sentences to convey the main idea of each paragraph. These parts of an American college essay are discussed in **1, Writing Processes,** on pages 10–11 and 18–22.

Tight structure: Although digressions into side issues and anecdotes enliven essays in many languages, your American college essays may require a more formal, straightforward structure. (See **1, Writing Processes,** pages 11–12 and 18–26.)

Clearly cited sources: In some languages, writers combine ideas from various texts without providing detailed information about their sources. In American academic writing, however, writers are expected to cite all sources of information completely. (See **2c, Use Your Sources Effectively,** pages 40–45 and **2d, Document Your Sources Correctly,** pages 45–53.)

Conciseness: In some languages, writers include long, eloquent passages that might be judged as wordy or inappropriate by American college teachers. (See **1d, Revising,** pages 22–26.)

Note: We would like to thank Paulette Swartzfager of Loyola University for her help with this section.

18b Articles and Nouns

In English, there are three articles, *a, an,* and *the,* small words that can cause big problems. English nouns—the words for persons, animals, places, and things—come in two basic types: proper nouns (*Sophia, Lake Erie*) and common nouns (*woman, lake*). The following sections concern the three articles, these two types of nouns, and the further division of common nouns into countable and uncountable nouns as well as general and specific nouns. These distinctions will help you to decide which nouns to capitalize, whether to use them in the singular or the plural, and which articles to use with these nouns. (For more information, see **19n, Nouns,** in Part Three, page 255.)

INDEFINITE AND DEFINITE ARTICLES

Articles indicate that a noun will follow and that any modifiers between the article and the noun apply to that noun: *a house, the big stick.*

A and *an* are called **indefinite articles** because they do not name one specific thing. Their meaning is similar to "one" or "any." They are always used with a singular noun:

➤ **I needed to find *a friend* when I started that new job.**

➤ ***A bagel* with cream cheese lay on the table.**

A is used before consonant sounds: *a book, a silly joke, a hospital. An* is used before vowel sounds: *an athlete, an awful movie, an hour.*

The is the **definite article**; it implies a specific reference to a known or identified person, place, or thing. It can be used with singular or plural nouns:

➤ ***The girls* at my high school often ran on *the track* near *the football field.***

PROPER NOUNS AND ARTICLES

Proper nouns begin with a capital letter, and they name a unique person, animal, event, or object:

Gabriel García Márquez	**Iowa State University**
Fluffy	**Tuesday**
Lake Erie	**September**

Most proper nouns are used with no article: *Selina left on Saturday to visit Europe and Africa.* There are, however, some exceptions, which are shown in the following box.

INSTANT ACCESS

EXCEPTIONS: PROPER NOUNS USED WITH *THE*

Although most proper nouns appear without an article, there are some exceptions. The following types of proper nouns are used with *the:*

Noun phrases that include *of*: the Fourth of July, the Declaration of Independence, the Statue of Liberty, the University of Kansas

Parts of the globe: the South Pole, the Equator, the West, the Southern Hemisphere, the Baja Peninsula

Names of countries that indicate a united group: the United Kingdom, the United States, the Philippines, the Bahamas

Oceans, seas, gulfs, and rivers: the Atlantic Ocean, the South China Sea, the Persian Gulf, the Nile River (Lakes, however, do not appear with *the:* Lake Michigan, Lake Winnipeg.)

Mountain ranges and deserts: the Rocky Mountains, the Ural Mountains, the Sahara Desert (Individual mountains, however, do not appear with *the:* Mount St. Helens, Mount Everest.)

Historical periods and events: the Renaissance, the American Revolution, the Industrial Revolution, the Cold War

Highway names (not numbers) and trails: the New Jersey Turnpike, the Long Island Expressway (but Route 66 or Interstate 10)

Buildings and hotels: the Empire State Building, the Sears Tower, the Alamo, the Taj Mahal, the Holiday Inn

Museums: the Museum of Modern Art, the Louvre

Web terms: the World Wide Web, the Web, the Internet, the Net, the Information Superhighway

As you can see, *the* is not capitalized when it is used with these proper nouns.

COMMON NOUNS AND ARTICLES

Unlike proper nouns, common nouns do not name a unique person, animal, place, or thing:

author	**university**
cat	**day**

To decide on the appropriate article to use with common nouns, you first need to consider two more characteristics of these nouns: they can be countable or uncountable, and they can be general or specific.

Countable Nouns

Countable nouns refer to things that can be counted; they have singular and plural forms:

➤ **Next term they hope to find an *apartment* off campus.**

➤ **Are there many *apartments* available near campus?**

Uncountable Nouns

Uncountable nouns refer to things that cannot be directly counted because they don't have plural forms.

➤ **The doctor said I should eat less *salt*.**

➤ ***Honesty* is the best policy.**

Some words in English, such as *equipment* and *jewelry*, seem as if they should be countable because they name separate units, but they do not have plurals and so they are uncountable nouns. They have to be combined with an *of* phrase to represent quantity: *two boxes of equipment, three pieces of jewelry.*

The box on page 201 lists some of the most common uncountable nouns. If you are not sure about other nouns that you encounter, you can look them up in a dictionary for nonnative speakers, such as *The American Heritage English as a Second Language Dictionary, The Cambridge Dictionary of American English,* or *The Longman Dictionary of American English.* Also check the online resources listed in the box on page 219.

Rules for Using Uncountable Nouns

When you have identified a noun as uncountable, you can follow these rules to use it correctly:

1. An uncountable noun is never used with *a* or *an.*

   ➤ **My teacher gave me ~~a~~ good advice.**

INSTANT ACCESS

COMMONLY USED UNCOUNTABLE NOUNS

Substances without definite shapes: air, dirt, flour, gasoline, rain, silver, snow

Food and drink: bread, butter, chocolate, coffee, milk, oil, rice, salt, sugar, tea, water

Abstract ideas or qualities: advice, anger, beauty, justice, wealth

Continuous processes: digestion, education, evaporation, pollution, time

Natural phenomena: electricity, heat, thunder, weather

Fields of study: biology, economics, mathematics, music

Languages: Chinese, French, Swahili, Vietnamese

Sports and games: chess, football, poker, rugby, soccer

Other: clothing, equipment, furniture, garbage, hardware, homework, information, input, jewelry, money, news, work

2. An uncountable noun is never used with a number, a plural word like *these* or *those,* or a plural quantity word such as *a few, several, both,* or *many.*

   ➤ **Lauralee bought ~~several~~ bread at the store.**

3. An uncountable noun can be used

   — without an article:

   ➤ ***Liberty* is a basic right.**

   — with a singular word like *this* or *that:*

   ➤ **I don't like *that music.***

   — with a quantity word such as *no, any, some, a little, more, much,* or *all:*

   ➤ **Add *some water* and *some sugar* to *a little snow* to make snow cream.**

   — or with a quantity phrase, such as *a small amount of, a cup of, a gallon of, a great deal of, a large amount of,* or *a lot of,* that allows you to count the substance:

   ➤ **In the evening, *a cup of tea* and *a few verses of poetry* give me *a great deal of happiness.***

4. An uncountable noun as a subject must have a singular verb.

   ➤ **This *candy is* homemade.**

   If it appears with a quantity phrase, that phrase will determine the verb.

➤ **A large *amount* of garbage *is* sitting on the curb.**

➤ **Two *cups* of flour *are* needed to make this cake.**

General and Specific Nouns

To understand noun usage in English and to decide on the correct article in any given case, you will need to consider another important distinction: whether the noun is being used in a *general* or a *specific* sense.

General Nouns

➤ ***Doors* are available in many different materials and styles.**

➤ **Every room in my parents' house had a *door*.**

Specific Noun

➤ **Kim shut the *door* and locked it.**

General nouns occur in three situations.

1. They name an entire category:

   ➤ **My sister has an unnatural fear of *spiders*.**

   ➤ ***Air* is necessary for *life*.**

2. They name a representative member of a category, one whose specific identity is not known to the reader:

   ➤ **A *city* offers more services than a *town*.**

   ➤ **I am looking for a *car* to drive to Maine.**

3. They name a person, a place, or an object for the first time, one that will be identified in the essay:

   ➤ **In the shadows, I saw a *boy* that I didn't recognize. As I got closer, I realized that it was Jimmy.**

Specific nouns refer not to a general category or an unknown thing but to one particular thing (or group of things) that is known to the reader:

➤ **The *air* in this room is stale.**

➤ **Please hand me the ice *water* on Louisa's tray.**

➤ **Let's go to the *mountains* this weekend.**

➤ **The *spiders* we found were not poisonous.**

Four Rules for Using the Articles *A*, *An*, and *The* with Common Nouns

The next section explains the four rules that govern the choice of the indefinite article, the definite article, or no

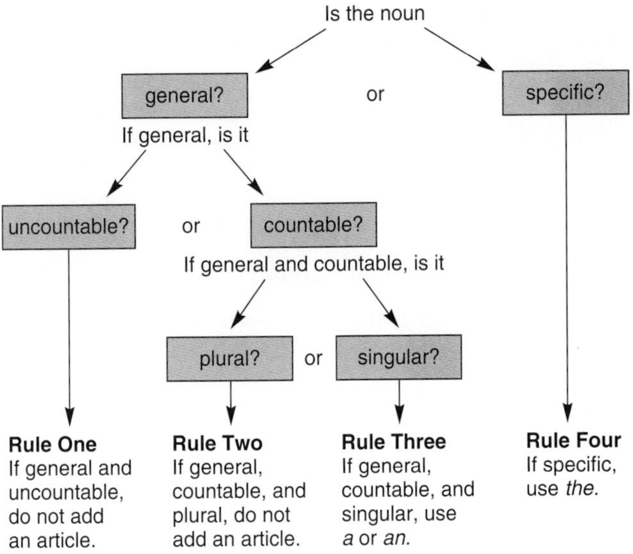

FIGURE 12. Flowchart and Summary of Rules for Using Articles with Common Nouns

article in English sentences. The rules rely on the previous section's definitions of countable and uncountable nouns (page 200) and of general and specific nouns (page 202). Figure 12 (above) will help you to see how these rules work.

Rule One: No Article before General, Uncountable Nouns

➤ **Alfredo has decided to study ~~the~~ economics.**

➤ **Jianyi went to buy ~~the~~ sugar.**

Rule Two: No Article before General, Countable, Plural Nouns

If you decide that a noun in a sentence is both *general* and *countable,* then you must decide whether it is *singular* or *plural.* If the noun is plural, it is not preceded by an article:

➤ **When Anna talks about ~~the~~ computers, she gets very excited.**

A

➤ **~~The~~ apples grow in North America.**

Rule Three: Use *A* or *An* before General, Countable, Singular Nouns

If you decide that a noun is *general, countable,* and *singular,* add *a* or *an.* If such a noun begins with a *consonant* sound, use *a.* If it begins with a *vowel* sound, use *an:*

➤ **James saw *a truck* in front of the dorm.**

➤ **Last week we read *an article* on the human genome.**

Rule Four: Use *The* before Specific Nouns

Specific nouns—words that clearly refer to one or more specific things—take *the* for an article. We return to the example used earlier:

➤ **Kim shut *the door* and locked it.**

Here *door* clearly refers to one specific door that is known to the reader; thus *door* is preceded by *the.* The plural, *doors,* would also be used with *the:*

➤ **Kim shut *the doors* and locked them.**

18c Adjectives

Adjectives modify (or add details about) nouns and pronouns. In English, they usually precede nouns, and they may also appear after linking verbs such as *appear, be, become, feel, look, seem, smell, sound,* and *taste.*

➤ **Corinne went to a *new* restaurant. The restaurant was *beautiful.***

Adjectives never have plural forms: *the new restaurant, the new restaurants.*

ORDER OF CUMULATIVE ADJECTIVES

Cumulative adjectives work together to modify the noun (and cannot logically be joined with *and*). These adjectives are not separated by commas.

➤ **I bought my *small antique marble table* at a yard sale.**

When several adjectives precede a noun, they generally appear in a specific order.

INSTANT ACCESS

ORDER OF CUMULATIVE ADJECTIVES

Articles, pronouns, quantity words, and possessives go first: *a, an, the, his, her, our, Laura's, several, few, every, two, fifty-seven,* and so on.

Evaluative words go next: *beautiful, ugly, handsome, pretty, committed, tasty, appealing,* and so on.

Words about size go next: *big, small, huge, tiny,* and so on.

Words about length and shape go next: *short, long, square, round, oblong, triangular, wide, narrow,* and so on.

Words about age go next: *old, young, fresh, stale,* and so on.

Words about color go next: *red, green, blue,* and so on.

Words about nationality go next: *Canadian, Irish, Mexican, Puerto Rican, Vietnamese,* and so on.

Words about religion go next: *Catholic, Protestant, Muslim, Buddhist,* and so on.

Words about material makeup go next: *concrete, wooden, brick, stone, steel-and-glass,* and so on.

Nouns used as adjectives go next: *swim* (as in *swim team*), *rope* (as in *rope ladder*), *fish* (as in *fish market*), and so on.

The noun being modified goes last: *teacher, student, house, books, ideas,* and so on.

-ING AND *-ED* VERBS USED AS ADJECTIVES

Adjectives can be formed from both the present participle (*-ing* form) and the past participle (*-ed* form) of verbs. The *-ing* form indicates that the word modified produces an effect; the *-ed* form indicates that something has affected the word modified:

➤ **The *exciting* movie is still playing.**

[The movie produces excitement.]

➤ **The *excited* girl waited in the lobby.**

[The girl has been excited: that effect has been produced in her.]

Produces an Effect	Has an Effect Produced on It
amazing	**amazed**
boring	**bored**
depressing	**depressed**
disappointing	**disappointed**
interesting	**interested**
satisfying	**satisfied**
surprising	**surprised**
worrying	**worried**

Even though you may not always hear the *-ed* ending in speech, remember not to omit it in your writing:

➤ **The *worried* girl waited for her mother.**

18d Adverbs

Adverbs modify (or add details about) verbs, adjectives, and other adverbs. They can be distinguished from adjective forms because they usually end in *ly:*

➤ **The *quick* runner went down the road.**

[*Quick* is an adjective describing the runner.]

➤ **The runner moved *quickly.***

[*Quickly* is an adverb adding information to the verb *moved.*]

Similarly, *successful, pretty,* and *careful* are adjectives; *successfully, prettily,* and *carefully* are adverbs. Other commonly used adverbs include *very, well, almost, always, often, soon, never,* and *not.*

(For more information, see **19a, Adverbs,** in Part Three, page 228.)

PLACEMENT OF ADVERBS

Adverbs modifying verbs appear in various positions: at the beginning or end of a sentence, before or after the verb, or between a helping verb and a main verb:

➤ ***Carefully,* he climbed through the window.**

➤ **She bought red roses *frequently.***

➤ **Bridget *usually* borrows my car on Saturday night.**

➤ **My physics teacher has *never* checked our homework.**

An adverb may not, however, be placed between a verb and a direct object:

➤ **Victor bathes ~~frequently~~ the dog** *frequently.* ^

[The adverb *frequently* can be placed at the beginning or end of the sentence or immediately before the verb.]

18e Prepositions

Prepositions appear in almost every English sentence, beginning phrases that provide information on time, location, and other specifics:

➤ **I left my books *in* the locker *below* the desk.**

➤ **Harold bought two books *concerning* Argentinian government.**

The difficulties that occur with using prepositions stem from their specific meanings and their combinations with nouns, adjectives, and verbs. (For a complete list of these words, see **19p, Prepositions,** in Part Three, page 262.)

PREPOSITIONS OF TIME AND PLACE

Prepositions that indicate time and place can be especially difficult to master because their use is idiomatic, not governed by clearly set rules. The following box lists the most common of these prepositions.

INSTANT ACCESS

FOUR COMMON PREPOSITIONS THAT SHOW TIME AND PLACE

ABOUT TIME

At at a specific time: *at 4:30, at noon, at lunch*

On on a specific day or date: *on Wednesday, on February 5*

In in a period of time: *in six months, in the twenty-first century*

in a part of a day: *in the morning, in the afternoon* (but *at night*)

(continued)

(Four Common Prepositions, continued)

In in a month or year: *in August, in 2002*

By by a certain time: *by this time tomorrow*

ABOUT PLACE

At at a certain place or location: *at the ballgame, at home, at the mall*

at the edge of something: *sitting at the table*

at a target: *throwing the ball at Phillip*

On on a surface: *on the wall, on the floor*

on a street: *on Broadway, on Martin Luther King Boulevard*

on an electronic medium: *on television, on the computer screen*

on a specific area: *on campus, on the farm, on the road*

In in an enclosed place: *in a box, in the basement, in the student union*

in a geographic location: *in Paris, in Puerto Rico, in the mountains*

in a print medium: *in a book, in a story, in a magazine*

By by a landmark: *by the pool, by the football field*

PHRASAL PREPOSITIONS

English has a number of phrasal prepositions, including the following:

according to	down from	out of
across from	in addition to	prior to

You can look up additional phrasal prepositions and get help with using them in a dictionary for non-native speakers (see page 200).

PHRASAL CONSTRUCTIONS: ADJECTIVES OR NOUNS + PREPOSITIONS

Several other *phrasal constructions* in English can be difficult if English is not your native language. These constructions usually follow a verb and take the form of an adjective (or a noun) plus a preposition:

afraid of	**identical to, with**	**superior to**
angry at, with	**independent of**	**suspicious of**
anxious about	**interested in**	**thankful for, to**
aware of	**jealous of**	**tired of**
capable of	**necessary for, of, to**	**worthy of, to**
content with	**proud of**	
fond of	**satisfied with**	

Because the meaning of the phrase depends partly on the preposition, you need to be careful to use the correct preposition in these constructions. If you're unsure of the correct combination, check a dictionary for non-native speakers during the finishing stage of your writing (see page 200).

18f Verbs

The errors that all writers make when choosing the correct English verbs are covered in **11, Verb Errors,** pages 142–51; **19v, Verbs,** in Part Three, pages 279–85, provides a complete description of all verb parts, tenses, and moods. The following sections expand that coverage by treating special problems encountered by ESL writers.

TWO-WORD VERBS OR PHRASAL VERBS

Many combinations of a verb and a preposition have a special (idiomatic) meaning in English. The following sentences illustrate these accepted combinations, including the ones in which the preposition can follow the object of the verb:

They were *accompanied by* their parents.
He was *accused of* a crime.
She can *adapt to* new situations.
The manager will never *admit to* his errors.
We never *agree on* the best vacation spot.
Do you *agree with* me?
Jana *called off* the wedding. [*Or* Jana *called* the wedding *off.*]
How much will he *charge for* admission?
How does this album *compare with* his last one? [The two albums are in the same category.]

He *compared* the crowd *to* an army of ants. [A figurative comparison is being made.]
We *differ on* that question.
She *differs from* her suitemates.
Carlos *dropped in* on his old roommate.
He always *gets up* early.
Come *join in* the singing of our school song.
Join with us in supporting Belinda for class president.
I will *look into* this problem.
My teacher asked me to *look up* the date that our school was built.
Sarah *objects to* your decision.
These seats are *occupied by* the dancers' families.
I have been *occupied with* raising children for ten years.
The clerk *waits on* the customer.
I will *wait for* a taxi.
Are you *worried about* the meeting?

Consult a dictionary for non-native speakers (see page 200) for the correct combinations when you are not sure about which preposition to use with a verb. These dictionaries give examples of sentences in which such combinations are used properly.

MISSING VERBS

In some languages, you can omit the verb if the meaning is clear without it. In English, this omission (usually of a form of *be*) is not allowed:

➤ **Cara ^is very pretty.**

➤ **Rosa ^is in the park near the corner.**

In English, neither the present participle (the *-ing* form) nor the infinitive (the *to* + *verb* form) may be used as the main verb of the sentence:

➤ **Prim ^is playing golf.**

➤ **Samuel ~~to be~~ ^is my friend.**

➤ **Samuel ^wants to be my friend.**

HELPING VERBS

Some verbs, called *helping* or *auxiliary verbs,* do not appear alone in sentences but instead are always combined with another verb, the main verb. The helping verb completes the meaning of the main verb:

h.v. m.v.
➤ **Khuyen can go to the party.**

h.v. m.v.
➤ **You should eat your vegetables.**

Some helping verbs, called *modals,* normally function *only* as helping verbs.

Modal Helping Verbs

can	**might**	**should**
could	**must**	**will**
may	**shall**	**would**

The other helping verbs, forms of *do, have,* and *be,* can also appear as main verbs.

Helping Forms of *Do*

do	**does**	**did**

Helping Forms of *Have*

have	**has**	**had**

Helping Forms of *Be*

be	**am**	**is**	**are**
was	**were**	**been**	**being**

(For more information on helping verbs, see **19v, Verbs,** in Part Three, page 284.)

Do, Does, and *Did*

Like the modal helping verbs, the forms of the helping verb *do* occur only with the base forms of verbs. However, unlike the modals, *do* changes to agree in number with the subject:

➤ **I *do* like pepperoni.**

➤ **He *does* like pepperoni.**

The various forms of *do* are combined with a base form of a verb for the following purposes:

- To express a negative meaning along with *not:*

  ➤ **You *do* not need that green registration form.**

  ➤ **He *did* not want to stay with his parents.**

- To ask a question:

    ➤ ***Do* you want your dessert?**

    ➤ ***Does* it ever rain in the winter here?**

[Note that in these questions only the helping verb moves forward.]

- To emphasize a main verb:

    ➤ **You *do* look delightful today.**

    ➤ **This makeup *does* make your face look more round.**

Have, Has, and *Had*

The helping verbs *have, has,* and *had* are used with the past participle form of the verb (usually ending with *ed*):

Regular Past Participles—Formed with *ed*

Base Verb	*Past Participle*
like	liked
receive	received
talk	talked

Irregular Past Participles—Ending in the Sound of *t, n,* or *d*

Base Verb	*Past Participle*
break	broken
bring	brought
build	built
buy	bought
catch	caught
choose	chosen
do	done
eat	eaten
get	gotten
keep	kept
read	read
say	said
sing	sung
speak	spoken
take	taken
teach	taught
throw	thrown

The combination of *have, has,* or *had* plus the past participle creates the *perfect tenses,* which indicate action that was or will be completed before another action or time:

➤ **We *had eaten* all the cake before Sam arrived.**

➤ **They *have worked* for a plumbing company for ten years, so they feel ready to start their own business.**

➤ **I *will have finished* my part of the report before George and Joe even begin to write.**

(For more information on principal parts of verbs, see **19v, Verbs,** in Part Three, pages 280–82.)

VERBS IN CONDITIONAL SENTENCES

Conditional sentences use two clauses to express the dependence of one action or situation on another action or situation.

➤ **When I return to college in the fall, I will speak to a counselor about applying to law school.**

The clause containing the condition begins with *if, unless,* or *when;* it can be placed at the beginning or end of the sentence. The four types of conditional sentences—statements of fact, prediction and advice, unlikely possibilities, and nonfactual conditions and wishes—use different verb forms:

- **In factual conditional sentences** (such as those that state scientific truths or describe habitual behaviors), the present tense is used in both clauses:

  ➤ **If the temperature *drops* below thirty degrees, ice *forms* on this bridge.**

  ➤ **When Mary *enters* her father's study, he always *puts* his books away.**

- **In conditional statements that predict the future or offer advice or opinions,** the *if* or *unless* clause contains a present tense verb, and the main clause contains the modal *will, can, may, might,* or *should* followed by the base form of the verb:

  ➤ **If you *marry* him, you *will please* your parents.**

  ➤ **Children *will* not *rest* unless you *remind* them to do so.**

- **In statements speculating about an unlikely condition in the present or the future,** the *if* clause has a past tense verb. The main clause contains the modal *would, could,* or *might* followed by the base form of the verb:

> **If I *won* the lottery, I *would retire* immediately.**

> **Tandra *could make* the team if she *ran* the mile twenty seconds faster.**

- Conditional sentences are also used to discuss **events that are not factual,** such as wishes that cannot be granted. These sentences, called *subjunctive,* have *were* (not *was*) in the *if* clause even though they do not concern the past. The main clause contains *would, could,* or *might* followed by the base form of the verb:

> **If I *were* king for a day, I *would provide* health care for everyone.**

> **If my father *were* still alive, he *would walk* me down the aisle.**

VERBS FOLLOWED BY GERUNDS AND INFINITIVES

The *gerund* is the *-ing* form of the verb used as a noun, as in the sentence "I like *swimming.*" The infinitive is the base form of the verb preceded by *to,* as in "I like *to swim.*" Either form can serve as the subject or the object of a sentence.

Verb + Gerund or Infinitive

Some verbs can be followed by a gerund or an infinitive without any change in meaning:

begin	**like**
continue	**love**
hate	**start**

"I hate *driving,*" for example, means the same as "I hate *to drive.*"

With other verbs, such as *stop* and *remember,* the meaning changes depending on whether the verb is followed by a gerund or an infinitive. That is, "I *stopped calling* my mother" means "I no longer called her," but "I *stopped to call* my mother" means "I interrupted what I was doing to call her." A dictionary for non-native speakers (see page 200) can help you with these distinctions. (See the box on page 219 for online ESL resources.)

Verb + Gerund

Some verbs may be followed by a gerund but not by an infinitive:

appreciate	**enjoy**	**practice**
avoid	**finish**	**recall**
deny	**miss**	**resist**
discuss	**postpone**	**suggest**

➤ **He finished ~~to play~~** *playing* **golf by noon.**

➤ **She enjoys ~~to study~~** *studying* **for her finals.**

Verb + Infinitive

Verbs that describe something anticipated or planned may be followed by an infinitive but not by a gerund:

agree	**decide**	**mean**	**promise**
ask	**expect**	**offer**	**wait**
beg	**have**	**plan**	**want**
claim	**hope**	**pretend**	**wish**

➤ **He offered ~~helping~~** *to help* **me.**

➤ **We planned ~~leaving~~** *to leave* **after the ceremony.**

Verb + Noun or Pronoun + Infinitive

With some verbs that take an infinitive, a noun or a pronoun must come between the verb and the infinitive in order to name the person who is affected by the action:

advise	**encourage**	**require**
allow	**instruct**	**tell**
cause	**order**	**urge**
command	**persuade**	

➤ **He caused** *me* **to quit my job.**

➤ **Treena encouraged** *Lucinda* **to return to college.**

➤ **She often tells** *Pablo* **to turn down the music.**

NOTE: *Tell* is used with a noun or pronoun to name the person addressed, but *say* is not used with a noun or pronoun:

➤ **He *told his sister* that he was tired of practicing the guitar.**

➤ **He *said that* he was tired of practicing the guitar.**

(For more information, see **19v, Verbals,** in Part Three, pages 278–79.)

18g Sentence Structure

The regular order for an English sentence is *subject/verb/object: She/sent/a letter.*

Indirect objects can follow the verb or be replaced with a prepositional phrase that follows the direct object:

➤ **She sent *her new roommate* a letter.**

➤ **She sent a letter *to her new roommate.***

You will find a thorough discussion of this order and of each type of English sentence in **19s, Sentences,** in Part Three, pages 270–72. What follows here are explanations of several trouble spots in sentence structure.

UNDERSTOOD SUBJECTS

In some languages, the subject of a sentence may be omitted if the writer judges that readers will know it. In English, the subject may be omitted only in *imperatives,* second-person constructions that state commands. In these sentences, the second-person pronoun *you* may be omitted as an *understood subject:*

Understood Subject

➤ **Go get the car.**

➤ **Clean your room.**

In any other situation, you need to be sure that the subject of the sentence—however familiar you think it may be to the reader—is stated:

the catalyst

➤ **Next, we will add a catalyst to the mixture; ^ *will speed up* the reaction.**

IT AND *THERE* STRUCTURES

Sentences can begin with *it* or *there* and a *be* verb if the subject has been moved to another position in the sentence. In these sentences, the *it* or *there* performs an important function and cannot be omitted:

> There are
> ➤ ~~**Are**~~ **many ways to speed up this chemical reaction.**

> It is
> ➤ ~~**Is**~~ **Luis's turn to record the procedure.**

DIRECT AND INDIRECT QUOTATIONS AND QUESTIONS

When you want to include a *direct quotation* (either a few words, a sentence, or a question), you must place the exact words in quotation marks. When you use an *indirect quotation* or *question,* which summarizes or paraphrases the speaker's words, however, you report the speaker's words without quotation marks.

Direct and Indirect Quotations

The following examples illustrate some of the changes you must make to turn a direct quotation into an indirect quotation:

- The indirect quotation has no quotation marks and requires an inserted *that.*

  Direct Quotation: **Our teacher said, "The guest enjoyed our class."**

  Indirect Quotation: **Our teacher said *that* the guest enjoyed our class.**

- When direct quotations use the first person (*I*), this pronoun changes to the third person (*her* or *she*) in the indirect quotation.

  Direct Quotation: **"I'm ready to leave," she announced.**

  Indirect Quotation: **She announced that *she* was ready to leave.**

- Direct quotations of commands become indirect quotations with the addition of *to* before the verb.

  Direct Quotation: **The camp counselor said, "Shut that window."**

  Indirect Quotation: **The camp counselor said *to* shut that window.**

- Creating indirect quotations may require some rewriting of time expressions or rephrasing of conversation.

  Direct Quotation: **His grandmother said, "You know, Bob, I think I should begin buying your school clothes tomorrow."**

  Indirect Quotation: ***Bob's* grandmother said that she *would* begin buying *his* school clothes *on Wednesday*.**

Direct and Indirect Questions

When you change a direct question to an indirect question, the word order is no longer that of the direct question, and the verb tense and the person may change (from *I* to *he* or *she*). Add *if, whether,* and question words such as *why* and *when* to introduce indirect questions:

Direct Question: **Nguyen asked, "Are the cookies done?"**

Indirect Question: **Nguyen asked if the cookies were done.**

Direct Question: **"Should I go home during the Thanksgiving break?" wondered Rachel.**

Indirect Question: **Rachel wondered whether she should go home during the Thanksgiving break.**

Direct Question: **The child asked, "Why can't I go to the circus?"**

Indirect Question: **The child asked why she couldn't go to the circus.**

(For additional help with incorporating quoted material into your writing, see **2c, Use Your Sources Effectively,** pages 40–45; for more information on quoting correctly, see **19q, Quotation Marks,** in Part Three, pages 264–68.)

INSTANT ACCESS

ONLINE RESOURCES FOR ESL WRITERS

If you simply type "ESL" into the text box of a search engine such as Yahoo!, you should find plenty of ESL resources on the Web. Listed here are some of the best sites:

- To review the Test of English as a Foreign Language (TOEFL) for free, try <http://testwise.com/review.html>, a service of Teletext USA, a TOEFL preparation company.
- For general ESL resources, take a look at ESL Net <http://esl.net/>.
- Dave Sperling's ESL Help Center <http://www.davescafe.com/help/> allows students to send in ESL questions via e-mail and receive answers online.
- A great list of ESL links, presented in an interesting format, can be found on the "Frizzy University Network" (that's "FUN" for short) at <http://thecity.sfsu.edu/~funweb/Welcome.html>.
- Finally, you can dive into a whole "ring" of ESL pages that have been joined together into "The ESLoop" (that's a clever way of spelling "the ESL loop"). Once you get to any page in the loop (in Web terminology, it's actually a "ring"), such as the loop's home page <http://www.linguistic-funland.com/esloop/>, you automatically have access to all the other pages.

RELATIVE CLAUSES

An adjective clause that modifies a noun or a pronoun and begins with *who, that,* or *which* is called a relative or dependent clause. An adjective clause should be placed right after the noun it modifies:

➤ **Gretel entered the plane, *which was a new 747 jet,* with her son.**

➤ **Tzusheng returned the book *that he had borrowed* to the library.**

Omission of *That*

Although the general rule is that relative clauses begin with a relative pronoun (*who, that,* or *which*), the pronoun *that* may be omitted when there is no possibility of misreading:

➤ **At the Comedy Club last night, Marta showed her audience [that] she knows how to make people laugh.**

Repeated Objects

When you use a relative clause to describe the object of a sentence, you do not need a pronoun at the end of the clause:

➤ **Pedro saw the tennis racket that he wanted ~~it~~.**

19

Grammar, Punctuation, and Mechanics from A to Z

A

ABBREVIATIONS

Abbreviations, shortened versions of words or phrases, enable writers to save space.

Personal and Professional Titles

Common personal and professional titles can be abbreviated when they precede a proper name. These abbreviations are followed by periods:

Dr. Cameron Jameson	**Mr. Morgenstern**
Mrs. Lazarra	**Ms. Martinez**

Ms. designates either a married or an unmarried woman, and it is followed by a period even though it is not an abbreviation. *Miss* is not followed by a period.

Religious, military, academic, and governmental titles should be abbreviated only if they are followed by a complete name (both a first and a last name):

Rev. Jesse Jackson	**the Reverend Jackson**
Gen. Douglas MacArthur	**General MacArthur**
Prof. Rami Adeleki	**Professor Adeleki**

When abbreviations for **family designations, titles, or academic degrees** follow a name, they are preceded by a comma:

Fredson Franks, Jr.	**Clara Parkinson, J.D.**

Numerals following a name, however, appear with no comma:

Jamel R. Williams III

Familiar Abbreviations and Acronyms

An acronym is an abbreviation that can be pronounced as a word, such as *UNICEF, NATO, NOW,* and *AIDS*. These familiar terms are commonly written without periods. Familiar abbreviations, such as *NFL, SAT,* and *CBS,* also appear in writing without being spelled out or explained. When these abbreviations stand for three words or more, they are commonly written without periods: FBI, CD-ROM.

Unfamiliar Abbreviations and Acronyms

If a new term (with an unfamiliar abbreviation or acronym) appears only once or twice in your paper, you may choose to write it out each time. If you use it frequently, however, cite the abbreviation or acronym in parentheses right after you introduce the term, omitting the periods if the abbreviation is of three or more words. Thereafter use the abbreviation or acronym by itself:

> **The new program, called *Writing Across the Curriculum (WAC),* has funding from a local foundation. *WAC* provides computer labs and tutorial services for students, staff, and faculty.**

Abbreviations with Numerals

The following abbreviations are acceptable when they are used with numerals:

450 B.C. [BC] or 450 B.C.E. [BCE]	**"before Christ" or "before the common era"**
A.D. [AD] 70 or C.E. [CE] 70	***anno Domini* (Latin for "in the year of the Lord") or "common era"; either one precedes the date**
11:15 A.M. [a.m.]	***ante meridiem;* Latin for "before noon"**
12:15 P.M. [p.m.]	***post meridiem;* Latin for "after noon"**
225° F	**Fahrenheit scale**
24° C	**centigrade or Celsius scale**

Do not abbreviate these terms when you use them without numerals:

before the birth of Christ.

➤ **The Roman Empire began to falter ~~B.C.~~**

morning.

➤ **He has trouble getting up in the ~~a.m.~~**

Geographic Locations

In formal writing, spell out names of cities, states, countries, and continents. Also spell out words such as *street, avenue, road, park, mount,* and *river* when they are used in proper names: 198–99

In *New York City* this summer, ice skaters from *New Hampshire* will study with experts from *Russia.*

The house on *Marmsley Road* is famous for its high walls, which protect it from the frequent overflowing of the *Ressem River* near *Mount Frederick.*

The abbreviation *U.S.* (or *US*) can be used for *United States*—but only as an adjective:

As a Noun	As an Adjective
I was glad when my uncle finally came to the *United States.* [not U.S.]	**The *U.S. team* slowly entered the hockey rink.**

Days and Months

Spell out days of the week and the names of months:

On *December* 15, Corinne finally finished the quilt she had begun on the first *Monday* in *January.*

Units of Measurement

Except in tables and graphs, spell out all units of measurement:

John, who is six *feet* tall, lost forty *pounds* after he began eating fewer *ounces* of meat and reducing the *grams* of fat in his diet.

Publication References

Except in bibliographies, spell out terms concerning books and journals, such as *chapter* and *page:*

In the second *edition* of the first *volume,* Jorge changed the *preface* to acknowledge his wife's contributions.

On the last *page* of the last *chapter,* Sherlock Holmes finally identified the murderer.

Latin Abbreviations

Reserve the common Latin abbreviations for use in bibliographies and for informal comments placed in parentheses.

These abbreviations generally do not appear in formal writing:

cf.	*confer*	**compare**
e.g.	*exempli gratia*	**for example**
et al.	*et alii*	**and others**
etc.	*et cetera*	**and so forth**
i.e.	*id est*	**that is**
vs. or v.	*versus*	**versus**

Company Names

Company names can generally be written without the final *Inc., Ltd., Co., Bros.,* or *Corp.* (*Sears* or *Sears Roebuck* instead of *Sears Roebuck & Co.*). If you want to cite the full name, you may use the appropriate abbreviation. No comma is needed between the company name and the abbreviation:

> **The new advertisements portray Ford Motor Co. [*or* Ford] as an all-American business.**

Symbols

Symbols such as @, +, =, #, ¶, and ¢ are not used in formal writing although they may appear in graphs and tables. Use of the dollar sign ($), however, is acceptable with numbers (*$125, $350 billion, $11.98*) although you should spell out the word *dollars* with numbers that can be expressed in one or two words. Similar use of the percent sign (%) with a figure is usually acceptable:

> **So far, we have spent less than *three percent* (*or* 3%) of the *$240,000* that was budgeted for this project.**

> **I bet you *five dollars* that Carlos will not bring back even *ten cents* from his vacation.**

ABSOLUTE PHRASES

An absolute phrase, consisting of a noun or pronoun and a participle, modifies a whole sentence instead of a single word. It is separated from the rest of the sentence by a comma:

> ***Her bags packed,* she was ready to leave for the airport.**

> ***Other things being equal,* he would prefer to hire someone with database experience.**

(See **Phrases,** page 260, for more examples of absolute phrases.)

ACTIVE VOICE

A sentence is in active voice if the subject of the sentence is the doer of the sentence:

Kathryn hit the free throw.

In passive voice, the subject receives the action of the doer:

The free throw was hit by Kathryn.

(For a discussion of active and passive voice, see **1d, Revising,** pages 22–23.)

ADJECTIVES

Adjectives modify nouns or pronouns, adding specific descriptive information about them:

The *pale* child stood by his mother.

***That dented* Toyota has 100,000 miles on it.**

When *several small* bubbles floated to the surface, we knew the diver was still alive.

Most adjectives have comparison forms (called **positive, comparative,** and **superlative**). The comparative of short adjectives is usually formed by the addition of *er,* and the superlative is usually formed by the addition of *est.* Adjectives of two or more syllables are usually made comparative with the addition of *more* (or *less*) and are made superlative with the addition of *most* (or *least*).

Comparison Forms of Adjectives

Positive	*Comparative*	*Superlative*
bad	worse	worst
careful	more careful	most careful
good	better	best
lucky	luckier	luckiest
quick	quicker	quickest
tough	tougher	toughest
weak	weaker	weakest

Some adjectives also have ordinal forms, which allow you to place things in an ordered sequence (*first, second, third, . . . last*).

Several types of pronouns can also be used as adjectives:

Pronouns as Adjectives

Type of Pronoun	*Example*
Personal	*his* jalopy
Demonstrative	*this* cable
Indefinite	*few* friends
Interrogative	*Which* show should I watch?

204–06

When two or more adjectives relate equally to the noun they modify, they are called **coordinate adjectives.** If you can put *and* between the adjectives and not change the meaning, they are coordinate. When you use coordinate adjectives, separate them with commas:

The Fordson was a *small, inexpensive, reliable* tractor.

When two or more adjectives work together to modify a noun (and could not logically be combined with *and*), they are called **cumulative adjectives** (or unit modifiers), and they are not separated by commas:

The Russian tractor offers *few optional* features.

ADVERBS

Adverbs modify verbs, adjectives, other adverbs, or an entire clause:

He strolled *confidently* through the shopping mall.

[The adverb *confidently* modifies the verb *strolled.*]

The *very* big dog did not respond to his owner's commands.

[The adverb *very* modifies the adjective *big.*]

They *almost never* leave before the bingo game ends.

[The adverb *almost* modifies the adverb *never,* and *never* modifies the verb *leave.*]

Many adverbs are formed by adding *ly* to an adjective: *pretty, prettily; quick, quickly; terrible, terribly; bad, badly.* (Note that a *y* at the end of an adjective becomes an *i* when *ly* is added.) Other commonly used adverbs include *very, well, almost, soon, never,* and *not.*

Like adjectives, some adverbs have **positive, comparative,** and **superlative forms.** One-syllable adverbs are typically made comparative with the addition of *er* and made superlative with the addition of *est.* For longer adverbs, *more* (or *less*) is used to form the comparative, and *most* (or *least*) to form the superlative.

Comparison Forms of Adverbs

Positive	*Comparative*	*Superlative*
carefully	more carefully	most carefully
far	farther, further	farthest, furthest
happily	more happily	most happily
well	better	best

AGREEMENT

The verb in a predicate should agree in number with its subject:

> ***Carolina and Margaret are* friends.**

Pronouns should agree in number, person, and gender with their antecedents:

> **The *women* are demanding to see *their* lawyers.**

(See also **11b,** pages 145–48, for subject-verb agreement and **13c,** pages 171–72, for pronoun-antecedent agreement.)

ANTECEDENTS

An antecedent is the noun to which a pronoun refers.

> **When Bill saw his coat, he wondered what the cleaners had done to it.**
>
> [*Bill* is the antecedent of *he,* and *coat* is the antecedent of *it.*]

(See also **13c,** pages 171–72.)

APOSTROPHES

The apostrophe has the following uses:

To indicate possession	**Lula's kitchen**
To mark omissions in contractions	**can't [cannot]** **I'll [I will]**
To form plurals of letters, numerals, and abbreviations ending in periods	**B.A.'s**

(See also **14,** pages 175–180.)

APPOSITIVES

An appositive is a noun or a noun phrase that is placed near another noun and renames it in some way:

> **Dr. Tran's yacht, *Windward II,* won the race.**

Appositives can be one word or a group of words; they can also be **restrictive** (essential) or **nonrestrictive** (nonessential). Restrictive appositives, which are essential to the meaning of the sentence, are not set off by commas:

> **Restrictive Appositive: George Lucas's movie *Star Wars* has become an American classic.**

Nonrestrictive appositives, which contain information that is not essential to the meaning of the sentence, are set off by commas.

Nonrestrictive Appositive: Ralph's truck, *a new Ford Ranger*, has a Texas Longhorns sticker on the back.

Here, the kind of truck Ralph drives is just extra information, a nonrestrictive appositive set off by commas.

ARTICLES

198–204

The articles *a, an,* and *the* precede nouns or the adjectives that modify nouns. *A* is used before nouns or adjectives beginning with consonant sounds:

***a* dog** ***a* silly joke**

An is used before nouns or adjectives beginning with vowel sounds:

***an* antelope** ***an* hour** ***an* ugly duckling**

A and *an* imply an indefinite reference; *the* implies a specific reference:

***A* thimble fell under the rug.** [one unspecified thimble]

***The* thimble fell under the rug.** [one particular thimble]

B

BASE FORMS

209–16

The base form of the verb is the form listed in a dictionary, the infinitive without the marker *to,* such as *shout, dance, be,* and *sing.* (For more examples of the base form of verbs, see **19v,** pages 280–82.)

BIASED USES OF LANGUAGE

The way language is used can suggest or reveal bias—discrimination against people on the basis of gender, age, race, religion, ethnic group, or physical abilities. When you write, you should look for and eliminate bias in your language.

Gender-Biased Uses of Language

Avoid using gender-biased language, which can stereotype or demean both women and men.

Degrading and Patronizing Language

➤ **Martha Blair ~~a pert little blonde~~ is running for city council.**

office staff is
➤ **The ~~girls in the office, including that new one with really great legs, are~~ taking up a collection to pay for the party.**

Occupational and Social Stereotypes

shirts come out of the dryer smelling fresh.
➤ **With the new fabric softener, ~~women can get their husbands' shirts to smell fresh.~~**

their work schedules are
➤ **Because ~~his work schedule is~~ ever changing, ~~a doctor~~**
doctors need patient spouses.
~~needs a patient wife.~~

➤ **A dental assistant should always wear ~~her~~ gloves while**
working.
~~she works.~~

Use of *He* to Designate Both Genders

A singular pronoun must be used with a singular construction like *everyone* or *each student*. *He* is appropriate if you are clearly talking about a male student, as is *she* for a female student. But if you mean to include both women and men, then you should not use *he*. To be inclusive, you have three options:

1. Use *he or she* (*him or her* or *his or her*):

   ***Each child* should write about *his or her* personal experience.**

2. Change the construction to a plural and use *they* (*them, their*):

   The *children* should write about *their* personal experiences.

3. Rewrite the sentence so that it does not need a pronoun:

   ***Each child* should write about *a* personal experience.**

Overusing the phrase *he or she* can make writing awkward ("He or she should bring his or her books to his or her classes"). Carefully plan your use of all three options to incorporate nonbiased language without interrupting the flow of your writing. (See also **13e,** pages 173–74.)

Age

Be careful to avoid negative stereotypes and sentimentalized depictions of any age group—babies are not always angelic, and older people are not always forgetful. Do not make unnecessary references to age:

➤ **We are seeking a number of new~~,~~ ~~young~~ employees who will bring fresh ideas to this year's sales effort.**

Race

If identifying people by race or ethnic group is relevant to your topic, use the most specific term you can. For example, if a person is Mexican American, use that term rather than the more general *Hispanic* or *Latino.* Do not mention race or ethnic identity, however, when it is not relevant:

➤ **Our new history teacher, ~~a bright young black man~~** *Clifford Reilly* **from the University of Chicago, will assist Sarah Perkins in the Guidance Office this year.**

Religion

Avoid generalizations about belief systems and organized religions. If you are writing about a particular religion or an individual's religious practices, use the terminology preferred by that group or person and try to maintain a neutral tone:

➤ **The coach lectured us at halftime about our poor play on defense with ~~all the~~** *so much* **fervor ~~of a Bible-thumping preacher who had discov-ered the seven deadly sins.~~** *that the veins stood out on his forehead, sweat rolled off his arms, and he finally lost his voice.*

Ethnic Group

Avoid ethnic stereotypes—such as the Jewish mother or the inscrutable Asian—as well as expressions that originated with a negative characterization of a particular group.

it would be unacceptable for her to take back the video

➤ **I told LaShondra ~~if she took back the video game she~~** ^

game she had given me as a gift.

~~had given me, she would be no better than an Indian giver.~~

Physical Abilities

Do not define people by their disabilities or impairments. Instead of *an arthritic,* write *a person with arthritis.* Avoid language that characterizes a person with a disability as a victim. Instead of *a person confined to a wheelchair,* write *a wheelchair user* or *a person who uses a wheelchair.*

➤ **We will make special provision at our restaurant for**

people with disabilities.

~~the disabled and the handicapped.~~
^

BRACKETS

Brackets are used to enclose an explanatory comment within a quotation or within parentheses.

Within a Quotation

Use brackets to add your own words to a quotation to make it grammatically complete, especially in cases where an ellipsis mark indicates that part of the quotation has been omitted. The added words should not alter the original meaning of the complete quotation:

> **Murray Ross thinks that fans idealize football players: "they tend to . . . [become] embodiments of heroic qualities such as 'strength,' 'confidence,' 'perfection.'"**

With *Sic*

When you must use a quotation that contains a spelling error, you need to let your readers know the error is the original author's, and not yours. Place the word *sic* (Latin for "just so") in brackets after the misspelled word. (Because *sic* is Latin, many writers put it in italics.)

> **According to Louis Strauss, Fred Newton Scott of the University of Michigan "had at his command, beside his spendid [*sic*] background in English literature and**

his thorough mastery of the history of rhetoric, a wide knowledge of the arts of painting and music and of many literatures."

Within Parentheses

Use brackets to supply additional information to statements made within parentheses:

Aubrey's will excluded all his family members (including his only son, Paul Frontmain [from his first marriage]).

C

CAPITALIZATION

The First Word in a Sentence

Capitalize the first word of a sentence, either your own or one being quoted:

Can you meet me tomorrow?

Erica's cleaning will be ready in an hour.

Lucia finally blurted out, "Aren't you ready to go?"

Sentence within Parentheses

A full sentence within parentheses should begin with a capital letter and be punctuated as a separate sentence within the parentheses:

The plant growth was generally slow in the first year. (See Table 1.)

Place the darts of the armhole and sleeve together. (The sleeve's darts will be one inch longer.)

Proper Nouns and Adjectives

Capitalize proper nouns (names of specific persons, places, or things) and proper adjectives (those created from proper nouns). Do not capitalize common nouns (names of general classes or types of persons, places, or things) unless they begin a sentence or appear as part of a title or proper noun:

Proper	Common
Darwin, Darwinian	**scientist, scientific**
America, American	**nation, national**
Lake Pontchartrain	**lake**

Titles of Books, Movies, and Other Works

Capitalize the titles of books, magazines, articles, essays, movies, plays, poems, television shows, songs, and paintings. Articles (*a, an, the*), prepositions, conjunctions, and the *to* of infinitives are not capitalized unless they begin the title:

> ***I Know Why the Caged Bird Sings***
>
> **"Stopping by Woods on a Snowy Evening"**
>
> **Handel's *Messiah***
>
> **Van Gogh's *Sunflowers***

Personal Titles

Capitalize titles when they appear before a proper name. When they are used alone or after a proper name, they should not be capitalized:

> **Governor George E. Pataki—*but* George E. Pataki, governor of New York**
>
> **Professor Mikiso Hideki—*but* Mikiso Hideki, a history professor**
>
> **Senator Mary Landrieu—*but* Mary Landrieu, senator**

EXCEPTION: Many writers capitalize the word *president* when it appears alone if it refers to the president of a national government.

Academic Institutions and Courses

Capitalize the names of specific universities, departments, and courses, but not the common nouns for schools or departments. *English, French,* and names of other languages are always capitalized, but names of other subject fields are capitalized only in official course titles:

> **University of Washington—*but* a good university**
>
> **Department of English—*but* the department office**
>
> **Physics 122—*but* an introductory physics course**

Do not capitalize words used to designate school terms:

fall term	**spring semester**
winter quarter	**summer school**

Names of Relatives

Common nouns such as *mother, father,* or *brother-in-law* are not capitalized. When they are used as proper nouns—either as substitutes for a name or as part of a name—they are capitalized:

My father and his sister grew up in Africa.

When they were first married, Father and Mother were avid hockey fans.

After the party, Aunt Laura, Uncle Stephen, and Dad rode down to the coast with my cousin.

Geographic Regions

Capitalize terms for specific regions of the United States and for people from those regions. Do not capitalize compass directions, such as *north* and *south:*

La Niña caused hurricanes in the South and severe drought in the Midwest.

Johnson lives west of town, south of Highway 68.

Seasons

Do not capitalize seasons. Although months and days of the week are capitalized, seasons of the year are not.

CASE

Nouns and pronouns in English can be used as subjects, as objects, or as modifiers in possessive forms. These uses correspond to three cases:

- subjective case (the subject form)
- objective case (the object form)
- possessive case (the possessive modifier form)

Nouns in English change form only for possessive case (*girl, girl's*), but pronouns have different forms for each case.

PRONOUN CASES

	Subjective	*Objective*	*Possessive*
Singular	I	me	my, mine
	you	you	your, yours
	he	him	his
	she	her	her, hers
	it	it	its
Plural	we	us	our, ours
	you	you	you, yours
	they	them	their, theirs

(For more on the possessive case, see **14b,** pages 177–79.)

CLAUSES

A clause is a group of words that has a subject and a verb. There are two kinds of clauses, independent and dependent (sometimes called main and subordinate).

An **independent clause**—with a subject and a predicate—can stand alone as a sentence:

She left home.

The young mother had taken her son to the park.

A **dependent clause** also has a subject and a predicate, but it is introduced by a word such as *that, while,* or *when* and needs an independent clause to complete its meaning: 219–20

Independent Clause	Dependent Clause
The rain fell in big, heavy drops.	***While* the tourists ran to escape the downpour.**

The dependent clause, if left by itself, would be a sentence fragment. It needs to be combined with an independent clause to make a grammatically complete statement. (For more on fragments, see **8,** pages 130–32.)

Combined: **The rain fell in big, heavy drops while the tourists ran to escape the downpour.**

The words that introduce dependent clauses are relative pronouns or subordinating conjunctions.

Relative Pronouns

that	**whichever**	**whomever**
what	**who**	**whose**
whatever	**whoever**	
which	**whom**	

Subordinating Conjunctions

after	**even though**	**that**
although	**how**	**though**
as	**if**	**unless**
as if	**in order that**	**until**
as soon as	**in that**	**when**
as though	**once**	**whenever**
because	**since**	**where**
before	**so that**	**wherever**
even if	**than**	**while**

CLICHÉS

Clichés are phrases that have been used so much that their meaning is no longer clear and forceful:

nose to the grindstone

with his heart in his hands

You should avoid clichés because they blunt your meaning rather than sharpen it.

COLONS

A colon can be placed after a complete sentence to indicate that it will be further explained by an example, a list, or a quotation. Colons also have other uses, such as separating numbers in time designations, as in *8:30*.

Colons between Two Independent Clauses

A colon can be used between two independent clauses as a substitute for a semicolon if the second clause further explains the first one or provides an example:

Luisa is so disorganized: yesterday she lost her briefcase and the file cabinet key.

(For more examples, see **9c,** page 137.)

Colons to Introduce Lists

A colon is used to introduce a list placed at the end of a sentence containing a subject, a verb, and an object or complement:

For our camping trip, we need to rent the big items: backpacks, tents, sleeping bags, and a stove.

NOTE: If the list follows a verb instead of an object or a complement, you do not use a colon:

For our camping trip, we need to rent backpacks, tents, sleeping bags, and a stove.

Colons with an Appositive (or One-Item List)

A colon can also be used to introduce an appositive:

Keith had forgotten only one thing: his plane tickets.

Colons with Direct Quotations

A colon should be used to introduce either a short quotation or a longer, indented quotation following a complete sentence:

> **This is what the consultant actually said: "People in other parts of the world will not like this ad series."**
>
> **Here are the consultant's exact words:**
>
> > **If your ad assumes people "read" pictures from left to right, you're going to be in trouble in cultures that "read" graphics from right to left.**

COMMAS

The comma is a mark of punctuation that separates elements within a sentence. As illustrated in the following examples, these elements can be words, phrases, or clauses:

> **When Luther left for college, he took his stereo, computer, and microwave oven.**
>
> **After hearing the weather report, Carmelita went to find her raincoat, galoshes, and umbrella.**
>
> **New mothers and fathers quickly learn how to make funny faces, how to keep walking on aching feet, and how to operate a wind-up swing.**

(See **12,** pages 152–66.)

COMMA SPLICES

A comma splice is a sentence error that occurs when two independent clauses are separated only by a comma:

but
➤ **The flood waters were rising more each hour, ^ many families refused to evacuate.**

(See also **9,** pages 133–37.)

COMPARISONS

Make Comparisons between the Same Types of Items

Two things being compared must be logically comparable:

He drove his
➤ ^ **~~His~~ *race car* ~~came~~ around the track quicker than any other driver I have ever seen.**

➤ **His *race car* came around the track quicker than any other ~~*driver*~~ *race car* I have ever seen.**

[The comparison should be between two drivers or two race cars, not between a car and a driver.]

(For additional examples, see **16e,** page 191.)

Make Comparisons Complete

A complete comparison clearly indicates the two items being considered:

➤ **Jana is happier/** *than she was last week.*

➤ **This margarine is better tasting/** *than butter.*

➤ **Carmen looks more like Thania than Juana/** *does.*

Indicate Degrees of Comparison Properly

Remember that comparative words ending in *er* and comparative phrases using *more* (*lovelier, more cooperative*) are used for comparing two items. Comparison words formed with *est* and comparative phrases using *most* (*loveliest, most cooperative*) are for comparing more than two:

She is *stronger* than her cousin.

She is the *strongest* athlete in her class.

She is *more helpful* than her brother.

She was the *most helpful* worker at the convention.

You can look the correct comparative form of any word up in the dictionary. (These forms are discussed in **Adjectives,** pages 227–28, and **Adverbs,** page 228.)

COMPLETE VERBS

The complete verb is the entire verb in a clause:

Because she *was running* quickly, she *was able to reach* her bus.

[The complete verb of the dependent clause is *was running;* the complete verb of the independent clause is *was able to reach.*]

(For a full discussion of verbs, see pages 279–85.)

COMPLEX SENTENCES

A complex sentence is one with both an independent clause and a dependent clause:

> **Thoreau did much of his writing while he was at Walden Pond.**
>
> [In this complex sentence, the independent clause is *Thoreau did much of his writing,* and the dependent clause is *while he was at Walden Pond.*]

(For more on the construction of complex sentences, see page 137.)

COMPOUND-COMPLEX SENTENCES

A compound-complex sentence has two or more independent clauses and at least one dependent clause:

> **Even though we were exhausted, Carla had to study, and I had to drive back to Des Moines.**
>
> [In this compound-complex sentence, the dependent clause is *Even though we were exhausted,* and the independent clauses are *Carla had to study* and *I had to drive back to Des Moines.*]

COMPOUND SENTENCES

A compound sentence has two or more independent clauses:

> **Wind erosion is destructive, but tropical deforestation is deadly.**
>
> [In this compound sentence, the two independent clauses are *Wind erosion is destructive* and *tropical deforestation is deadly.*]

(For more on the construction of compound sentences, see **9c,** pages 135–37.)

CONJUNCTIONS

Conjunctions connect words or groups of words to one another. There are three kinds of conjunctions: *coordinating, correlative,* and *subordinating.* (For information on using conjunctions to correct comma splices and run-on sentences, see **9c,** pages 135–36, and **10c,** pages 140–41.) One kind of adverb, the *conjunctive adverb,* is also used as a conjunction, but it has to be preceded by a semicolon to join two independent clauses. (See also page 243 for further discussion of conjunctive adverbs.)

Coordinating Conjunctions

Coordinating conjunctions (*and, but, or, nor, for, so,* and *yet*) can connect words, phrases, or clauses:

> **Shaquille O'Neal *and* Kobe Bryant have profited from Phil Jackson's emphasis on teamwork *and* defense.**
>
> **She will have to clean up her room soon *or* evacuate it.**
>
> **Carmella felt nervous about moving away, *so* she decided to go to a community college in her hometown.**

When a conjunction joins two words or phrases, no comma appears between them ("Shaquille O'Neal and Kobe Bryant"; "clean up her room soon or evacuate it"). In a series of three or more words or phrases, a comma separates each item ("techniques of acting**,** lighting**,** and set design"). When a coordinating conjunction joins two independent clauses, as in the final example, a comma precedes it.

Correlative Conjunctions

Correlative conjunctions (*either . . . or, neither . . . nor, not only . . . but also, both . . . and*) can join words, phrases, or clauses:

> ***Not only* the boys *but also* their parents are expected to participate in each Tiger Cub activity.**
>
> **All applicants for the directorship should have *either* studied geriatrics *or* worked with senior citizens.**
>
> ***Either* you should begin doing the work, *or* you should drop the class.**

Subordinating Conjunctions

Subordinating conjunctions can be used to introduce a dependent (or subordinate) clause, which consists of the subordinating conjunction, a subject, a complete verb, and its object or complement ("when I left home last week"). The subordinating conjunction generally explains the connection between the main clause and the additional information given in the dependent clause. (For information on using subordinating conjunctions to correct comma splices and run-on senences, see **9c,** page 137, and **10c,** page 141. For a list of common subordinating conjunctions, see page 237.)

CONJUNCTIVE ADVERBS

Conjunctive adverbs are transition words such as *however.*

Conjunctive Adverbs

accordingly	**however**	**next**
also	**incidentally**	**nonetheless**
anyway	**indeed**	**otherwise**
besides	**instead**	**similarly**
certainly	**likewise**	**specifically**
consequently	**meanwhile**	**still**
finally	**moreover**	**then**
furthermore	**nevertheless**	**therefore**

When two independent clauses are joined by a semicolon, a conjunctive adverb is often used at the beginning of the second clause to provide a transition. The adverb is preceded by a semicolon and followed by a comma.

She studied carefully for the test; *however*, no amount of review could have prepared her for question five.

(For information on using conjunctive adverbs and semicolons to correct comma splices and run-on senences, see **9c,** page 136, and **10c,** pages 140–41.)

CONNOTATIONS AND DENOTATIONS OF WORDS

Words that have similar dictionary definitions (denotations) may have different connotations, a different emotional impact and set of associations. For example, *sports car* is defined as "an automobile equipped for racing," but it may connote rich, young people on exciting adventures. What connotations do the following words have for you?

surgeon	college	politician	red
cigarette	home	graveyard	pumpkin pie

(See also **Word Choice (Diction),** page 286.)

CONTRACTIONS

A contraction is two words condensed into one by omitting one or more letters and adding an apostrophe in their place: *isn't* for *is not, aren't* for *are not, couldn't* for *could not.*

(For a list of contractions, see **14c,** page 179.)

D

DASHES

The dash is dramatic; it draws the reader's attention to a word or a phrase. It can signal a sudden change, or it can emphasize an introductory list or parenthetical material.

To Signal a Sudden Change

Use a dash as a strong signal of a sudden change in thought or tone, a new direction in the sentence:

> **I'm sure we will get our raises soon—or never.**

After an Introductory List

Use the dash between an introductory list and the main part of the sentence. This construction leads the reader to consider an emphasized list of traits and then apply it to the subject:

> **Cold, calculating, ruthless, conniving—our boss is commonly described with these terms.**

To Emphasize Parenthetical Material

Use the dash (or two dashes if the addition occurs within the sentence) to emphasize an added explanation, illustration, or comment. If the added material contains commas, the dashes help mark its separation from the rest of the sentence:

> **Liechtenstein—not quite as large as Washington, D.C.—is a constitutional monarchy located in the Alps between Austria and Switzerland.**

DEPENDENT CLAUSES

Although it may contain a subject and a predicate, a dependent clause cannot stand on its own as a sentence because it begins with a word such as *when* or *if* that makes it dependent on some other clause to complete its meaning:

> **When the snow melts, there may be floods.**
>
> [*When the snow melts* is a dependent clause.]

(For further discussion of dependent and independent clauses, see **Clauses,** page 237.)

DICTION

Diction means the choice of words. Criteria for choosing the right words to express your ideas include appropriateness, specificity, and conciseness. (For help with diction, see **Word Choice (Diction),** page 286, and **Revising Sentences** in **1d,** pages 22–26.)

DIRECT OBJECTS

The direct object is the word that receives the action of a verb in a sentence in which the subject is doing the action. In such a sentence, the subject names the doer, the verb names what is done, and the direct object names who or what the verb acts upon:

Susan bought new *boots.*

[*Boots* is the direct object in this sentence.]

DOUBLE NEGATIVES

A double negative is the nonstandard use of two negatives in a sentence that is intended to have a negative meaning. To correct this error, one of the two negative words must be eliminated:

anything
➤ **Shakespeare *can't* have ~~*nothing*~~ like that in mind in this play.**

E

ELLIPSIS MARKS

Three spaced periods (the ellipsis mark) are used to indicate omissions from quotations or to mark a hesitation.

For Omissions in Quotations

The ellipsis mark indicates that a word, phrase, sentence, full paragraph, or more has been left out of a quotation. If the omission follows a sentence, the period ending the sentence precedes the ellipsis mark (making, in effect, four dots).

Use ellipses to emphasize the key lines and ideas from a source, not to modify the author's arguments:

Original: **There has always been a poignancy in watching human activity and settlement crowd out existing animals and plants so that their numbers gradually dwindle and disappear. The dodo, the passenger pigeon, and the golden parakeet are examples of animals that were once abundant and have now vanished. The buffalo, the whooping crane, the rhinoceros, the tiger, the African elephant, the sperm whale, and many other large animals may soon follow them. No one wants to see such rare and exotic creatures driven to extinction.**

—William Tucker, *Progress and Privilege*

Shortened Quotation with Ellipsis Mark: **After naming animals that are now extinct, William Tucker mentions another sad possibility for Americans: "the buffalo . . . may soon follow them."**

Shortened Quotation with a Period and Ellipsis Mark: **William Tucker maintains that recent extinctions have frustrated human observers: "There has always been a poignancy in watching human activity and settlement crowd out existing animals and plants so that their numbers gradually dwindle and disappear. . . . No one wants to see such rare and exotic creatures driven to extinction."**

An ellipsis mark is not necessary to indicate that material preceded or followed your excerpt. Your reader will understand that the quotation, whether a few words or a few paragraphs, is part of a larger work. (See also **2c,** pages 40–45.)

For a Pause or Hesitation

The ellipsis mark can indicate a pause, a reluctance to speak further, or an intentionally unfinished statement. If the omission follows a complete sentence, the ellipsis mark should be preceded by a period:

He remembers many joyous moments from his marriage . . . and too many fights over nothing.

It's a bird. . . . It's a plane. . . . No, it's Superman!

END PUNCTUATION

Three punctuation marks can signify the end of a sentence: the period, the question mark, and the exclamation point.

Period

The period is normally used at the end of a declarative sentence (one that makes a statement):

Sandy approved the revised schedule gladly.

With Indirect Questions and Exclamations

A sentence that reports a question but does not ask it is an indirect question, which ends with a period: 217–218

Kerry asked if Tanesha's signature was legible.

Mustapha wondered where all the people had gone.

Similarly, if a sentence reports an exclamation, it should end with a period.

Question Mark

Question marks are used after direct questions:

Where are Ben and Amy today?

As discussed above, *indirect* questions (such as "Linda asked if I was finished with her book") do not end with question marks but with periods.

With Quotations

The question mark is placed either inside or outside the quotation marks that set off a direct quotation, depending on whether the material within the quotation marks is a question or the question is about the material within the quotation marks:

"Where are you going?" Juanita asked.

[The material within the quotation marks asks the question; thus the question mark is inside the quotation marks.]

Was it Bill Clinton who said, "I didn't inhale"?

[The material outside the quotation marks asks the question (the quotation itself is not a question); thus the question mark is outside the quotation marks.]

Exclamation Point

Exclamation points are used after sentences or other groups of words that express strong feelings:

Shoot the ball!

Home at last!

F

FAULTY PREDICATION

Faulty predication is the use of a predicate (the complete verb plus any object, predicate adjective, or predicate noun and all their modifiers) that does not fit with the subject of the sentence. "One test *is* an infrared spectrometer" is an example of faulty predication. The sentence should be revised to read "One test *involves the use of* an infrared spectrometer." (For more on mismatched subjects and predicates, see **17b,** page 193.)

FIGURATIVE LANGUAGE

A *figure of speech,* or figurative language, is an expression in which words are used in an imaginative rather than a literal sense. The two chief figures of speech are the simile and the metaphor.

A *simile* is an explicit comparison between two things that are essentially unlike, usually introduced by the word *like* or *as.* Humorist Dave Barry chooses the simile, for example, to complete a description of his son's new haircut:

> **The hair on the top was smeared with what appeared to be transmission fluid and sticking up in spikes, which made it look like a marine creature striking a defensive posture.**

A *metaphor* is an implied comparison of unlike things, made without *like* or *as,* as in this Dave Barry comment on his sons' messiness:

> **Little boys are Pod People from the Planet Destructo.**

Both similes and metaphors can enhance your writing by bypassing strict logical connections and providing instead a more forceful and imaginative expression of meaning.

FORMAL WRITING

Formal writing is the kind required for the papers you will prepare for college classes, the articles you will write for publication, and the letters and reports that will be a regular part of your career work. The grammatical and stylistic usage discussed in this book is an essential component of formal writing. For your personal letters or daily journals, a more informal, colloquial style may be appropriate.

FRAGMENTS

A fragment is a part of a sentence punctuated as though it were a complete sentence with a capital letter for the first word and with end punctuation. For a complete discussion of fragment types and methods of correcting them, see **8,** pages 130–32.

FUSED SENTENCES

A fused sentence is an error caused by placing two independent clauses in one sentence with no punctuation between them:

➤ **The chef put the milk and butter into the hot pan. ~~t~~Then she stirred the mixture for five minutes.**

(This error, also called a *run-on sentence,* is discussed fully in **10,** pages 138–41.)

G

GERUNDS

A gerund is the *-ing* form of the verb used as a noun: 214–15

> ***Writing*** **is more difficult than math.**
>
> **Many sports build character, but sailboat *racing* builds characters.**

H

HELPING VERBS

Helping, or auxiliary, verbs, such as *can, would, have,* and *do,* combine with the principal forms of verbs to create the different tenses in English. (For a complete discussion, see **Verbs,** page 284.) 211–13

HYPHENS

A hyphen is used to divide a word at the end of a line and to link compound words or word parts.

Hyphen at the End of a Line

To divide a word at the end of a line, make the break between syllables (*break-fast, mor-ning*) and put a hyphen at the end of the first unit to indicate that the rest of the word will appear on the next line.

Hyphen with Compound Words

A hyphen is often used to join two or more words that function as a single word:

double-jointed, long-range, off-key [adjectives]

double-decker, Johnny-come-lately [nouns]

double-park, hand-feed, pinch-hit [verbs]

If you are not sure whether a compound has a hyphen, check a dictionary. Many compounds are written as one word without a hyphen or as two words.

With Compound Adjectives

When you use a compound adjective not listed in a dictionary, insert a hyphen if the compound adjective precedes the noun; do not hyphenate the compound if it follows the noun:

Hyphen before Noun	No Hyphen after Noun
The exterminator entered the *rat-infested* warehouse.	**The exterminator entered the warehouse, which was *rat infested.***
She no longer buys those *ill-fitting* discount dresses.	**She no longer buys those discount dresses, which are *ill fitting.***
The *well-respected* attorney refused to take the case.	**The attorney who refused to take the case is *well respected.***

With *Very* and with Adverbs Ending in *ly*

Do not hyphenate compounds that contain *-ly* adverbs or *very* plus an adjective:

The *plainly visible* lighthouse led us to the shore.

The *very large* orchestra could not fit onto the school's stage.

Hyphen with Numbers and Fractions

Use hyphens if you spell out numbers from *twenty-one* to *ninety-nine,* both when the numbers stand alone and when they are part of a larger number:

twenty-seven	**thirty-two thousand**
forty-eight	**ninety-five billion**

To spell out a fraction as an adjective, place a hyphen between the fraction's two parts. Hyphenation is not required when the fraction is used as a noun:

As Adjective	As Noun
***one-eighth* full**	**containing *one eighth* of the liquid**
a *two-thirds* majority	**a majority of *two thirds***

I

INDEPENDENT CLAUSES

An independent clause is a group of words that contains a subject and a predicate and can stand alone as a sentence:

When Phish performed an encore, many people started to dance.

[The independent clause is *many people started to dance.*]

INDIRECT OBJECTS

Some verbs, such as *buy, bring, lend,* and *sell,* may have a direct object and an indirect object. The indirect object is who or what receives the direct object and the action of the verb. The indirect object usually precedes the direct object in the sentence:

Mai sold *Dave* her used history *book.*

[*Dave* is the indirect object, and *book* is the direct object.]

An indirect object can also be replaced by a prepositional phrase following the direct object:

Mai sold her used history book to *Dave.*

INFINITIVES

The infinitive is the base form of the verb preceded by the infinitive marker *to,* as in *to shout, to dance,* and *to sing.* (For information about infinitive phrases, see **Phrases,** page 259.)

INTERJECTIONS

Interjections—such as *oh, wow, ouch, ah,* and *all right*—are exclamations used to express surprise or emotion. They are generally followed by a comma or an exclamation point:

Wow!

Oh, what a lovely day!

INTERNET ADDRESSES

Uniform Resource Locators (URLs) should be placed within angle brackets (< >) wherever they appear as part of a paragraph:

<http://www.mhhe.com/keene3>

If angle brackets are used, breaking the address across two lines is acceptable, but the break should be made after a slash.

INTERROGATIVES

Interrogative pronouns, adjectives, and adverbs—such as *what, where, why, whose,* and *which*—are used to ask questions:

Whose car are we taking?

INTRANSITIVE VERBS

Intransitive verbs are verbs that do not take objects (for example, "The fish *died.*") *Go, laugh, persevere, sit,* and *tremble* are other examples of intransitive verbs. (Transitive verbs, page 278, are those that can take objects.)

ITALICS (OR UNDERLINING)

When you write longhand or use a typewriter, use underlining as the equivalent of the italics found in word-processed documents and printed materials. The following sections discuss the appropriate uses of italics or underlining.

With Titles

Use italic type (or underlining) for titles of complete works: books, magazines, newspapers, plays, long poems, movies, television shows, CDs or record albums, ballets, operas, musical compositions, and works of art:

> **In *Rolling Stone,* reviewer Peter Travers praised *Mission: Impossible* and *M:I-2* for their stunts and special effects, but he was less impressed with their confusing plots.**

For Foreign Words and Phrases

Foreign words or phrases—those that are not also English words—should be italicized (underlined):

> **When he hears *"Sicilia est insula"* coming from the class next door, Mr. Mauldin knows that the first-year Latin students have begun their oral drills.**

For Names of Ships, Aircraft, Spacecraft, and Trains

> **The U.S.S. *Nautilus,* an atomic submarine, made the first voyage under the polar ice cap in 1958.**

For Special Uses of Words, Letters, Numbers, or Phrases

Italicize (underline) words, letters, numbers, and phrases used as such:

> **The letter combination *ough,* which is pronounced differently in *dough* and *cough,* confuses many young readers.**

You can also use italics (underlining) occasionally to emphasize a word or a phrase. If you employ this technique too frequently, though, it will lose its effect.

> **Why don't *you* see who's at the door?**

> **If Roger had been on time to his appointment, *he* would have witnessed the robbery.**

J

JARGON

Within scientific and technical circles, the controlled and careful use of a specialized vocabulary can serve an important purpose: to convey information quickly and exactly.

But for other audiences, such words may obscure meaning. Jargon, the special vocabulary of a trade or a profession, should be used only within the group for which it is appropriate (and then only in moderation). Music historians, for instance, might discuss the polyphony or dodecaphony of a certain symphony, but they need to either avoid or define that vocabulary when they address other audiences. (See also **Word Choice (Diction),** page 286, and **Revising Sentences** in **1d,** pages 22–26.)

L

LINKING VERBS

Linking verbs link, or join, a subject with a predicate noun or a predicate adjective:

Josepha *is* a teacher.

She *appears* friendly.

Common linking verbs include *appear, be, become, feel, look, seem, smell, sound,* and *taste.*

M

MODAL AUXILIARIES

211–13

Modal auxiliaries—such as *will, would, shall, should, may, might, must, can,* and *could*—are a subset of the helping verbs. These verbs do not change form as they change number. They are used with the principal parts of verbs to show ability (*can*), possibility (*may*), intent (*shall*), obligation (*should*), or necessity (*must*).

MODIFIERS

A modifier is a word or word group that describes, limits, or qualifies another word or word group. Modifiers include words, phrases, and clauses that function as adjectives or adverbs.

The *hungry* customers harassed the waiter.

The grass grew *quickly*.

I own the car *that has a dented fender.*

(See also **15,** pages 181–87.)

N

NOUNS

Nouns are words that name persons and animals (*teacher, daughter, brontosaurus*), places (*town, ocean*), things (*table, incubator*), and concepts (*freedom, creativity*). 198–204

Common nouns name people, animals, objects, places, things, or concepts in a general (nonspecific) way (*girl, dog, city, religion*).

Proper nouns name specific people, animals, places, things, or concepts (*Louisa, St. Louis, University of Wisconsin, Christianity*). Proper nouns begin with capital letters.

Collective nouns name groups: *team, crew, chorus.* When a collective noun refers to the group as a whole, it is treated as singular. When it refers to members of the group who are acting individually, it is treated as plural.

Common Collective Nouns

army	**clergy**	**enemy**	**jury**
audience	**committee**	**family**	**majority**
band	**company**	**flock**	**number**
class	**crowd**	**group**	**team**

Mass nouns name something that is not usually countable (*sugar, sand, gravel*) or qualities (*peace, tranquility, fortitude*). They usually do not have a plural form.

Plural forms of most nouns are made by adding an *s* or *es* (*pictures, heroes*). A few nouns use irregular endings for their plurals (*child—children; man—men; mouse—mice*).

Nouns can also be written in **possessive forms** to indicate ownership. You form the possessive by adding an apostrophe plus *s* to a singular noun, an apostrophe to a plural noun, or an apostrophe plus *s* to a plural noun that doesn't end in *s* (*John's friend, the boys' dog, the children's classroom*).

NUMBERS

Write as words any numbers that can be expressed as one or two words; use numerals for numbers expressed in more than two words:

one friend	**2,800 years ago**
seven times	**$197.50**
twenty-two boxes	**2,970,000 pebbles**

Large round numbers can be written with words or numerals. To emphasize the size of the amount, use numerals:

thirty-seven million dollars or **$37 million** or **$37,000,000**

In most scientific and technical disciplines, the practice is to write out numbers from one to nine and to use numerals for ten and above and with units of measurement. Be sure to be consistent.

Special Uses

- At the beginnings of sentences, always write numbers as words:

  Ninety-two
  ➤ ~~**92**~~ **contestants chose the first answer.**
  ^

- Write **pages** and **divisions of books and plays** as numerals:

  part 3
  page 97
  chapter 7
  act 1, scene 6 *or* Act I, Scene vi

O

OBJECT COMPLEMENTS

An object complement follows and modifies a direct object. The complement may be a noun, an adjective, or a word group functioning as a noun or an adjective:

Meleta declared the party a *disaster*.

[*Disaster* is the object complement; it modifies the direct object *party*.]

P

PARALLELISM

Parallelism refers to similarity of form in pairs or series of words, phrases, or clauses:

We tried *hiking the trails, rafting the rivers,* and *exploring the backcountry* on our vacation.

(For help with correcting faulty parallelism, see **16,** pages 188–91.)

PARENTHESES

Parentheses to Set Off Supplementary Material

Parentheses separate information from the main part of the sentence and minimize its importance. If the information is significant to the meaning of the sentence, place it within dashes (which provide emphasis) or commas:

> **There are 110,000 species of moths and butterflies (one thousand butterfly species in the United States alone).**

Parentheses to Enclose Letters or Numerals in a List within a Sentence

> **Three actions will solve our budget problems: (1) disconnect the office WATS lines, (2) discontinue spending for entertainment, and (3) suspend travel allocations.**

Punctuation with Parentheses

When parentheses enclose an element within a sentence, commas and periods are placed after the closing parenthesis:

> **When we entered the main entrance (called the Thompson Lobby), we saw the large signs for the City Consortium of Actors (CCA).**

When parentheses enclose an entire sentence, the sentence should begin with a capital letter and end with a period or other end punctuation placed before the closing parenthesis:

> **Columbus made four voyages to the New World, visiting what are now the Bahamas, Jamaica, Cuba, Puerto Rico, Trinidad, and Venezuela. (He first came in search of a westward route to India.)**

PARTICIPLES

A participle is a verb form that functions as part of a verb phrase (Paulette is *leaving;* the guests have *eaten*) or as an adjective (the *required* course; the students *waiting* in line). When it is functioning as an adjective, the participle is a verbal and can combine with other words to make a participial phrase. In "The cars sitting in the showroom were too expensive," the participial phrase is *sitting in the showroom.* (For more on participles, see **Verbals,** page 279, and **Verbs,** pages 280–82. For help with misplaced participles and modifiers, see **15,** pages 183–84.)

205–06
212–13

PARTS OF SPEECH

There are eight parts of speech:

- **Nouns**—words that name a person, animal, place, or thing
- **Pronouns**—words that substitute for nouns
- **Verbs**—words that express action or state of being
- **Adjectives**—words that modify nouns or pronouns
- **Adverbs**—words that modify verbs, adjectives, or other adverbs
- **Prepositions**—words that show a relationship between their object and the rest of the sentence
- **Conjunctions**—words that connect words, phrases, or clauses
- **Interjections**—exclamation words

(Each part of speech is discussed more fully in its own entry here in Part Three.)

PASSIVE VOICE

A sentence is in the passive voice if the subject of the sentence receives the action of the doer:

The mayor was surrounded by shouting reporters.

In the active voice, the subject of the sentence is the doer, as in "Shouting reporters surrounded the mayor." (See **1d,** pages 22–23.)

PHRASES

A phrase is a group of grammatically related words that lacks either a subject or a complete verb. There are eight kinds of phrases.

Noun Phrases

198-204 A noun phrase includes a noun and its modifiers:

Judy took off *her very old raincoat.*

Verb Phrases

209-216 A verb phrase includes a main verb and helping verbs:

Judy's raincoat *is dripping* on the floor.

The phrase *is dripping* contains no subject; the verb phrase in combination with the noun phrase *Judy's raincoat* does make a complete sentence, however. The combination of the auxiliary, or helping, verb *is* with the participial form *dripping* creates a complete form of the verb *drip*. (For a complete discussion, see **Verbs,** pages 279–85.)

Prepositional Phrases

A prepositional phrase consists of a preposition (such as *to, at,* or *of*) and its object (a noun or pronoun and any modifiers): 207–09

I took my shoe *to the repair shop.*

***At the shop,* a new heel costs ten dollars.**

(See **Prepositions,** page 262, for a list of prepositions.)

Gerund Phrases

The gerund is a verb form that ends in *ing* and functions as a noun. Here are some examples of gerund phrases: 214–16

***Replacing heels* is a lucrative business.**

I seem to specialize in *wrecking shoes.*

(See also **Verbals,** pages 278–79.)

Infinitive Phrases

The infinitive is the base form of a verb preceded by *to*—*to run, to fly, to dream.* Infinitives can be combined with other words to form infinitive phrases: 214–16

She woke up at 7:00 A.M. *to practice her free throws.*

***To be drafted by the WNBA* was her only goal.**

(See also **Verbals,** pages 278–79.)

Participial Phrases

The participle is the *-ing* or *-ed* form of the verb used as a modifier. Present participles are the *-ing* forms of verbs; past participles are the *-ed* forms of regular verbs. (See also **Verbs,** pages 280–82.) Participles combine with other words to form phrases that add details to sentences:

Lupe turned down my invitation to dinner, *cracking a smile* and *breaking my heart.*

***Laughing loudly,* she asked me to meet her the next day.**

Appositive Phrases

An appositive is a noun or a noun phrase that renames another noun or noun phrase in some way. An appositive phrase is a group of words functioning as an appositive:

> **Faculty objected when the trees in the parking lot, *Chinese elms,* were removed to create a walkway.**
>
> **The big box of sixty-four crayons introduced several generations of children to the colors *burnt umber and sienna.***

(See also **Appositives,** pages 229–30.)

Absolute Phrases

An absolute phrase, consisting of a noun or pronoun followed by a participle, modifies a whole sentence instead of a single word. It should be set off from the rest of the sentence by commas or dashes:

> **Then we left the stadium—*Celeste catching the subway for home and me walking on air.***
>
> ***The rain having freshened the air,* we went for a walk.**

Phrases and Sentence Fragments

A common writing error is to treat a phrase as if it were a complete sentence—to start it with a capital letter and end it with a mark of end punctuation (a period, a question mark, or an exclamation point). Here's what this kind of sentence fragment looks like:

> **Dripping on the floor.**   **Opening the door.**
>
> **To the game.**   **Having finished dinner.**
>
> **That she could be interested in me.**

In each case, the phrase needs to be joined to a complete (independent) clause. (For more on recognizing and correcting fragments, see **8,** pages 130–32.)

PLAGIARISM

To plagiarize means to claim authorship falsely. Giving the impression that another person's words, ideas, images, or data are your own constitutes plagiarism. (For guidelines for acceptable uses of other people's words and ideas, see **2c,** and **2d,** pages 40–53.)

POSSESSIVES

The possessive case shows ownership or a comparable relationship: *Lucia's car, a day's pay.* It replaces a phrase beginning with *of: the car of Lucia, the pay of a day.*

The possessive case of singular nouns and indefinite pronouns is indicated by an apostrophe plus *s* (*the child's braces, somebody's galoshes*).

Plural nouns ending in *s* are followed by an apostrophe to indicate possession (*the singers' recital*), and plurals not ending in *s* are followed by an apostrophe and *s* (*men's attitudes*).

Personal pronouns (such as *he, she,* or *it*) have their own possessive case forms (*his, hers,* or *its*). They never use apostrophes to show possession.

(For more on possession and the apostrophe, see **14b**, pages 177–79. For more on forms of pronouns, see **Pronouns,** pages 263–64.)

PREDICATE ADJECTIVES

A predicate adjective follows a linking verb (such as *is, looks, smells, becomes, appears, seems*) and modifies the subject:

Jim Carrey's films are *funny.*

[*Funny* is the predicate adjective; it modifies the subject *films.*]

PREDICATE NOUNS

A predicate noun, also known as a predicate nominative, follows a linking verb (such as *is, looks, smells, becomes, appears, seems*) and renames the subject:

The Beatles were *George, Paul, John, and Ringo.*

[The series *George, Paul, John, and Ringo* is the predicate noun; it renames the subject *The Beatles.*]

PREDICATES

The predicate of a sentence is the complete verb plus any object, predicate noun, or predicate adjective and all their modifiers. Thus it is everything in the sentence except the subject and its modifiers. In "My best friend Vick likes to spend Sunday afternoons watching football and playing the piano," the predicate is *likes to spend Sunday afternoons watching football and playing the piano.* (For information on faulty predication, see **17b,** page 193.)

PREPOSITIONS

A preposition expresses the relationship that its object (a noun, pronoun, or noun clause) has to the rest of the sentence:

The Cheshire cat perched *in* the tree.

Jamie reached the finish line *before* her friend.

In the first example, the preposition *in* describes a spatial relationship: it tells where the cat perches. In the second, *before* shows a time relationship. The object of *in* is *tree;* the object of *before* is *friend.* The entire unit—the preposition, its object, and the object's modifiers—is called a prepositional phrase.

Some Common Prepositions

about	**as**	**beyond**
across	**before**	**concerning**
against	**below**	**down**
among	**beside**	**except**
for	**onto**	**toward**
in	**outside**	**underneath**
into	**past**	**until**
near	**since**	**upon**
off	**throughout**	**within**

207–09

Some Common Phrasal Prepositions (consisting of more than one word)

according to	**due to**	**in spite of**
along with	**except for**	**instead of**
aside from	**in addition to**	**next to**
because of	**in front of**	**out of**
by way of	**in place of**	**with regard to**

PRINCIPAL PARTS OF VERBS

The principal parts of verbs are their basic forms. Except for *be,* all verbs in English have five forms.

Parts of Verbs

The base form—the one that combines with *to* to form the infinitive: *walk, ring*

The *-s* form—the third-person-singular form: *walks, rings*

The past tense—as in "Last night they *walked* around the track" or "Last night we *rang* the bell twice."

The past participle—as in "We have *walked* together many times" or "We have *rung* the bell before."

The present participle—as in "They are *walking* here now" or "They are *ringing* the bell now."

The irregular verb *be* has eight different forms: *be, is, am, are, was, were, been, being*. (A full discussion of verbs appears on pages 279–85.)

PRONOUNS

Most pronouns substitute for nouns or noun phrases and function in sentences as nouns do. They allow writers to continue discussing a person or a thing without repeating the noun:

Dauphine looked for *her* biology textbook, but *she* could not find it.

In this example, *her* stands for *Dauphine's,* and *she* stands for *Dauphine;* the writer uses *it* to avoid repeating *biology textbook.* In other words, *Dauphine* is the antecedent of *her* and of *she; textbook* is the antecedent of *it.*

(Errors in using pronouns are discussed in **13,** pages 167–74.)

Types of Pronouns

- **Personal pronouns** (*I, you, he, she, it, we, they* in the subjective case; *my, mine, your, yours, his, her, hers, its, our, ours, their, theirs* in the possessive case; and *me, you, him, her, it, us, them* in the objective case) refer to specific people or things:

  I* am sorry that *you* don't like *his* friends and that *you* refuse to play music with *them.

- **Reflexive pronouns** (*myself, yourself, himself, herself, itself, oneself, ourselves, yourselves, themselves*) refer to the subject of the sentence or clause, indicating that it receives the action of the complete verb:

  If that rope breaks, you will hurt *yourself.*

- **Intensive pronouns** have the same forms as reflexive pronouns. They are used to emphasize a noun or a pronoun:

  The manager *himself* could not open the safe.

- **Indefinite pronouns** (including *all, anybody, anyone, both, each, either, enough, everybody, everyone, everything, few, many, most, neither, none, no one, one, ones, other,* *others, some, somebody, someone*) do not substitute for specific nouns, but they function as nouns:

Common Indefinite Pronouns

all	**each**	**much**	**other**
another	**either**	**neither**	**some**
any	**everybody**	**nobody**	**somebody**
anybody	**everyone**	**none**	**someone**
anyone	**everything**	**no one**	**something**
anything	**few**	**nothing**	**such**
both	**many**	**one**	

(The use of indefinite pronouns as subjects is discussed in **11b,** pages 147–48.)

- **Demonstrative pronouns** (*this, that, these, those*) point to nouns, clarifying the group under discussion:

  ***Those* are the presents that should be taken to the homeless shelter.**

  Kahlil bought *that* swing set for *these* children.

- **Interrogative pronouns** (*who, whom, whose, which, what*) are used to ask questions:

  ***Who* is the rabbi at your synagogue?**

  ***Whose* mittens and boots are those?**

- **Relative pronouns** (*who, whom, whose, which, that, what, whoever, whomever, whichever, whatever*) introduce dependent clauses by relating the additional information to the rest of the sentence. Each relative pronoun should refer to a specific noun:

  You look like the boy *who* came to the party last week.

  I will do *whatever* it takes to attend one of Tiger Woods's golf clinics.

Q

QUOTATION MARKS

Quotation marks set off source materials, some types of titles, and words intended in a special sense. You will need to understand not only the correct use of quotation marks but also the correct punctuation to go along with them. (For more on the use of quotation marks for quoting source materials, see **2c,** pages 40–45. The specific requirements of MLA, APA, and *Chicago Manual of Style* documentation are found in **3, 4,** and **5,** pages 54–109.)

When to Use Quotation Marks

With Short Quotations from Source Materials

Use double quotation marks (") to enclose brief direct quotations from written or oral source material—four lines or less of prose or three lines or less of poetry for Modern Language Association (MLA) documentation style, less than forty words for American Psychological Association (APA) documentation style, or less than eight lines for *Chicago Manual of Style.*

> **"The first mistake," writes Isaac Asimov, "is to think of mankind as a thing in itself."**
>
> **According to Alexander H. Leighton, residents described the bomb that hit Hiroshima as "a black smoky mass, lit up with color."**

With Longer Quotations from Prose and Poetry

Unlike short quotations, longer quotations are not enclosed in quotation marks. Instead, they are set separately from the main text and indented. If the author of the quoted passage includes quotations, copy the quotation marks as they appear in the original:

> **In his essay "Side Effects," Steve Martin satirizes the long lists of warnings that come with today's prescription drugs:**
>
>> **If a fungus starts to grow between your eyebrows, call the *Guinness Book of Records.* Do not operate heavy machinery, especially if you feel qualified for a desk job; that's good advice anytime. May cause famines and pustules. There may be a tendency to compulsively repeat the phrase "no can do." (36)**

With Short Excerpts of Dialogue

Like quotations from source materials, dialogue is put in quotation marks. Generally each person's lines are written as a separate paragraph:

> **"Should we walk into the park here?" Cara asked her mother, indicating a small gap in the hedge.**
>
> **"No," her mother replied, "Let's wait until we come to the main entrance where the lighting is better."**

With Paragraphs of Dialogue

If a speaker's words continue for more than one paragraph, use quotation marks at the beginning of each paragraph but at the end of only the last one.

With Thoughts

To state a thought as though you or another speaker were saying it internally, use quotation marks, as with a direct quotation:

> **I finally said to myself, "I am so tired of this vacation."**
>
> **"How can I stop this log from rolling down the hill?" Bradley wondered.**

With Titles

Use quotation marks to cite the title of a short work or a part of something larger—a short story; an essay or article from a book, magazine, or newspaper; a short poem; a song; an episode of a television or radio show; or a chapter or subdivision of a book.

> **In the article entitled "On Impact," Stephen King wrote about his near-fatal accident and his slow return to writing.**

With Words Intended in a Special or Ironic Sense

You may—infrequently—place a word or a phrase in quotation marks to indicate that you are modifying its usual meaning:

> **Her "perfect man" turned out to have two children and a wife in New Jersey.**
>
> **She found out the truth about his "big promotion."**

Do not use quotation marks to enclose a cliché or slang. Instead, avoid such words or phrases in your writing.

> Faulty: **That "dude" was "sitting on the fence."**
>
> Better: **That man remained neutral.**

With Word Usage and Definitions

Use quotation marks (or italics) when you discuss a particular word or its definition:

> **The word "friendship" was not in his vocabulary.**
>
> **"Slink" means "to move in a quiet, furtive manner."**

With Quoted Material That Contains Quotation Marks

If the quotation contains material within quotation marks (such as a quotation, a title, an ironic phrase, or a definition), you will need both double and single quotation marks. The single quotation marks enclose the material that the author placed in quotation marks. The double marks enclose the entire passage being quoted:

Original	Quoted
America has given the Negro people a bad check, a check which has come back marked "insufficient funds." **—Martin Luther King, Jr.**	**When Martin Luther King called justice "a check which has come back marked 'insufficient funds,'" he was describing America's lack of commitment to equality under the law.**

Punctuation with Quotation Marks

- Place **periods** and **commas** within quotation marks:

  "Come on," he said. "You don't fool me."

  "When I go to baseball games," she told me, "I start getting nervous right after 'The Star-Spangled Banner.'"

- Place **colons** and **semicolons** outside quotation marks:

  In the nineteenth century, quiltmaking was popularly known as "patchwork"; this practical use of fabric scraps provided one of the few creative outlets for women.

  Emily Dickinson wrote about the fine sewing required for "esthetic patchwork": "I'll do seams—a Queen's endeavor / Would not blush to own."

- **Question marks** and **exclamation points** should be placed *inside* quotation marks when they are part of the quotation:

  The short-order cook leaned over the counter and asked me, "Do you take your eggs over easy?"

  Why was Laura yelling, "Can I eat now?"

  [With a question within a question, only one question mark is used, and it is placed within the quotation marks.]

  When Mary asked if she could join the boys' hockey team, the coach first said, "Absolutely not!"

When a question mark, an exclamation point, or a dash is not part of the quotation, it belongs *outside* the quotation marks:

Why did you yell "Fire"?

Don't expect me to listen to your xylophone version of "Home on the Range"!

"And Richard Cory, one calm summer night, / Went home and put a bullet through his head"—those final lines of Edwin Arlington Robinson's poem have always shocked me.

- When **parenthetical documentation** (MLA style) is used for a *short* quotation, the page numbers (or line numbers of poetry) that are placed in parentheses come after the quotation marks and before the period:

  "Tread softly," wrote William Butler Yeats, "because you tread on my dreams" (8).

QUOTATIONS

To quote a person or another source is to repeat the words of that person or source. Quotations can be presented word for word (*direct quotation*) or rewritten in your own words (*paraphrase*). (For more on using quotations, see **2c,** pages 40–45.)

R

RELATIVE CLAUSES

A relative clause is a dependent clause that begins with a relative pronoun (*which, that, what, who, whoever, whomever, whom, whose, whatever, whichever*).

The President defended the estimates *that he had made before.*

[The words *that he had made before* are a relative clause.]

RESTRICTIVE AND NONRESTRICTIVE CLAUSES

The presence or absence of commas helps readers distinguish between modifying clauses or phrases that are essential to the meaning of a sentence (restrictive) and those that are not essential (nonrestrictive). Nonrestrictive elements are set off by commas; restrictive elements are not.

Commas with Nonrestrictive (Nonessential) Clauses or Phrases

The car, a 1965 yellow Mustang convertible, caught my eye immediately.

The test of adulthood, as my neighbor likes to say, is the ability to say no.

No Commas with Restrictive (Essential) Clauses

➤ **The bank robber, whose picture was shown on television last night, was recognized today by his neighbors.**

➤ **The book, that I haven't been able to find all year, has been recalled by the library.**

Appositives (nouns or noun phrases renaming a noun) may also be classified as essential or nonessential; for more on restrictive and nonrestrictive appositives, see **Appositives,** pages 229–30.

RUN-ON SENTENCES

A run-on, or fused, sentence is the combination of two independent clauses into one sentence with no punctuation between the two clauses:

The battle over salary increases seemed to be deadlocked neither side wanted to compromise.

(See **10,** pages 138–41, for ways to correct this error.)

S

SEMICOLONS

The semicolon can join two or more independent, or main, clauses that are not linked by a coordinating conjunction (*and, but, for, nor, or, so,* or *yet*). It is used when the two clauses are closely related in meaning:

He can't stop worrying; he can't seem to control any part of his life.

Stella peered out the window; she was surprised by what she saw in the street below.

Semicolons with Conjunctive Adverbs

If the second of two independent clauses begins with a conjunctive adverb such as *however,* you still need the semicolon. These adverbs are generally followed by a comma:

People use words like *Kleenex, Dramamine, Band-Aid,* and *Coke* to refer to product types; *however,* these terms are actually trademarks of specific manufacturers.

(For a full list of conjunctive adverbs, see **Conjunctive Adverbs,** page 243; for help with correcting errors, see **9c,** page 136, and **10c,** pages 140–41.)

Semicolons with Complex Sentences

The semicolon can combine not only two independent clauses but also two or more complex sentences (sentences that contain both an independent and a dependent clause):

> **When the mechanic crawled under the car, he saw a corroded muffler and shaft; when he crawled out, the car owner saw a large bill to be paid.**

Semicolons with Coordinating Conjunctions

If the independent clauses you are joining are long and complicated, perhaps having several commas or conjunctions, you can use a semicolon along with a coordinating conjunction to create a clear division between the two main parts:

> **The warm-water ocean and endless sunny weather, heralded in the state's tourist advertisements, make southern California's beaches popular for swimmers; *and* the high, straight waves, which rival Australia's, make these beaches a mecca for surfers.**

Semicolons with Series

For clarity, use semicolons to separate items in a series when the items are long and contain commas:

> **Leading the meeting were Frederica Nipp, president; Raul Garcia, vice president; Louisa Lane, secretary and treasurer; and Laura Holmes, student representative.**

SENTENCES

A sentence is a group of words that (1) makes sense on its own, (2) includes a subject and a predicate, and (3) begins with a capital letter and ends with a period, a question mark, or an exclamation point. Omission of the subject or the verb creates a sentence fragment. (For help recognizing and correcting sentence fragments, see **8,** pages 130–32.)

Parts of Sentences

- The main parts of sentences in English are the *subject* (usually built around a noun or a pronoun) and the *predicate* (built around a complete verb):

  Rain fell.

- The **subject** of a sentence is a noun or a pronoun about which the predicate asserts or asks something. It may also include modifiers (usually adjectives) of the noun or pronoun:

  ***The dusty, summer-smelling rain* fell.**

Some sentences, such as instructions or commands, begin with an understood subject—*you:*

> **[*You*] Insert the address into your file with the "Merge Files" command.**

- The **predicate** of a sentence is the part that says something about the subject. The predicate includes the complete verb and its modifiers. The predicate may also include a direct object, an indirect object, a predicate adjective, or a predicate noun.

  The rain *was falling lightly.*

- The **direct object** receives the action of the complete verb:

  The rain hit *Bob's just-washed car.*

Here *car* is the direct object, receiving the action of the predicate verb, *hit; Bob's* and *just-washed* are adjectives that modify the direct object.

- The **indirect object** tells to or for whom or what something is done:

  Lucia gave *Simon* her book.

  Lucia gave her book *to Simon.*

Here *book* is the direct object, receiving the action of the complete verb: it is what Lucia gave. *Simon* and the prepositional phrase *to Simon* are both indirect objects, telling for whom the action was performed.

- The **object complement** follows and modifies a direct object:

  Officials considered the town *a disaster area.*

Here *area,* the object complement, modified by *a disaster,* renames and further describes the direct object, *town.*

- The **predicate adjective** follows a linking verb (such as *is, looks, smells, becomes, appears, seems*) and modifies the subject:

  The rain was *gray against the sky.*

Here *gray* is a predicate adjective, modifying the subject *rain,* and *against the sky* is a prepositional phrase modifying *gray.*

- The **predicate noun** follows a linking verb (such as *is, looks, smells, becomes, appears, seems*) and renames the subject:

  The rain was *a deluge.*

Here *deluge* is a noun, renaming *rain*—it is not some aspect or attribute of the rain (as *gray* was in the previous example) but rather another name for the same thing.

Structures of Sentences

Sentences may be classified as simple, compound, complex, or compound-complex, depending on how many independent and dependent clauses they contain. An independent clause is a subject-verb unit that makes a complete statement and can stand on its own. A dependent clause begins with a subordinating word (such as *when, if,* or *since*) and thus needs to be linked to an independent clause to complete its meaning.

- A **simple sentence** contains only one independent clause:

  Drug abuse clearly is destroying our cities.

- A **compound sentence** has two (or more) independent clauses:

  Elementary-school teaching provided some employment opportunities for nineteenth-century women, but high-school teaching was reserved for men.

- A **complex sentence** contains an independent clause and a dependent clause:

  When drug-related crime makes whole neighborhoods unsafe after dark, drug abuse clearly is destroying our cities.

- A **compound-complex sentence** has two or more independent clauses and one or more dependent clauses:

  When you first enter the master's degree program in public administration, you may find America's foreign policy difficult to understand, but the professor's lectures will clarify it for you.

- A sentence is in **inverted order** when the verb appears before the subject for effect:

Inverted Order	Usual Order
Then came the day of reckoning.	**Then the day of reckoning came.**

SIMPLE SENTENCES

A simple sentence contains only an independent clause:

Cole is playing a video game.

SLASHES

Use the slash to separate two or three lines of poetry quoted within your text. Add a space before and after the slash:

> **W. H. Auden's poem "The Unknown Citizen" concludes with these ironic lines: "Was he free? Was he happy? The question is absurd: / Had anything been wrong, we should certainly have heard."**

You can also use the slash to indicate a pair of options, with no space before or after the slash:

> **Internships are generally offered as pass/fail courses.**

SPELLING

Knowing basic spelling rules can help you avoid mistakes. However, you should always use a dictionary when you are writing and check it whenever you are not sure about the spelling of a word.

Keep a list of the words that you frequently misspell and then review it as you proofread. For particularly troublesome words, you might also jot down the reason for the spelling to help you understand the correct choice.

COMPUTER NOTE: SPELL CHECKERS

The spelling checkers provided with most word-processing programs can help you avoid many errors, but they have some limitations: they cannot tell you how to spell words not listed in their dictionaries, such as many proper nouns, or words that are commonly confused, such as *belief* and *believe*. If you make an error in typing but write a real word, typing *cash* for *case*, for example, the spelling checker won't help you find the error. You still need to proofread carefully.

Spelling Rules

Many of the difficulties involved in commonly misspelled words can be solved through an understanding of spelling rules.

Words with *ie* and *ei*

The full rule can help you determine which spelling to choose:

I before e

believe, friend, field, piece, relieve, niece, brief, grief, chief, hygiene, yield, siege, cashier, frontier

Except after *c*

receive, deceive, perceive, conceive, deceit, ceiling, conceit

Or When Pronounced *ay*

neighbor, weigh, eight, freight, beige, vein, sleigh

Or in Weird Exceptions Like *Either* and *Species*

neither, leisure, seize, weird, foreign, height, caffeine, forfeit, ancient, conscience

Suffixes

Suffixes are placed at the ends of words to form new, related words. For example, you can build on the word *love* by adding suffixes:

lov*able*	**love*liest***
lov*er*	**love*less***
love*ly*	**lov*ing***

Spelling Rules for Suffixes

- **Drop an unpronounced *e*** at the end of a word if the suffix starts with a vowel:

  grade → gradation

  create → creator

  love → lovable

EXCEPTIONS: The final unpronounced *e* may be maintained

(1) to distinguish homonyms:

dye + ing = dyeing [*not* dying]

singe + ing = singeing [*not* singing]

(2) to clarify pronunciation:

shoe + ing = shoeing [*not* shoing]

be + ing = being [*not* bing]

(3) to keep the sound of *c* or *g* soft:

notice + able = noticeable

courage + ous = courageous

- **Keep an unpronounced *e*** if the suffix starts with a consonant:

  arrange → arrangement

  fate → fateful

EXCEPTIONS: judgment, argument, ninth, likable, truly, wholly

- **Change *y* to *i*** before all suffixes except *ing:*

  try → tries, tried (trying)

  carry → carries, carried, carrier (carrying)

EXCEPTIONS: Verbs ending in *y* preceded by a vowel do not change the *y* before *s* or *ed:* play, plays, played; destroy, destroys, destroyed.

- **Double the final consonant** in the following cases:

  When the word ends in a vowel and a consonant and has one syllable:

  hop → hopping

  hit → hitter

  When the word has an accented last syllable and the suffix begins with a vowel:

  begin → beginning

  refer → referring

- **Do *not* double the final consonant** in the following cases:

  When the final consonant is preceded by more than one vowel or another consonant:

  wait → waiting

  report → reporter

  When the suffix begins with a consonant:

  red → redness

  master → masterful

  When the word is not accented on the last syllable:

  benefit → benefited

  panel → paneled

  When the accent shifts from the last syllable to the first after the suffix is added:

  confer → conference

  refer → referee

- **Use *ly* to form the adverb** if the base word does not end in *ic*. If the word ends in *l*, keep the *l* when you add *ly:*

  slow → slowly

  forceful → forcefully

  formal → formally

- **Use *ally* to form the adverb** if the base word ends in *ic:*

  basic → basically

  characteristic → characteristically

EXCEPTION: public + ly = publicly

Plurals

Most nouns are made plural by adding an *s* to the singular form:

dogs, lamps, schools, problems

brothers-in-law [in such compounds, the chief word is made plural]

- **For nouns ending in *f* or *fe*,** change the ending to *ve* before adding *s:*

  thief → thieves

  life → lives

EXCEPTIONS: chief → chiefs; belief → beliefs.

- **For nouns ending in *y* preceded by a vowel,** add an *s* to form the plural:

  joy, joys

  holiday, holidays

- **For nouns ending in *y* preceded by a consonant,** change the *y* to *i* and add *es:*

  company, companies

  specialty, specialties

- **For nouns ending in *o* preceded by a vowel,** add an *s:*

  rodeo, rodeos

  zoo, zoos

- **For nouns ending in *o* preceded by a consonant,** you will need to memorize the spelling or consult a dictionary for the plural because some add *es* and some add *s*. Here are the plurals of some of the most common of these words:

hero, heroes

potato, potatoes

veto, vetoes

memo, memos

- **For nouns ending in *s, ch, sh,* or *x*,** add *es* to form the plural:

  Jones, the Joneses

  class, classes

- Some nouns, many of which were derived from other languages, have **irregular plurals:**

  woman, women

  man, men

  child, children

STANDARD ENGLISH

There are many forms and dialects of English. Some are geographically based; others are racial or ethnic in origin (such as Black English, sometimes called Black English Vernacular, or Spanish Influenced English). The form of English used for communication in education, business, industry, government, and the professions in the United States is called **Standard American English** (SAE). The standards established by colleges and universities for student writing are often those of SAE. When prospective employers look at your writing, chances are they are looking for SAE.

Writing in Standard American English (or revising your writing to conform to it) involves selecting particular options in vocabulary, grammatical forms, spelling, capitalization, and punctuation. SAE avoids slang, vernacular (spoken) forms, and regional or ethnic dialects. (For a discussion of nonstandard forms, see **11c,** pages 149–50.) When you are writing (or speaking formally) in an academic setting or in business or government, Standard American English needs to guide the choices you make. (See also Formal Writing, page 248.)

SUBJECTS

216–17 The subject of a sentence is a noun (or a substitute for a noun) that performs the action expressed in the predicate of the sentence:

> **The *contractor* offered the mayor a bribe.**
>
> [The subject, *contractor,* is performing the action of offering.]

SUBORDINATE CLAUSES

The term *subordinate clause* is another name for a dependent clause:

> ***When Avia entered the lab,* all the tutors were eating at the counter.**
>
> [The subordinate, or dependent, clause is *When Avia entered the lab.*]

(For a list of words that begin subordinate clauses, see **Clauses,** page 237.)

T

TRANSITIVE VERBS

A transitive verb is a verb that can take an object; verbs such as *bring, give, hit, insert,* and *take* are transitive verbs. (**Intransitive verbs,** page 252, do not take objects.)

V

VERBALS

Verbals are forms of verbs that function as nouns, adjectives, or adverbs. There are three types of verbals: *gerunds, infinitives,* and *participles.* They can take subjects, objects, and complements and can be modified by adverbs, but they cannot be used as complete verbs.

- **Gerunds** end in *ing.* Thus they have the same form as present participles. Gerunds and gerund phrases always function as nouns:

> **Camilla loved *skating.***
>
> ***Eating at authentic Mexican restaurants near the hotel* consumed all his time at the Santa Fe conference.**

- **Infinitives** are the base form of the verb plus *to.* Infinitives and infinitive phrases can function as nouns, adjectives, and adverbs:

  To graduate **was his only goal. [noun]**

  Taking a quick straw vote would be a good way *to assess the group's general preferences.* [adjective]

  To improve your golf game, **watch the instructional series available at your video store. [adverb]**

- **Present** and **past participles** are the *-ing* and *-ed* verb forms. The past participle of some irregular verbs ends in *en, n,* or *t.* Participles and participial phrases function as adjectives:

  The *freezing* children finally saw a rescue truck. 205–06 212–13

  Running quickly, **they got away from the fumes.**

  Exhausted from the two-hour session, **the young debaters waited to hear their scores.**

(For more on gerunds, infinitives, and participles and how they are used, see **Phrases,** page 259.)

VERBS

The verb is the part of a sentence that connects the subject with everything else. The verb may tell what the subject does, name an action done to the subject, or describe the subject's state of being. 203–16

Subjects and verbs always need to agree in *number*—singular or plural:

> ***Jamel likes*** **Christina, but *he doesn't like* the arguments *they have.***

They also need to agree in *person*—first, second, or third:

> ***You are*** **sure that *he has* his driver's license.**

No matter where the subject appears in the sentence, the number of the subject determines whether the verb will be in the singular or plural form:

> **The *weeds* growing in the garden behind the shed *are* the healthiest plants in the yard.**

(For a full discussion of subject-verb agreement, see **11b,** pages 145–48.)

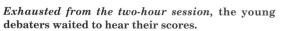

Principal Parts of Verbs

The principal parts of verbs are their basic forms. Except for the verb *be,* all verbs in English have five forms.

Five Principal Parts of Verbs

Base Form: **I (*talk, swim*). [The base form is usually the present tense of the first person singular.]**

-s Form: **He/she/it (*talks, swims*).**

Past Tense: **Last week they (*talked, swam*).**

Past Participle: **We have (*talked, swum*) many times before.**

Present Participle: **They are (*talking, swimming*) now.**

The verb *be* has eight parts:

be, am, are, is, was, were, been, being

Irregular Verbs

All regular verbs have past tense and past participle forms that are the same: they end in *ed* or *d.* Irregular verbs, however, have irregular past tense and past participle forms. As you can see from this list, many irregular verbs are used frequently.

Principal Parts of Irregular Verbs

Base	*Past Tense*	*Past Participle*
arise	**arose**	**arisen**
awake	**awoke, awaked**	**awoken, awaked**
be	**was, were**	**been**
become	**became**	**become**
bid	**bid [or bade]**	**bid [or bidden]**
build	**built**	**built**
burst	**burst**	**burst**
come	**came**	**come**
cost	**cost**	**cost**
cut	**cut**	**cut**
deal	**dealt**	**dealt**
dive	**dived, dove**	**dived**
dream	**dreamed, dreamt**	**dreamed, dreamt**
eat	**ate**	**eaten**
fight	**fought**	**fought**
flee	**fled**	**fled**

forget	**forgot**	**forgotten, forgot**
get	**got**	**got, gotten**
hang (suspend)	**hung**	**hung**
hang (execute)	**hanged**	**hanged**
have	**had**	**had**
hurt	**hurt**	**hurt**
lay (put)	**laid**	**laid**
lead	**led**	**led**
lend	**lent**	**lent**
let (allow)	**let**	**let**
lie (recline)	**lay**	**lain**
make	**made**	**made**
prove	**proved**	**proved, proven**
read	**read**	**read**
rise (get up)	**rose**	**risen**
set (place)	**set**	**set**
sit (be seated)	**sat**	**sat**
slide	**slid**	**slid**
spin	**spun**	**spun**
spring	**sprang, sprung**	**sprung**
steal	**stole**	**stolen**
strike	**struck**	**struck, stricken**
swing	**swung**	**swung**

If you are not sure whether a verb is irregular, consult a dictionary. When you look up the base form of an irregular verb, it will be followed by its principal parts. (See also **11c,** pages 148–50.)

Lie and *Lay*

Writers often confuse *lie* and *lay* because their principal parts are similar. *Lay,* a transitive verb, means "to put or place something"; *lie,* an intransitive verb, means "to recline or rest in a flat position." After choosing the right verb, you must use the correct principal part.

Forms of *Lie* and *Lay*

Base	*Past Tense*	*Past Participle*	*Present Participle*
lay (put)	**laid**	**laid**	**laying**
lie (recline)	**lay**	**lain**	**lying**

She was *lying* on the floor.

Have you seen where I *laid* the silverware?

He has *lain* in that bed for a week.

Tense

The three **simple tenses** are *present, past,* and *future.* The three **perfect tenses** are *present perfect, past perfect,* and *future perfect.* Each of these tenses has a **progressive** form.

Simple Tenses

- The **simple present** indicates action occurring as it is being mentioned or occurring regularly. This tense uses the base form or, for third-person singular, the *-s* form:

SIMPLE PRESENT

	Singular	*Plural*
1st person	I talk	we talk
2nd person	you talk	you talk
3rd person	he/she/it talks	they talk

- The **simple past** (the *-ed* form for regular verbs) indicates action completed in the past:

SIMPLE PAST

	Singular	*Plural*
1st person	I talked	we talked
2nd person	you talked	you talked
3rd person	he/she/it talked	they talked

- The **simple future** (*will* or *shall* plus the base form) indicates action that will occur in the future:

SIMPLE FUTURE

	Singular	*Plural*
1st person	I will talk	we will talk
2nd person	you will talk	you will talk
3rd person	he/she/it will talk	they will talk

Perfect Tenses

The perfect forms indicate action that was or will be completed before another action or time. They consist of a form of *have* plus the past participle:

PRESENT PERFECT

	Singular	*Plural*
1st person	I have talked	we have talked
2nd person	you have talked	you have talked
3rd person	he/she/it has talked	they have talked

PAST PERFECT

	Singular	*Plural*
1st person	I had talked	we had talked
2nd person	you had talked	you had talked
3rd person	he/she/it had talked	they had talked

FUTURE PERFECT

	Singular	*Plural*
1st person	I will have talked	we will have talked
2nd person	you will have talked	you will have talked
3rd person	he/she/it will have talked	they will have talked

Progressive Forms

Each of the six tenses just explained has a progressive form to indicate a continuing action. These verbs consist of a form of *be* plus the present participle:

PRESENT PROGRESSIVE

	Singular	*Plural*
1st person	I am talking	we are talking
2nd person	you are talking	you are talking
3rd person	he/she/it is talking	they are talking

PAST PROGRESSIVE

	Singular	*Plural*
1st person	I was talking	we were talking
2nd person	you were talking	you were talking
3rd person	he/she/it was talking	they were talking

FUTURE PROGRESSIVE

	Singular	*Plural*
1st person	I will be talking	we will be talking
2nd person	you will be talking	you will be talking
3rd person	he/she/it will be talking	they will be talking

PRESENT PERFECT PROGRESSIVE

	Singular	*Plural*
1st person	I have been talking	we have been talking
2nd person	you have been talking	you have been talking
3rd person	he/she/it has been talking	they have been talking

PAST PERFECT PROGRESSIVE

	Singular	*Plural*
1st person	I had been talking	we had been talking
2nd person	you had been talking	you had been talking
3rd person	he/she/it had been talking	they had been talking

FUTURE PERFECT PROGRESSIVE

	Singular	*Plural*
1st person	I will have been talking	we will have been talking
2nd person	you will have been talking	you will have been talking
3rd person	he/she/it will have been talking	they will have been talking

Helping or Auxiliary Verbs

211–13 The base form of the verb can also combine with helping, or auxiliary, verbs, such as *do, can, could, may, might, will, would, shall, should,* and *must:*

The boys do run. **She can go.**

Active and Passive Voice

The voice of a verb indicates how the subject relates to the action expressed by the verb. When the subject is the actor (the doer), the sentence is *active.* When the subject receives the action expressed by the verb, the sentence is *passive:*

Active	Passive
Marcos kicked the ball.	**The ball was kicked by Marcos.**

Mood

The mood of a verb tells whether the verb expresses a fact or a factual condition (*indicative mood*); expresses doubt, a condition wished for, or a condition contrary to fact (*subjunctive mood*); or expresses a command (*imperative mood*):

Indicative

His bike *had been stolen* for the third time.

Her essay *won* the prize for this year.

Subjunctive

If it *were* mine to give, it would be yours.

I wish Cheryl *were* here to see this.

Imperative

***Look* over here!**

***Take* the dog home!**

The Subjunctive

The form of the subjunctive is the base form of the verb (the one the dictionary gives first—the infinitive form without the marker *to*). The only exception involves the verb *be,* which has a present subjunctive form (*be*) and a past subjunctive form (*were*). 213–14

The subjunctive is used in four instances:

1. To express conditions of doubt, conditions wished for, or conditions contrary to fact:

   I wish I *were* a rich person.

2. In *if* clauses that describe conditions that are contrary to fact, hypothetical, or improbable:

   If I *were* in charge, things would be different.

3. In *that* clauses following verbs of asking, insisting, requesting, making a motion, or wishing:

   I move that Dorothy *be* elected.

4. In a few common expressions:

   As it *were* . . . | **that we might *be* free of . . .**

   ***Be* that as it may** | ***Come* what may**

VOICE

Voice refers to the relationship between the subject and the action expressed by the verb. If the subject acts, the sentence is in **active voice.** If the subject receives the action of the verb, the sentence is in **passive voice:**

Active	Passive
The staff must wear uniforms.	**Uniforms must be worn.**

(For help with choosing between active and passive voice, see **1d,** pages 22–24.)

W

WORD CHOICE (DICTION)

Choosing Specific Language

Word choices range along a continuum from the most general to the most specific:

General ⟵		⟶ Specific
mammal	**dog**	**German Shepherd**
food	**appetizer**	**steak tartare**
people	**children**	**Darlene and Tommy standing in the mud and rain with dirt caked all over them**

You generally want to use the most specific and appropriate words possible and avoid needless abstraction and wordiness.

AVOIDING PRETENTIOUS WORD CHOICES

Try to avoid flowery or stilted phrases, overwriting that calls attention to the words instead of the ideas. Especially in prose, this type of phrasing sounds affected:

Overwritten	Improved
When the last glimmer of the sun fell behind the horizon, in the long ago days of my youth, I felt the shiver of fear as I climbed the stairs to my room.	**When I was a child, I was afraid to go upstairs to bed at night.**

Considering Your Reader

In choosing the right words for any piece of writing, you also should consider the nature of the audience. Different levels of formality and different kinds of word choice are appropriate for different readers. (See **1a,** page 6, for more on adjusting your writing to the reader. Further discussion of problems with word choice can be found in **1d** on pages 22–26 and in **Jargon,** pages 253–54.)

20

GLOSSARY OF USAGE

a, an Use *a* before a consonant sound; use *an* before a vowel sound: *a dog, an animal.*

accept, except *Accept* is a verb meaning "to receive willingly." *Except* is a preposition meaning "excluding":

> I will accept all the nominations except the last one.

adapt, adopt *Adapt* means "to adjust to a situation":

> She will adapt to college life easily.

Adopt means "to take into the family" or "to accept a course of action or belief":

> We adopted a child.
>
> She adopted a new code of ethics for all employees.

advice, advise *Advice* is a noun meaning "guidance"; *advise* is a verb meaning "to counsel":

> We advised him to seek advice from a college counselor.

affect, effect *Affect* is a verb meaning "to influence":

> Her performance affected me.

Effect is generally used as a noun meaning "the result":

> She explained the effects of that drug.

Effect can also be a verb meaning "to bring about":

> The new diplomat immediately effected important changes.

ain't *Ain't* is nonstandard. Use *am not, isn't,* or *aren't.*

all right *All right* should always be written as two words, never as *alright.*

a lot *A lot* is always two words:

> She has a lot of friends.

already, all ready *Already,* an adverb, means "before" or "previously." *All ready,* an adjective, means "completely prepared":

> I already told you that I am all ready to leave for the camping trip.

altogether, all together *Altogether* means "entirely, completely." *All together* means "in a group":

> I altogether agree with you that we cannot go all together to the wedding.

among, between Use *among* for three or more items; use *between* with two:

> The tasks were divided among the ten volunteers.
>
> Park your car between these two posts.

amount, number *Amount* refers to items in bulk or mass; *number* is for countable items:

> You will need a larger amount of flour, baking soda, and sugar to make a large number of cakes.

an See *a, an.*

and etc. A redundant phrase: use *etc.* by itself. See also the entry for *etc.*

and/or Avoid this construction because it can be awkward and confusing:

> The decision will be made by the teacher and/or the adviser.
>
> [If you mean *both,* use *and.* If you mean *either one,* use *or.* If you mean *either one or both,* write "by the teacher, by the adviser, or by both."]

anybody *Anybody* is singular.

anyone *Anyone* is singular.

anyone, any one *Anyone* means "any person at all." *Any one* refers to a member of a group:

> Anyone can purchase any one of the paintings in the show.

anyplace Nonstandard for *any place* or *anywhere.*

as Do not use *as* to mean "because" or "since": the resulting sentence may be confusing, since *as* can also mean *when.*

> We left the pool because [not *as*] it was raining.
>
> See also *like, as.*

bad, badly *Bad* is the adjective form; *badly* is the adverb:

The bad wound healed badly.

being as, being that Nonstandard for *because.*

beside, besides *Beside* means "by the side of"; *besides* means "in addition to" and "other than":

She sat beside the bed.

He is getting a monthly living allowance besides his regular salary.

She has few friends besides those she made in the army.

be sure and Use *be sure to* in formal writing:

Be sure to [not *and*] bring in the dog tonight.

between See *among, between.*

biannual, biennial *Biannual* means "twice a year"; *biennial* means "once every two years."

breath, breathe *Breath* is a noun meaning "the air inhaled and exhaled." *Breathe* is a verb meaning "to inhale and exhale":

When her breath became regular, I began to breathe more easily.

burst, bursted, bust, busted *Burst* is the standard verb form:

The balloon burst.

Bursted, bust, and *busted* are nonstandard forms.

capital, capitol *Capital* means "a city that is a government seat." *Capitol* means "a building where a legislature meets":

As soon as our train arrived in the capital, we looked up to see the dome of the capitol.

cite, sight, site *Cite* is a verb meaning "to refer to." The noun *sight* means "the ability to see" or "something that is seen." The noun *site* means "a location":

Remember to cite your sources in your research paper.

He lost his sight when he was five.

The vacant lot was the site of the new parking lot.

complement, compliment *Complement* means "to make whole or bring to perfection." *Compliment* means "praise":

That color complements your eyes.

Her new haircut received many compliments.

continual, continuous *Continual* means "of frequent recurrence." *Continuous* means "without stop."

> The continual ringing of bells at nearby churches bothered the office staff, but they never noticed the continuous hum of the copy machine.

could of Nonstandard for *could have:*

> She could have [not *could of*] been a wonderful president.

council, counsel *Council* is a noun that means "an assembly of leaders." *Counsel* means "advice" (noun) or "to give advice" (verb):

> The student council offered to counsel the new freshman class.

data, datum *Data* is, technically, the plural form of *datum.* In many fields, *data* is now treated as the only form, as singular or plural depending upon the context.

disinterested, uninterested *Disinterested* means "impartial, objective." *Uninterested* means "not interested":

> Umpires should be disinterested.
>
> Fans often become uninterested when their team falls behind.

due to *Due to* should be used to mean "because of" only after a form of the verb *be:*

> Darla left the house because of [not *due to*] her husband's violence.
>
> Freida's success was due to hard work.

each *Each* is singular.

effect See *affect, effect.*

either *Either* is singular.

emigrate from, immigrate to *Emigrate from* means "to leave one country or region":

> Many people emigrated from England in search of religious freedom.

Immigrate to means "to enter another country and live there":

> He left Sarajevo and immigrated to Italy.

etc. In formal writing, avoid the Latin abbreviation *etc.* (for *et cetera,* meaning "and so forth"). Instead of ending a list with *etc.,* begin it with *such as, for example,* or *for instance.*

everybody, everyone *Everybody* and *everyone* are singular.

everyday, every day *Everyday* is an adjective meaning "ordinary." Do not confuse it with the phrase *every day* meaning "each day":

> On every day except Sunday, I use my everyday plates and silverware.

everyone, every one *Everyone* is an indefinite pronoun. *Every one,* the pronoun *one* modified by the adjective *every,* means "each individual or thing in a particular group":

> Everyone waited until every one of the jewels was found.

except See *accept, except.*

farther, further *Farther* refers to additional distance. *Further* refers to additional time, quantity, or extent:

> As we drove farther from home, I told Dennis that I didn't want to discuss the matter any further.

fewer, less *Fewer* refers to items that can be counted; *less* refers to bulk or mass amounts:

> fewer days, less time; fewer cups, less sugar

firstly *Firstly* sounds stilted, and it leads to the awkward series *firstly, secondly, thirdly, fourthly,* and so on. Use *first, second, third* instead.

get In formal writing, avoid using *get* to mean the following: "to evoke an emotional response" (*That song gets to me* or *Her pouting gets to me*); "to take revenge on" (*I plan to get her back*); "to finish" (*We got done*); "must" (*I've got to study*); and "have" (*I've got three tests this Friday*).

good, well *Good* is an adjective, and *well* is nearly always an adverb:

> The good friends dance well together.

Well may be used as an adjective to refer to health:

> She is well.

good and Nonstandard for *very:*

> I am very [not *good and*] angry with you.

had ought The *had* is unnecessary:

> She ought [not *had ought*] to finish college.

hanged, hung *Hanged* is the past tense and the past participle of the verb *hang* meaning "to execute":

In the nineteenth century, many petty criminals were hanged.

Hung is the past tense and past participle of the verb *hang* meaning "to fasten or suspend":

The large decorations were hung on piano wire.

hardly Avoid expressions such as *can't hardly* and *not hardly,* which are considered double negatives:

I can [not *can't*] hardly wait for the party to begin.

he/she, his/her In formal writing, use *he or she* or *his or her.*

hisself Nonstandard for *himself.*

hopefully *Hopefully* means "in a hopeful manner":

We waited hopefully while Tran was in surgery.

Do not use *hopefully* to mean "it is to be hoped":

I hope that [not *Hopefully*] you will get the lead part in the play.

if, whether Use *if* in a statement of condition and *whether* to express alternatives:

If you go to college, whether to a private or a state school, you will need to fill out financial aid forms.

immigrate to See *emigrate from, immigrate to.*

imply, infer *Imply* means "to suggest without stating directly"; *infer* means "to draw a conclusion":

The lawyer implied that her client had been treated unfairly, but the judge inferred that the defendant had lied.

irregardless Nonstandard for *regardless.*

is when, is where These constructions are often incorrectly used in definitions:

A beefalo is a hybrid between an American buffalo and a domestic cow.

[Not "A beefalo *is when* an American buffalo is bred with a domestic cow."]

Washington, D.C., is the capital of the United States.

[Not "Washington, D.C. *is where* the capital of the United States is."]

its, it's *Its* is a possessive pronoun; *it's* is a contraction of *it is:*

It's pleasing to see that dog leave the pound with its new owner.

later, latter *Later,* referring to time, is the comparative form of *late. Latter* refers to the second named of two; the first is called the *former:*

I had hoped to see Naomi and Chris, but only the latter was home. Naomi wasn't expected until much later.

lay, lie *Lay* is a transitive verb meaning "to put or place." Its principal parts are *lay, laid, laid. Lie* is an intransitive verb meaning "to recline or rest in a flat position." Its principal parts are *lie, lay, lain:*

Where did I lay those leather gloves?

Do you need to lie down?

lead, led *Lead* is a noun referring to a metal and a verb meaning "to go before." *Led* is the past tense of the verb *to lead:*

The tests led to the conclusion that the child had lead poisoning.

less See *fewer, less.*

liable *Liable* means "obligated" or "responsible." Do not use it to mean "likely":

You're likely [not *liable*] to fall if you walk on that high wall.

like, as *Like* is a preposition. It should be followed by a noun or a noun phrase. *As* is a subordinating conjunction that introduces a dependent clause:

You look like a friendly person.

You don't know her as I do.

loose, lose *Loose* is an adjective meaning "not fastened." *Lose* is a verb meaning "to misplace" or "to fail to win":

Rosa began to lose the race when her rear wheel became loose.

lots, lots of *Lots* and *lots of* are slang substitutes for *many, much,* or *a lot.* Avoid using them in formal writing.

media, medium *Media* is, technically, the plural form of *medium. Media* is often treated now as the only form, as singular or plural, depending upon the context.

moral, morale *Moral* is an adjective meaning "conforming to standards of goodness." *Morale* is a noun meaning "the spirit of an individual or group":

His moral decision to stand up for his staff increased the morale of the whole group.

most *Most* should not be used to mean *almost:*

Almost [not *Most*] everyone enjoyed the concert.

myself, yourself, himself, herself, ourselves, themselves The *-self* pronouns are reflexive or intensive pronouns and thus must have an antecedent.

Reflexive: I hurt myself.

Intensive: I will teach you myself.

Do not use *myself* in place of *I* or *me:*

The police next questioned Trudy and me [not *myself*].

neither *Neither* is singular.

none *None* is singular.

number See *amount, number.*

of Use the verb *have,* not the preposition *of,* after the verbs *could, should, would, may, might,* and *must:*

You should have [not *of*] seen her new interview suit.

off of The *of* is unnecessary. Use *off:*

She fell off [not *off of*] the balcony.

OK, O.K., okay All three spellings are acceptable, but you should avoid these slang expressions in formal writing.

passed, past *Passed* is the past tense of the verb *to pass;* thus it means "went by" or "received a passing grade." *Past* means "of a former time" or "beyond in time or position":

She passed her test.

He passed the car driven by our past president.

The accident occurred just past the new entrance ramp.

plus Do not use *plus* to join two independent clauses:

The oleander bushes need clipping, and [not *plus*] the roses need fertilizer.

precede, proceed *Precede* means "to come before." *Proceed* means "to go onward" or "to move in an orderly fashion":

> As Juana proceeded to the final turn of the walk race, she realized that three contestants had preceded her.

principal, principle *Principal* is a noun meaning "the head of a school" or "a sum of money." It is also an adjective meaning "first in importance." *Principle* is a noun meaning "a basic truth or standard":

> The principal asked the school board, "Do we have the principal to rebuild the science building?"
>
> My principal reason for leaving home was that I disagreed with my stepfather's principles of discipline.

proceed See *precede, proceed.*

provided, providing *Provided* can serve as a subordinating conjunction meaning *if. Providing* cannot be used this way:

> We will begin providing a larger budget for urban housing provided we receive a new federal grant.

raise, rise *Raise* is a transitive verb meaning "to move upward." It takes a direct object:

> She raised the banner above her head.

Rise is an intransitive verb meaning "to go up." It does not take a direct object:

> When the sun comes up, the temperature rises.

real, really *Real* is an adjective; *really* is an adverb. *Real* is sometimes used informally as an adverb, but you should avoid this use in formal writing:

> They were really [not *real*] tired.

reason is because, reason why Both of these phrases are redundant. Use *reason is* or *reason is that* instead.

> The reason [not *The reason why*] he chose a technical college is unclear.

respectfully, respectively *Respectfully* means "in a manner that shows respect." *Respectively* means "each in the order given":

> She acted respectfully toward her older cousins.

> The three childhood friends, Margaret, Paula, and Suelinda, became a college teacher, a lawyer, and a counselor, respectively.

rise See *raise, rise.*

set, sit *Set* is a transitive verb meaning "to put" or "to place." Its principal parts are *set, set, set. Sit* is an intransitive verb meaning "to be seated." Its principal parts are *sit, sat, sat:*

> She set the tray of cucumber sandwiches near the bench where her mother-in-law sat.

should of Nonstandard for *should have:*

> He should have [not *should of*] filled the tank with gas before he left town.

sight, site See *cite, sight, site.*

sit See *set, sit.*

somebody, someone *Somebody* and *someone* are singular.

sometime, some time, sometimes *Sometime* is an adverb meaning "at an indefinite or unstated time":

> The plane will leave sometime soon.

Some time is two words (a noun and its modifier) that mean "a period of time":

> I had not seen my sister for some time.

Sometimes is an adverb meaning "now and then":

> Sometimes I go jogging at the track.

stationary, stationery *Stationary* means "not moving." *Stationery* is a type of writing paper:

> Stationary and alone, Rodney waited while the dean pulled out her stationery to write his parents.

suppose to Nonstandard for *supposed to.*

than, then *Than* is a conjunction used in comparisons; *then* is an adverb meaning "at that time in the past" or "next":

> Then he decided that he liked contact lenses more than glasses.

that, which *That* introduces essential (or restrictive) clauses. *Which* can introduce either essential or nonessential (nonrestrictive) clauses, but many writers reserve *which* for nonrestrictive clauses. (For further discussion of restrictive and nonrestrictive clauses, see pages 268–69.)

theirselves Nonstandard for *themselves.*

there, their, they're *There* is an adverb meaning "in that place" and an expletive (or filler word) in the phrase *there is:*

There is a homeless man lying over there.

Their is a possessive pronoun. *They're* is a contraction of *they are:*

They're sure that they left their skates near the door.

thru In formal writing, avoid this colloquial spelling of *through.*

to, too, two *To* is a preposition usually meaning "in a direction toward"; *too* is an adverb meaning "also"; *two* is a number:

Gerald went to the soccer game.

Two famous Argentinians were playing, and pro scouts were there too.

try and Nonstandard for *try to:*

We agreed to try to [not *try and*] stop arguing about our in-laws.

uninterested See *disinterested, uninterested.*

use to Nonstandard for *used to.*

wait for, wait on *Wait for* means "to be in readiness for" or "to await." *Wait on* means "to serve":

We are waiting for [not *on*] the rain to slacken.

ways Use *way* when referring to distance:

Her house is a long way [not *ways*] from her garden.

well See *good, well.*

whether See *if, whether.*

who, whom *Who* is used for subjects; *whom* is used for objects.

Who wrote the sentence?

She is the woman whom I love.

who's, whose *Who's* is a contraction of "who is"; *whose* is a possessive pronoun:

Who's going to your graduation?

Whose bedspread is this?

your, you're *Your* is a possessive pronoun; *you're* is a contraction of "you are":

Your dog has won the first prize.

You're the best trainer at the meet.

INDEX

DIRECTORY of INSTANT ACCESS BOXES

LIST OF FIGURES

A Checklist for Finishing Documents

Before you hand in anything you've written, take a few minutes to make one final check:

- Does your introduction interest readers in your subject?
  (**1d, Revising,** page 20)

- Is the main point or thesis of your paper clearly expressed?
  (**1b, Planning,** pages 10–11; **1d, Revising,** page 18)

- Does the paper have a structure your reader will be able to follow?
  (**1b, Planning,** pages 11–14; **1d, Revising,** pages 18–19)

- Does the conclusion discuss the topic's significance or provide a call to action?
  (**1d, Revising,** page 22)

- Is your paper prepared according to the assignment's guidelines for margins, line spacing, use of source material, and so on?
  (**1e, Finishing,** pages 27–29; **2d, Document Your Sources Correctly,** pages 45–53; **3, MLA Documentation Style,** pages 54–71; **4, APA Documentation Style,** pages 72–87; **5, *Chicago Manual of Style* (*CMS*) Documentation Styles,** pages 88–109); **6, Document Design,** pages 110–16)

- Have you checked your spelling?
  (**1e, Finishing,** page 28; *Spelling* in **Grammar, Punctuation, and Mechanics from A to Z,** pages 273–77)

- Have you carefully proofread the final version of your paper?
  (**1e, Finishing,** pages 27–29)

- Have you kept a copy for yourself?